An Invi

GW00633394

LUNCH, DINE, STAY & VISIT

SOMERSET & AVON

Including the Exmoor National Park
Second Edition

INNS, PUBS, HOTELS, RESTAURANTS

Potted History of Areas, Exciting Attractions, and Places to Visit
Great Venues, Great Food and Comfort, Great Value

By
JOY DAVID

"The book as a whole will not date: National Trust concur that with their knowledge of a substantial proportion of the hostelries, they rank the contents very highly"

National Trust 'Oakleaves'

THE PERFECT COMPANION FOR LOCALS & VISITORS, YOU CAN NOT AFFORD TO BE WITHOUT

The Author wishes to thank the team who have made this book possible in a very short time from its inception to publication.

My thanks to Patricia Hayes for the writing of Chapter 5. To Hassina Carder, Adrian Carey and Christine Scobling in Production. The Field Researchers, Rose Dennis, Nancy Pavey and Victoria Sprott. The 'In-House' Researchers, Hilary Kent, Sue Loomes, Cathy Mitchell, Ruth Bowden & Alison Troth.

Thanks are also given to Emma Macleod-Johnstone, Will Goodall, David Williams, Stephen Tait, Paul Worth, David Moore, Carlos Escobar, Gareth Howell, Kevin Evans and Hassina Carder for all the drawings.

And finally thank you to Jamie Macleod-Johnstone, who is the constant source of ideas for this series of books and for the new books in 1994.

The Roman Baths, Bath

ISBN 1 873491 50 6
First published in 1993
Copyright Joy David

Typeset by Invitation Press Ltd, Devon. Tel: (0752) 256177 / 256188
and Typestyle (The P.C. Bureau), Devon. Tel: (0752) 698668
Printed and bound in Great Britain by Short Run Press Ltd, Devon. (0392) 211909

INCLUDES

'Strange to see how a good dinner and feasting reconciles everybody'
Samuel Pepys

SOMERSET & AVON

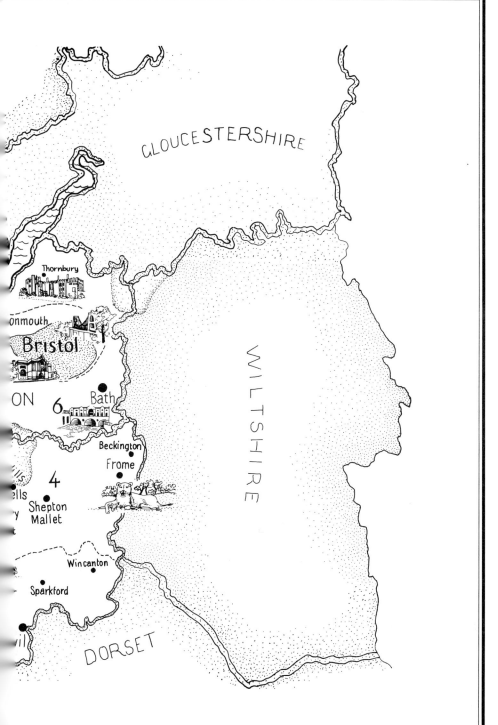

GLOUCESTERSHIRE

Thornbury

onmouth

Bristol

ON   6   Bath

Beckington

Frome

lls   4

ells
y   Shepton
Mallet

Wincanton

Sparkford

ll

DORSET

WILTSHIRE

5

an invitation to
LUNCH, DINE, STAY & VISIT IN
SOMERSET & AVON

INTRODUCTION

It was a family discussion about where we should go for lunch on the Sunday before Christmas that prompted the writing of this series of books. I thought we knew the local area well enough to make it a fairly simple choice but when it came down to brass tacks this was definitely not the case.

We did not mind whether it was a hotel, a restaurant or a good pub but with the gathering of the clan for the festive season, the group's demands were somewhat exacting. It had to be somewhere that children were welcome and grannies would not be out of place; the men wanted a decent pint of Real Ale and to be well fed. Log fires, old beams, and a good malt Scotch were added to the list with the request for provision of some kind of activity after lunch to help one's system limber up for the annual Christmas gorge. Either a scenic walk near the venue if the weather was kind or an indoor entertainment if it were not, and to add to this ever growing list of requirements, one of our number was a vegetarian!

Having got together all the ingredients that were required to make a successful outing the question still remained unanswered, Where?

We dug out old newspapers, looked through Yellow Pages but not once did we discover, listed, the information that we sought. Finally we did find a super pub, had an excellent lunch and walked along the banks of the river enjoying a matchless December day; but what an effort!

This book has been designed to help you find easily a suitable establishment to answer your needs, whether it be for lunch, dinner, a stay or a visit. Some are simple down to earth pubs, others are more sophisticated but every venue has its own dedicated page which tells you exactly what you can expect in the way of food, the sort of establishment it is, the opening hours, if they take credit cards, have access for the disabled, if children are welcome, if there are letting rooms and finally if there is a garden.

The beginning of every chapter is devoted to what there is to do and see around the pubs, restaurants and hotels. Some places you will know, others may be new.

This is an all year round book, as pertinent in summer as in winter. Useful to couples looking for somewhere different, for families and perhaps, a secretary wanting to find somewhere for her boss to take a visiting client.

I have tried to make sure there is something for everyone which is almost an impossibility but hope that readers will be kind enough to write to me and tell me about their favourite spots so that they can be included in the next edition.

The Timeless Packhorse Bridge, Allerford, Minehead

EXMOOR NATIONAL PARK

INCLUDES

"And Noah he often said to his wife when
he sat down to dine,
I don't care where the water goes if
it doesn't get into the wine"

G.K. Chesterton

EXMOOR NATIONAL PARK

 Exmoor straddles the borders of Devon and Somerset with a determination to be recognised for its own worth and not solely as a part of either county; a place of magical beauty, enchanting vistas, and not a little sinister in parts. Its villages are timeless and, once visited, it will always beckon you back to discover more. The word moor may suggest it is inland but this is not so of Exmoor; part of its grand beauty is its coastline, where every twist of the road will give you a sometimes tantalising glimpse through leaf laden branches of trees to the sparkling sea, and at other turns of your path you will be left gasping at the sheer clarity of the ocean splendour. The coastline takes the full force of the winter's gales which are ferocious and menacing but to the well wrapped onlooker, the frightening majesty sends the adrenalin coursing through the body.

In 1954 Exmoor became a National Park, somewhere to be protected for future generations. It is one of our smallest National Parks, yet within its 267 square miles lies English natural beauty of incomparable variety. Its wild magnificence has been recognised and the ever increasing number of people who fall under its spell each year, seem to have harmonised with those lucky enough to live here, establishing a code which simply underlines the need, for everyone who loves Exmoor, to be responsible for its future.

Britain's National Parks oddly enough do not belong to the nation, even though the title suggests that they do. It is true that some areas of the parks are managed by public bodies like the Forestry Commission, protected by the Nature Conservancy Council, or owned by the Crown, the National Park Authorities and National Trust.

Most of the land however, is privately owned, as it has been for centuries; and nearly all of it represents somebody's livelihood. On Exmoor, for instance, over 80% of the national park's 267 square miles is privately owned. Most is devoted to farming - Exmoor is famous for its sheep and beef cattle - and the farmer's land, even the open moorland, is as private as your back garden.

Traditionally, however, we are privileged to enjoy considerable freedom within the open countryside of Exmoor, particularly on the moor; and there are over 600 miles of public footpaths and bridleways as well. This freedom will only remain while the public respect the life of the countryside and the rights of those who make a living from it.

Exmoor's ever changing scenery, rich in history, colour and wildlife, is readily available to all who decide to leave their cars and explore the countryside on foot. For the well-equipped and experienced rambler the moor's steep-sided and wooded combes and switchback paths along the precipitous coastline and coastal valleys offer challenges to satisfy even the most zealous and enthusiastic walker.

For those of us not quite so energetic - or someone like me who sees something special through a car window and decides to explore further - Exmoor offers endless and rewarding opportunities, and always with the sure knowledge that sooner or later one is going to come across a village with a marvellous hostelry!

Many of the 600 miles of footpaths and bridleways are waymarked with coloured arrows or squares. Linked with signposts, they help you to find your way between points without trespass. The colours should not be confused with waymarks in other areas which denote path status. These are purely to keep you on the right track. You will find few waymarks or signposts on open moorland because, obviously, they detract from the experience of wilderness, something rare in Southern England and much valued. This means that to walk across open moorland you should have a good walking map or booklet and, of course, the ability to use it! The National Park Authority publishes a range of walking literature and provides advice. Just call at one of its Visitor Centres at Dulverton, Dunster, County Gate, Lynmouth and Combe Martin. In 1993, as an experiment, five Exmoor village shops are providing a basic information service with the idea of broadening the information network and encouraging wide use of these vital elements of our rural communities. The shops are in Wootton Courtenay, Brompton Regis, Withypool, Challacombe and Parracombe. I have discovered that the shopkeeper may not always be able to advise you but you will certainly get a warm welcome.

There are bus services running on Exmoor which will help you get to places of interest. You can get timetables from the Visitor Centres but if it is easier then I have listed below the bus companies and their telephone numbers to help you enquire further:

Red Bus, North Devon Ltd. (0271) 45444
Lyn Valley Bus (0598) 53320 or 52470
The Garage, Withycombe (0984) 40246
Exmoor Community Bus (03984) 352
Kingdom's Tours, Tiverton (0884) 252373

Scarlet Coaches, Minehead (0643) 704204
W Ridler & Son, Dulverton (0398) 23398
Terraneua's Tours, South Molton (07695) 2139
Southern National, Taunton (0823) 272033
Bryant's Coaches, Williton (0984) 32551
County Council Transport Advice (0392) 382800

One should always be aware of, and know about, the excellent work of the Exmoor Ranger, who probably contributes more to the public face of the National Park than anyone else. There are four Rangers, each responsible for an area of Exmoor and, living close to their work, with a wealth of local knowledge and experience. They are supported by three seasonal and one voluntary Ranger and led by the Head Ranger, who is based at Exmoor House in Dulverton - the National Park Administrative base. There is also an Educational Ranger, who works alongside them. On their travels about Exmoor the Rangers talk to residents, visitors, farmers, sportsmen and many people, not all of them with a common belief of how the park should be run! They listen, advise and endeavour to see that everyone's point of view has a hearing. They check on National Park owned property, from moorland and woodland to car parks and loos, and undertake survey and monitoring work to assist other National Park staff. As a part of the Visitor's Services team they are an important contact for the Park's five visitor centres.

Their tasks are multifold. They provide muscle for 'swaling' - the controlled burning, to ensure healthy regrowth of the National Park's own grass and heather moorland and help to look after the Park's herds of Exmoor ponies. They find themselves acting as 'the veterinary' to quote 'All Creatures Great and Small'. People bring them injured buzzards, ask for help in securing a badger sett. They have to catch runaway horses, unblock drains, mend gates, discourage motorcyclists from using the bridleways, deal with the problems of rave parties in the open countryside and illegally encamped travellers. They are always there to answer your questions and will also have to stop to pick up thoughtlessly discarded litter.

As with the police and the local emergency services they are fast on the scene of an accident. Their Land Rovers and mobiles frequently make them the first one on the spot if a rider has been injured or there is a lost walker. Where the Land Rover cannot get through a mounted Ranger can. One of the tasks they love most is taking people on guided walks throughout the year, sometimes helped by volunteers. Overseas visitors are on the increase including the number of European school children who want to discover the countryside. The Rangers arrange a special walk for them, indeed as they do for all manner of official visitors from travel agents to conservationists. The Education Ranger has a special role. He is the one who advises groups and responds to the many equiries from schools and teachers, students and school children. He deals with people doing the Duke of Edinburgh orienteering exercises, liaises with voluntary groups, and organises the work of the now thriving Exmoor Conservation Volunteers. You will sometimes find these dedicated Rangers at the County Shows telling people about their work.

One of the most exciting days in the Exmoor Calendar year is the annual gathering of the Exmoor ponies on Withypool Common. It is an occasion when you need cameras at the ready. It is a moving experience and brings home the natural continuity of life on the moor. The ponies are quietly rounded up by just three riders and as you watch you will see some 40 ponies and their foals brought in giving you a rare opportunity to see them at such close quarters. The whole free living pony population on Exmoor is only around 120 and when free, they naturally graze in small groups. Each pony will have been branded in previous years but it is quite difficult to see under their new coats the distinguishing mark. However each owner is quite sure which pony belongs to whom.

As you listen to the 'Gatherers' talking you will begin to understand what a task this is. You will hear how the riders eventually found the main herd on farmland bordering the moor and how good it was to see a third stallion who had been unexpectedly gathered, proving to be one that had been missing for three years. These are not stray animals but a true race of ponies, marginally influenced and managed by humans, but essentially still native fauna rather than domestic stock.

One of the finest ways to see Exmoor is on horseback but for those who prefer to keep their feet on the ground and go fishing, the rivers and streams offer excellent sport for the freshwater fisherman. They flow through some of the most beautiful scenery in the country and abound with wild brown trout which average at two or three pounds and are good fighters.

There are runs of salmon and sea trout in most main rivers with the large sea trout - 4-6lbs - entering the rivers from late May onwards and the school peal in July.

The main runs of salmon come in the spring and the autumn and range from 7-12lbs. The seasons do vary between rivers, something you will need to check when booking, at which time you will also need to check on the permitted catching methods for each species. Still-water trout fishing has grown in popularity in recent years with more and more waters becoming available. Although Exmoor is primarily a game fishing area, there is coarse fishing available not far from the National Park.

Excellent sea fishing can be had along much of the Exmoor coast, with cod, bass, whiting and conger eel, skate and mackerel in evidence. Some of the stony beaches and rocky headlands can be hard on tackle and many good places are limited by the state of the tide. Most of the harbour entrances, sea walls and open beaches offer good fishing and, for the heavier fish, boats can be hired at Watchet, Minehead, Porlock Weir and Combe Martin.

*Talking of Withypool Common just now gives me reason to take you to the village of **Withypool**. This small Exmoor village has wonderful thatched cottages which bravely stand firm against the storms driving over the hills around it. The old church has a round Norman font, simply decorated with grooved lines, and a silver cup and cover chased by a craftsman in the days of Queen Elizabeth I. Just outside the village, Landacre Bridge spans the River Barle with five ancient arches. At the heart of the village is THE ROYAL OAK INN which, whilst it has a varied mix of locals and visitors in its bar, might more properly be referred to as a 'residential inn and restaurant'. Run by Mike Bradley, an escapee from the rat-race, he has taken up the rustic life with enthusiasm and his attitude has a lot to do with the friendliness that greets everyone.*

In years gone by R.D. Blackmore wrote part of Lorna Doone here, the artist Alfred Munnings had a studio in the loft and in the 1940's General Eisenhower planned much of the D-Day Normandy landings within the pub. The hospitality is superb and so is the food and drink on offer in two bars and an Egon Ronay-recommended restaurant.

Withypool also has the excellent WESTERCLOSE COUNTRY HOUSE HOTEL, run by the Foster family who invite you to bring your horse with you if you wish; stable accommodation is there waiting for them. This comfortable, friendly establishment will cater for people with special diets if requested, will direct you to find some of the best spots for bird watching or invite you to join them for a walking weekend. Food is one of the pleasures of these weekends, a splendid picnic is produced whilst you are on the trail, tea, scones and clotted cream on your return and then a first class dinner in which the wine list offers wines from around the world, local wines and some that are organic.

It was while I was here that I went to take a look at the world famous TARR STEPS, close to **Dulverton***, and is place of infinite beauty and steeped in history. There are many opinions on how old the steps are but the general consensus is, medieval times. A wonderful man, Dr Sweetapple claims in his guide, written about 1928, that 'A visit to the old bridge of Tarr Steps is an event only to be compared to the first sight of Stonehenge. Both take us back to the mists of antiquity. There is always a fascination in calling on the imagination to picture some of the scenes which may have been witnessed by such historic stones'.*

Tarr Steps. Exmoor's Famous Ancient Clapper Bridge

Taking the view that the present bridge is medieval then it will have been built at much the same time as the 'Clapper Bridges' on Dartmoor. One historian says that 'An old British track is said to have crossed the Barle at Tarr Steps in 1219', but a bridge is not mentioned.

Many people wonder why this particular place was chosen, not just for the ford, but for the most spectacular bridge of its type in Britain. It is thought that it was a link track between the ridgeway over Winsford Hill with its Wambarrows and Caractacus Stone, presumably to the harbours on the Bristol Channel, with the other ridgeway over Molland Common via Anstey Barrows, White Post and over Fyldon Ridge and on to Barnstaple. The significant point in common is that both tracks have Bronze Age Round Barrows alongside, which date them around 2500 BC, making the bridge seem comparatively modern and the ford across the river of very ancient origin.

What a fascinating procession of travellers TARR FARM must have seen over the centuries. 600 years it has stood on the hill above the steps and must have been a welcome sight for those seeking shelter in times of snow and flood. Travelling is easy today and the visitors still come at all times of the year, but now it is to enjoy the food and the wine, and browse in the little gift shop. The walls are slate-stone and James Harrison, the owner, will tell you that there are slate mushrooms as well. What he refers to are the slate tables at which you can enjoy a meal outside, overlooking the steps.

Wherever my travels take me I am always dumbfounded by the skill and ingenuity shown by the builders of our cathedrals and places like Tarr Steps, all without the assistance of any kind of machinery. Nearly always there is a story to tell and here we have the case of Tarr Steps said to have been built by the Devil. He brought the stones in his apron and dropped them in a sequence so that he could cross the river. All this was done in one night! It was for his exclusive use and he announced that he would destroy the first creature crossing it. An unfortunate cat attempted it and was torn to pieces. The animal's untimely death appears to have broken the spell, for a Parson then crossed in safety, exchanging niceties with the Devil en route. The Devil called the Parson a black crow to which the Parson replied that he was not blacker than the Devil.

Red Deer at Exmoor

Deer are regularly to be seen, it is said that stags coming up the Barle usually jump up on the bridge at about the third slab from the Dulverton side, but hinds as a rule pass under it. Otters and mink used to

16

be seen but they are now a rarity. Salmon, however, can still be seen lying in the pool above, when there is a run of them, mostly in the autumn.

From Winsford Hill you can see Cornwall's Brown Willy and over the sea to the Welsh Mountains. Below is the incomparable Tarr Steps across the river Barle, and on other side of the hill is the Exe Valley. The Caractacus Stone on the hill is thought to have been inscribed in the Dark Ages. On the same hill are the Wambarrows - three buried mounds probably of the beaker period or Bronze age and between 2,500 and 4,000 years old.

Winsford *is arguably the prettiest village on Exmoor and it certainly has one of the most charming inns, THE ROYAL OAK INN, with an immaculately thatched roof, soft cream washed walls and a profusion of colourful hanging baskets on the outside. The pub dates from the 12th century and its open fireplaces and oak beams have been subtly combined with the modern facilities we all expect today. It is a superb place to stay, the hospitality is second to none. Winsford itself was described by W.H. Hudson in 1909 as 'fragrant, cool, grey green - immemorial peace - second to no English village in beauty, running waters, stone thatched cottages, hoary church-tower'. Little has changed over the centuries. I believe there is still one lady in the village who has seen aeroplanes and cars but never a ship or a train because she has never left the village. I must admit that Winsford and The Royal Oak are the sort of places one does not want to leave.*

The woods and hills of Exmoor close round **Dulverton** *on three sides, the Barle flows past its front doorstep. It is a place steeped in history and one of tranquillity. In the church are two memorials to the Sydenhams who lived from 1540 to 1874 at Combe, a beautiful Tudor House. The life of the moor has made great literature and Dulverton is a name often found in books. Here Jan Ridd met Lorna Doone. Richard Jefferies watched the red deer. If you come to Dulverton in the spring take a walk in Burridge Woods which becomes totally carpeted with bluebells.*

One very good reason for coming to Dulverton is to stay at THE CARNARVON ARMS HOTEL. Owned by Mrs Toni Jones who runs it with the help of her family, this is a hotel that provides good, old fashioned service, courtesy and very high standards. It is a sporting establishment where everyone who enjoys outdoor pursuits, and if shooting comes into that category for you, then a stay here becomes a must. Excellent shooting is arranged, fishing is available, there is an outdoor heated swimming pool and tennis courts. It is only a short drive from this comfortable, welcoming hotel, to reach the wild beauty of the moor itself, a sudden transition from sheltered, wooded combes, to springy clumps of heather, brilliant gorse, beautiful beech hedges, ferns, bracken and trees bent by the winds of centuries. Rare birds may be seen, butterflies, flowers and plants, the ubiquitous sheep, the endearing Exmoor pony and perhaps even a glimpse of the elusive red deer.

Dulverton Bridge

From here one can wander all over the place with great ease. Had I not made my way in this direction from Withypool and Winsford, I might well have taken the B3223 going west just a few miles and arrived at **Simonsbath***, an ideal stepping stone on your way to discover the wild, stark beauty of Exmoor. I cannot say that the village excites me for it does not but it is a wonderful foil to the exquisite scenery which surrounds it on every side. However, within the welcoming walls of the EXMOOR FOREST HOTEL you can plan expeditions to the many interesting places closeby, like Tarr Steps, of course.*

Had I been able to take the time to stay in Simonsbath I would have made a beeline for THE SIMONSBATH HOUSE HOTEL, with BOEVEYS RESTAURANT in its well kept grounds. This comfortable place is somehwere you can do anything you like, or nothing at all, if that is your wish. Well run, friendly and good value, it is a place to remember. Boeveys Restaurant is only open during the season but serves good food, at sensible prices, all day long.

My route from Dulverton took me north along the A396 first to one of my favourite places on Exmoor, **Luxborough,** *well hidden along a* *small road off the B3224. It is somewhere both solitary and lonely, every time I go there I wonder at the indomitable spirit of the men who built it. What makes it so special to me is THE ROYAL OAK, a truly rustic inn, set deep in the folds of the Brendon Hills. It is a place of uncontrived charm, with no intrusion of piped music, fruit machines or even matching furniture! The several rooms have flagstoned or cobbled floors, low beams, old kitchen tables and hardly a pair of matching chairs. It is quite remarkable. The garden is lovely, the food is honest and the extensive menu ranges from sandwiches and jacket potatoes, good home-made soup with big hunks of bread and non-packet butter, to gargantuan pasties. Main courses are to be relished especially the Beamish pie with tender, lean meat in a rich gravy. Quite wonderful.*

*Back on the A396 once more I stopped at **Wheddon Cross**, another delightful place tucked in the Brendon Hills. It is on the very steep hill between Minehead and Tiverton and has a well named pub, THE REST AND BE THANKFUL. Originally coaches were pulled up this hill taking passengers on their travels. One can just imagine the state of the horses and probably the passengers as well. When they arrived at the inn they were no doubt exhorted to 'Rest and be Thankful!' This is a fine pub with the old beams giving it a sense of permanency in this ever changing world You can stay here awhile if you wish and everyone who comes is welcomed with true Somerset courtesy. If you were feeling really energetic you might have climbed Dunkery Beacon before arriving here for lunch. It is a walk that would take you through woods in which woodpeckers are frequently to be heard and sometimes there is a rare glimpse of red deer.*

Dunster Castle

The coast is quite close from here and I would never miss the chance to stop or stay in **Dunster**. *At the west gate of Exmoor, it seems to belong to centuries past. It is unforgettable; a place to savour and about which to dream. DUNSTER CASTLE rises dramatically above the village and the sea. It dates from the 13th century and for over 600 years it has been the home of the Luttrell family. Colonel Luttrell gave it to the National Trust in 1975 and we are privileged in being able to visit it. The gardens and the grounds are wonderful especially the terraces where rare shrubs grow. The church is unique. It is two-in-one, the Monk's Church and the Peoples's Church dating back 500 years. In the High Street is THE YARN MARKET, a quaint octagonal building erected in 1609 when wool was made into cloth in this area and kerseymere, a fine twill cloth of local wool, was marketed here. I can sincerely recommend two excellent places to stay, OSBORNE HOUSE HOTEL and DUNSTER CASTLE HOTEL. One of my favourite places to have coffee, tea or a light lunch is THE TEA SHOPPE in the High Street. This cottage was built in 1495 during the reign of Henry VII. A considerable amount of the original fabric remains. The ceilings are pil reed and horsehair plaster. The reed was grown and cut by the Crown estates commercially until recent times, on land by the old manor house in the marsh area of Dunster. The back wall in the Oak Room is the original construction of oak beams and supports with cob infil. The facade of the Tea Shoppe was rebuilt about 1900 and is the only brick faced building in Dunster High Street. It became a Tea Shoppe in the 1930's and has delighted its clientele ever since.*

Dunster has a quiet unspoilt beach which is totally safe for children and has the great advantage of being the only beach you can drive onto in West Somerset. It also has one of the most valuable places for tourists. THE EXMOOR NATIONAL PARK'S NEW VISITOR CENTRE.

All visitors to Exmoor have a basic need for information about the area, but the role of effective information and interpretation goes beyond this. Encouraging visitors to take an interest in their surroundings may help them to enjoy their stay more, to develop a greater awareness of conservation and management issues, and to respect the interest of those who live and work within the Park. This is done, as I have written previously, mainly through information centres and publications but also, and effectively, through direct contact between visitors and the National Park Authority Ranger Service and others, informally and on organised events.

In the mid 1960's, the Authority operated only two information centres and provided a limited range of literature concentrating upon waymarked walks. By the late 1970's, four manned information centres, at Dulveton, County Gate, Lynmouth and Combe Martin attracted a total of 40,000 visitors per annum. By relocating the Lynmouth centre and opening a fifth permanent centre at Dunster, the throughput has risen to over 500,000. In addition, visitor contacts have been maintained 'out of hours' through computerised information systems, and a mobile information unit which tours local shows throughout the summer months. The free information newspaper 'Exmoor Visitor' introduced in 1985, has proved a popular medium both for the visitor and the local tourist providers who advertise in it. It has brought together a range of information about the Park which is seen by two thirds of all visitors to Exmoor.

*The Visitor's centre in Dunster is a must for any visitor. The town thrived in medieval times on the woollen industry. An eye-catching feature here draws attention to it. There are 30 metres of wool woven, exactly to the style of the medieval cloth, from almost 30 miles of yarn, supplied by Craftsman's mark of Wellington, the proprietor of which, Morfudd (pronounced Morveth) Roberts, also supervised the production of the cloth. The Yarn was woven at COLDHARBOUR MILL AT **Uffculme,** itself a museum of wool production and well worth visiting. Setting up the loom took several days and involved tying many hundreds of knots by hand before weaving could start.*

One length of the cloth has been left in its natural, slightly grubby looking state. This would be virtually identical to the woollen cloth worn by the monks of nearby CLEEVE ABBEY in the 13th century. Further lengths of the unique reproduction medieval materials have been dyed by Gill Dalby, a local specialist in the use of vegetable dyes. Indigo was used to create the blue, madder, the red, and weld, the yellow. The invitation to the visitor very definitely is PLEASE TOUCH.

In 1500, many of the homes in Dunster would have had a spinning wheel where the housewife and the unmarried daughters would have toiled ceaselessly for all the daylight hours. Their efforts would have earned them little more than a penny a day. An independent weaver would have kept a team of about five or six women fully employed spinning yarn to meet his needs. This woven cloth was washed and taken out to the Castle Tor to be dried in the open air at the Tenteryarde. It was stretched tight on tenterframes by means of tenterhooks. Now you know where the expression ' to be on tenterhooks' comes from. I certainly did not know this before. Another term came into being as well. When using a spinning wheel, women (never men) drew fibres from the distaff. This women's work has resulted in the ' distaff side' to indicate the female side of a family.

In the Visitor's Centre, a mounted Exmoor Horn ram - representing the source of wool - presides over the imaginative interpretation of the processes involved in producing woollen cloth in Dunster in 1500.

On quiet days, if there are any in this fascinating place, Dunster born Beryl Priddle, who is in charge of the National Park's Visitor's centre may find time to demonstrate to visitors the spinning of wool on a traditional spinning wheel.

Without question the EXMOOR VISITOR'S CENTRE is a great boon to the visitors and it could not be better situated than in Dunster. The story the Centre tells gives one an insight into so many things and into the history of Dunster which will heighten their enjoyment of this lovely place.

*There is one corner of **Minehead** where a steep flight of steps takes you up to the church of St Michael. It is quite charming and reminds me so much of scenic **Clovelly**. Until you have been to Minehead you cannot appreciate what a delightful place it is. Protected by the hills which rise behind it, the houses have flowers climbing over their doors and walls. It is still a little old-fashioned which is part of its charm. The people are courteous as you will find out when you visit AVILL HOUSE, instantly recognisable by the magnificent display of red and white hanging baskets. A welcoming, comfortable guest house with good food and hospitality. Then there is THE OLD SHIP AGROUND, one of the town's landmarks where you will find the beer excellent, the hotel welcoming and the restaurant full of interesting dishes. Here they can arrange for you to go Clay Pigeon Shooting, take to the water on Sea Angling trips or perhaps go horseriding - probably the most spectacular way to see Exmoor.*

Minehead is the home of the WEST SOMERSET RAILWAY where steam trains will take you on 20 miles of scenic delights. From the vale of Taunton Deane through the rolling Quantock Hills. Past the beaches of Blue Anchor Bay to Minehead or the reverse journey. There are nine restored stations at which you may break your journey, museums, displays and steam locos. To find out more details you are asked to send a stamped addressed envelope to West Somerset Railway PLC, The Station, Minehead TA24 5BG. All sorts of events take place during the year but for me it is the sheer beauty of the route that is the main interest.

*If you follow the A39 towards Minehead and bear left at a mini-roundabout on the A39 Porlock to Lynmouth road you will discover on the left hand side about a mile and a quarter along PERITON PARK at **Middlecombe**, a Country House Hotel and Restaurant where time seems to stand still. The house nestles in its own woodland and gardens on the northern edge of the Exmoor National park. The views are magnificent from its elevated yet sheltered position. This is a place in which you will be pampered and at the same time a wonderful base from which to explore all that Exmoor has to offer.*

*When I stayed here I used it as a base to journey to the west and to the east of Exmoor. My first journey was to the little port of **Watchet**. The harbour is so small that you wonder how any craft can safely manoeuvre in and out. This was the port where Colerdige first conceived the 'Ancient Mariner' It was on a walk from **Nether Stowey** with the Wordsworths that his mind was simmering with the story. Coleridge looked at the harbour and said 'this is where he shall set out on his fateful voyage'.*

The 15th century church stands above this miniature seaside town and has a 600 year old cross beside it. A family called Wyndham lived at Kentisford Farm near the church and a square 17th century pew bears their arms. One brass honours Florence Wyndham, an Elizabethan about whom a strange story is told. Whilst she was lying in her coffin in the church awaiting burial, a greedy sexton saw her rings and coveted them. He broke open her coffin and did it so roughly that he woke her from a trance. She arose from the coffin, went home and soon after gave birth to a child. History does not relate what happened to the sexton, was he a life-saver or hung for being a thief?

Looking for somewhere to eat and drink, then THE WEST SOMERSET HOTEL has a good reputation. Another attractive place is SEYBURNS RESTAURANT in Market Street, where you can both eat and drink all day long and well into the evening. The food is a good variety of home-made dishes, steaks, fish and some Oriental dishes as well. It is licensed and the price is right. Here too you can stay a night or two, very comfortably at reasonable prices.

From Watchet it is simple to reach firstly Monksilver which is full of romance for me and also Stogumber which I love for its name, let alone anything else.

Monksilver *is the home of that wonderful house COMBE SYDENHAM with its fine Country Park. You must make sure you allow time to spend at least a day here. It was here Francis Drake courted the beautiful daughter of the house Elizabeth Sydenham, who finally agreed to marry him. The dashing Sir Francis then sailed away to fight more battles and chase the Spaniards. His voyages were long and arduous and the lovely Elizabeth became despondent believing that he would never return. Encouraged by her father she finally agreed to wed another suitor. The day of her wedding arrived and she was driven to* **Stogumber** *church for her marriage. As she alighted from the carriage a cannon ball fell at her feet. Her heart leapt in excitement. It had to be a sign that Drake was back in harbour. She abandoned her unfortunate bridegroom and went home to await Drake. Drake came and they were married, probably in this church. The cannon ball can be seen even today at Combe Sydenham, which experts believe to be a meteorite in fact. It has become a symbol of good fortune for all those who touch it. It was this marriage that brought Buckland Abbey into Drake's possession. Their marriage lasted until Drake's death ten years later. Soon after she married Sir William Courtenay and became mistress of Powderham Castle in Devon. Her happiness lasted only a few months, until she too died.*

Before I tell you about Combe Sydenham Country Park, I must introduce you to a very good country inn, THE NOTLEY ARMS, in the village. Here the lively landlords, Alistair and Sarah Cade, have a charmingly simple establishment. The L shaped Bar is furnished plainly with wooden furniture, there are twin woodburning stoves. It is a delight and renowned for its excellent food, hence the star listing in so many guide books. However it is not just the food that draws people but the genuine warmth of the welcome. There is always someone in the bar who will add a bit of embroidery to the Elizabeth Sydenham story, which must almost rival Cinderella in the number of times it gets told in a year.

COMBE SYDENHAM COUNTRY PARK will give you a unique opportunity to see history restored and nature revived. It has taken forty years of dedication and planning to restore it. Owned by the Theed family, it is at last returning to self-sufficiency through forestry, trout farming and estate-produced delicacies.

What ever your age you will enjoy the celebration of nature that takes place at Combe Sydenham. Take a look at the restoration plan in action: from the 400 year old trout ponds to the west wing of the Hall, where you can see the remarkable Elizabethan Courtroom. The restored medieval Corn Mill is now back in production, milling their own stone ground flour. You can see it working most days. There are 500 acres of superb Country park for you to explore where you may glimpse the shy fallow deer in the Deer park, and find the deserted hamlet of **Goodley**, *thought to have been decimated by the Black Death in 1348.*

The network of woodland paths is shown on a map to help you get the best out of it. You are asked politely to keep your dog on a lead because of the wildlife about. Children find the leaflets about the Magic Story Trails wonderful. There is something special about taking a close view of nature while ambling through 'Alice in Wonderland' and 'Ancient Trail of Trees' Story Trails. The Children's play area is a favourite too.

You can fish on the more advanced Trout Lake if you know what you are doing but for beginners there is tuition. All tackle is supplied. Trout and in particular Somerset Rainbow Trout, are available for purchase, fresh and in freezer packs for you to take home. There is also smoked Salmon and smoked Trout pate plus Venison in season and smoked mature Cheddar Cheese all done with traditional smoking on the premises, using Oak wood chips. Marmalade and preserves are also available from the shop which is open throughout the year Monday-Friday, and in summer, Saturday mornings from 9-12noon.

The Tea Room is the place to relax and enjoy the excellent tea or coffee, home-made cakes and lunches.

Combe Sydenham opens one week before Easter until the end of October (Half term), Sunday to Friday 10am-5pm. Courtroom and gardens Monday to Friday. The Country Park is open on November Sundays for those who want to take the opportunity of seeing the stunning autumn colours.

Stogumber *is a wonderful name and goes down in history as the place where Cardinal beaufort, the wealthiest man in all England, came for hunting, when the church was new. It would have been about the time when he saw Joan of Arc burnt at the stake in Rouen and led the young King Henry to Paris to be crowned as King of France and England - two dramatic events in one year of his extraordinary life.*

Going back to Minehead and Periton Park, I was able to set off on the next stage of my thoroughly enjoyable tour of Exmoor. This time it was westwards. First of all to the lovely **Porlock Vale** *which stretches from* **Porlock Weir**, *the tiny harbour nestling beneath the wooded cliffs of*

25

Porlock Hill and Bossington near Hurlestone Point, to the hills of Tivington and Selworthy. Within the Vale, lie the villages of **Porlock, Bossington, Lynch, Allerford, Hornworthy, Selworthy** *and* **Luccombe**. *You can walk, ride, sail, fish or just relax. Marshlands in the sweeping bay offers rewarding walks. It is an area rich in nice old pubs, quaint shops and the romance of the moorland history.*

Cottage with Bread Oven in Stony Street, Luccombe

In the High Street of Porlock is the pretty and welcoming SHIP INN with its thatched roof surmounted by proudly strutting peacocks. It was here that the poet Robert Southey, caught in a shower, sheltered from the elements and whiled away the time writing this sonnet:

Porlock! I shall forget thee not,
Here by the unwelcome summer rain confined;
But often shall hereafter call to mind
How here, a patient prisoner, twas my lot
To wear the lonely, lingering close of day,
Making my sonnet by the alehouse fire,
Whilst Idleness and Solitude inspire
Dull rhymes to pass the duller hours away.

This village has friendly cottages crowding on the narrow twisting street, the green hills close it in on three sides and the sea is on the other. The church is 13th century and has the distinction of being dedicated to the saint who is said to have crowned King Arthur.

LOWERBOURNE HOUSE a little further along from the ship, is the home of a fascinating art and bookshop as well as a pretty tea room where you will find coffee and tea served in bone china. It is a simple place, where children and wellingtons are very much welcomed! Wonderful home-made cakes tempt the most strong minded. Also in the High Street is the very popular COUNTRYMAN, a licensed restaurant where you get breakfast all day long, lunch on a super steak or a simple sandwich. In the afternoon you may indulge in a wonderful cream tea, or the epitome of decadence, a luxury afternoon tea which consists of a round of sandwiches of your choice, home-made scone with jam and clotted cream, or toasted tea cake, a cake from the gorgeous selection, a pot of tea or coffee.

Still in the High Street you will come to PIGGY IN THE MIDDLE where the food is delicious, the waiter one of the most amusing people around, and everywhere there are pigs, even one that walks and oynks - not living ones of course. It is a fun place to be.

*There is a particularly nice small country house hotel set in its own grounds. You will find it at **West Porlock** on the way to Porlock Weir from the High Street. WEST PORLOCK HOUSE was once the local manor and now pleases everyone who stays there. There are only four double rooms, all en suite and so it feels much like a private house. The home-cooked meals are delicious enough to tempt the fussiest palate and the gardens are full of camellias, Azaleas and Rhododendrons. The garden canals boast the tallest magnolia in the country.*

Each time I leave one of the beautiful little pockets of Exmoor, I feel a wrench, a sense of loss, but this time, whilst I was loth to leave Porlock, I knew that I was making my way to the Doone Valley and on to Lynton and Lynmouth; somewhere for which I have a deep affection.

*Just off the coast road from Porlock to Lynmouth I never fail to stop at **Oare**. Hidden from the sea in a deep valley, it is surrounded by wild hills and an incredible silence broken only by the twittering of birds and the tinkling sound of Oare Water as it wanders along before it joins Badgworthy Water where they both become part of Devon.*

This is Lorna Doone country, it was from Oare that her lover walked to meet her. In the tiny, 15th century church of St Mary, they were married and through its windows was fired the shot that spilled her blood on the altar steps. You can almost hear the shot, the appalled, strangulated sound of the congregation as they witnessed her falling to the ground and the blood staining her simple, white wedding dress.. For many of us, our first introduction to Exmoor was the story of 'Lorna Doone', written by R.D.Blackmore in the 19th century but so powerful is his description of Exmoor that I have always found it hard to believe that he story of Lorna Doone is fiction. Once you enter this austere little church you will feel the wonderful atmsphere envelope you; take note of the plaques on the wall and you, like me, will want to believe the Doones and the Ridds did exist. The church with its medieval wagon roofs is open daily during daylight hours. It is odd to think that this beloved book almost faded into insignificance when it was published. It was not until Queen Victoria's daughter, Princess Louise, became engaged to the Marquis of Lorne that it became a best seller. Why? Because an over zealous and misinformed critic wrote in his column that the book was about the ancestors of the marquis. From that moment it became the fashionable thing to read 'Lorna Doone'

Lorna Doone Cottage

One place I discovered quite by chance is THE STAG HUNTERS HOTEL at **Brendon** *just off the A39 between Oare and Lynmouth. It is delightful with frontage to the East Lyn river noted for fishing, magnificent scenery and walks. The hotel retains the charm of a traditional Exmoor inn, yet offers the services and comfort of a well run, small family hotel. There is hunting within easy reach with both foxhounds and staghounds during the season. The hotel has stables available for guests who wish to bring their own horses. Just a short walk from the hotel is COUNTISBURY FORELAND, the highest cliff face in England and three miles of fishing with named pools, Salmon and Trout fishing are available in unrivalled* *beautiful surroundings. An ideal place to stay from which you can see and do so much.*

*   **Lynton** *and* **Lynmouth** *are linked together by a remarkable CLIFF RAILWAY which opened in 1890. It climbs 500ft above sea level along a 900ft track. Worked by water and gravity it must have seemed terrifying to the intrepid users when it first started, they never having seen anything like it before. Sir George Newnes was the driving force behind its construction because he saw the need for easier access between the two villages which had grown in popularity during the Napoleonic wars when the English were unable to travel abroad.*

*   Lynmouth is a gem; the River Lyn runs through Lynton and tumbles over moss strewn rocks and boulders, through thickly wooded hills as it falls to the sea at Lynmouth. The village has a picture postcard quality and where better to stay and enjoy it than HEWITTS COUNTRY HOUSE HOTEL. This wonderful house has a romantic history that is quite delightful to read about. It is the story of Sir Thomas Hewitt and his second wife. Few men are lucky enough to fall in love with a woman and a view at the same time and to be able to build a house to please one and capture the other from that very same spot. (I own up to taking the copy for this part of my book largely from a splendid small booklet produced by Hewitts Hotel, for which I hope they will forgive me) Thomas Hewitt married twice - both times for love. The first ended with the death of his wife, which drove him to work ceaselessly, making himself a considerable fortune. The second sustained him throughout his long and active life and it was for the love of this lady that the house called The Hoe, now Hewitt's Hotel, was built. Fanny, his second wife, was also his cousin. She had a delicious sense of humour and was an inspiration to him. They were married on the 15th September 1869, the ceremony being conducted by Canon Charles Kingsley, the famous author of 'The Water Babies'.*

*   Tom planned the honeymoon around Fanny's interests and a walking and riding holiday around Exmoor seemed perfect - certainly early autumn in this part of the world can be heavenly. The couple were happy and in love with both themselves and the area and Lynmouth, then still a tiny fishing village best approached by sea, was their favourite spot. They did not feel ready to return to their home in Walton-on-Thames and it is at this moment that the idea of a romantic house which is now Hewitt's Hotel was born. The couple were standing on the cliffs at Lynton North Walk looking out over Lynmouth Bay when Tom asked Fanny if she would like to have a summer house built especially to capture the view. Seeing her face light up with excitement Tom marked a stone and gave it to her saying 'wherever it lands I will build you your house'.*

The stone was thrown and landed on a steep rocky hillside then devoid of trees. The choice of a builder was easy since there was only one in the area - Mr Tom Jones, but fortunately the man was totally competent. What he thought of the chosen site is not recorded. What we do know is that a long narrow ledge was dynamited and a house of the same shape was dove tailed into it. No planning permission was required in those days, but looking at the building today no official interference could have improved the vision of the designers who also loved it, lived in it and added extensions as and when the need arose. Gardens, bowered walks, a terrace garlanded with flowers were developed over the years and the house echoed to the sound of children's laughter as the three sons of the marriage grew up.

The house has been altered very litte, its character and its happiness have remained. In fact many people who have stayed here will tell you that Hewitts remains like a private house. You can still stand and enjoy the view up the gently sloping tree-lined drive much in the way that Lady Hewitt did. The gardens have proved to be a haven for wildlife and visitors to the hotel sitting on the terrace can be assured of an excellent education in the field of natural history.

Right down on the harbour is another of my favourite places owned by the interesting and likeable Hugo Jeune whose family have been associated with Lynton for centuries. He is in fact the Lord of the Manor. A title passed down to him through his family but meaning little in to-day's world because the manor has long gone; it was sold to the Council in 1908. However the Lord of the Manor does have certain rights laid down in the deeds. For example he can own the sea shore as far as a knight can throw a lance! THE RISING SUN is where Blackmore is said to have written much of Lorna Doone and Shelley spent his honeymoon with his child bride, and Robert Southey dreamed. Lynmouth would inspire anyone who is not without soul.

Twelve years ago Hugo Jeune returned to Lynmouth and acquired the Rising Sun, he must have wondered if he would ever achieve the standard that he required. The place was a mess and in need of absolutely everything doing to it. How do you retain all that is beautiful and right about its antiquity and at the same time make good the wear and tear of 600 years? He described it to me as a cobweb which had to be worked around so that not one strand was broken. Miraculously and thankfully he has been successful.

It sits overlooking a small picturesque harbour at the mouth of the river Lyn where it joins the sea. Inside, the uneven floors, the crooked ceilings, thick walls and fine oak panelling in the dining room and bar endorse its age. When you climb the fairly steep stairs to your bedroom you will occasionally have to duck your head to avoid the old beams.

In the 14th century The Rising Sun would have been dispensing hospitality as it does today, and in later centuries, many of the customers were smugglers or seafaring men, mulling over their hauls, making brazen or surreptitious plans for the next smuggling run. You can feel the sense of history as you walk into this very pretty thatched inn, which today, not only upholds its innkeeping tradition but, without losing one ounce of its charm, has become a first class hotel.

It was just about ten years before the Manor was sold that Hugo Jeune's grandmother opened Sir George Newnes's fabulous railway. that climbs up the cliff vertically from Lynmouth to Lynton. The land on which the railway was built still belongs to Hugo. He also has half a mile of fishing rights where keen fishermen can catch some of the best salmon anywhere. It is free for anyone staying in the hotel apart from the local authority fee.

Two attractiver eateries are in the centre of Lynmouth. THE CORNER HOUSE RESTAURANT AND RIVERSIDE TEA GARDENS is charming. Its situation is idyllic at the meeting of the East and West Lyn where Exmoor joins the sea. One of the great pleasures is being able to sit on the terrace immediately alongside the river. There can hardly be a more tranquil place in Lynmouth on a sunny day. My other choice is THE SPINNING WHEEL. It is a delightful Cottage Tea Room during the day and then at night it changes into somewhere in which one can sit and enjoy a leisurely dinner.

I look forward to trips on the last sea-going paddle steamer in the world, the famous WAVERLEY, and the traditional cruise ship, BALMORAL which sail on day trips, afternoon and evening cruises from Minehead, Lynmouth and Ilfracombe. As you sail into **Ilfracombe** *remember this nice story. In 1797 four French ships were sighted off the port. Most of the towns 200 full time sailors were away serving with the Royal Navy. The women folk recognised that they were in imminent danger of being invaded. With ingenuity and courage they removed their traditional red petticoats and draped them round their shoulders like scarlet cloaks, then took up prominenet positions on high ground around the town. The French spotted them through their telescopes and believing the red cloaks meant the town was garrisoned with a large number of military, set sail with alacrity. The cruises provide a unique way to view the whole of the magnificent Exmoor coast: sail away to Wales or see*

LUNDY ISLAND and the Devon coast. For more information ask at the Tourist Information Centres or ring (0446) 720656.

*There are some wonderful walks between Lynmouth and **Combe Martin**. Some for the experienced walkers only but no one should miss the sheer splendour of the VALLEY OF THE ROCKS. Leave Lynmouth from Riverside Road with the RHENISH TOWER on the right, cross the road to turn left by the pavilion where there is a signpost 'To the Valley of the Rocks'. It winds uphill to join the path to the north of Hollerday Hill called NORTH WALK, a path cut to the Valley of the Rocks by a Mr Sanford in 1817. It is a brilliant feat of engineering. The first time I walked it, I spent much of the time bewitched by the scenic beauty and the sight of the Welsh coast. At times the path drops sheer away to the pounding sea below. The colouring is fantastic; rocks and boulders are covered with lichen, the mixture of colours heightened where the dark patches of ground ivy curl around tree stumps. Eventually the eye reaches the rock masses of RAGGED JACK and CASTLE ROCK guarding the entrance to the Valley of the Rocks. The Valley was created during the Ice Age some, 10,000 years ago - awe inspiring.*

Do you like brass rubbing? If you do, the EXMOOR BRASS RUBBING AND HOBBYCRAFT CENTRE in Watersmeet Road, Lynmouth, will give you hours of pleasure. There is no entry charge, you merely pay for your rubbing. The prices start from £1.35 with over 100 brasses and children's rubbing plates of Kings, Queens, Knights, Clergy, skeletons, Exmoor scenes, chidren's stories, animals, Oriental dancers and a'no-smoking' sign! Open normally from Monday to Friday, but seven days a week from Easter during the school holidays and half terms until the end of September plus the Autumn half-term, from 10.30am-5pm.

*The National Trust owns WATERSMEET now but once it belonged to the Hallidays. He was the heir to a merchant's fortune who fell in love with the wild beauty of this north-western corner of Exmoor and began buying land in the early part of the 19th century. He and his wife were philianthropists who planned to set up a patriarchal estate, peopled with tenants for whom they laid out farms and provided employment. This romantic couple built a dream mansion beside the sea at **Glenthorne**, two miles east of Countisbury, with a drive plunging ever more steeply from County Gate, 1,000 feet above, at the border of Devon and Somerset. In 1832 they constructed WATERSMEET HOUSE, in an equally romantic setting. It now accommodates the Trust's restaurant, shop and information point. Watersmeet is glorious, one of the two places in Britain where the*

Irish spurge is found. Revelling in the damp clean air so close to the sea, lichens, mosses and ferns abound, creating a site of national importance for ancient woodland flora.

I suppose that strictly speaking I should not include **South Molton** *in my Exmoor travels, but for me it has always been a starting and finishing place, a wonderful springboard at the beginning and a restful place at the end. It is an ancient sheep and cattle market town dating back to the 12th century. Until the 19th century it thrived as a centre of the wool trade. Today it is quietly charming with its fine Georgian houses and a nice early 15th-century parish church, St Mary Magdalen which you approach along an avenue of limes. For 300 years THE POLTIMORE ARMS, situated at* **Yarde Down** *between South Molton and Simonsbath, has been caring for travellers. A hospitable, friendly inn which serves food 7 days a week until 9.30pm. An ideal place for refreshment perhaps after visiting the SOUTH MOLTON MUSEUM which is housed in a 17th-century building. A fascinating place with a wealth of interesting displays, including 18th century wig making tools, cider presses and a wooden fire engine.*

HANCOCK'S DEVON CIDER at CLAPWORTHY MILL, in the beautiful Bray Valley is also worth a visit. Apart from being able to buy scrumpy, cider, honey and cream from the shop there is also a craft shop. You will be invited too to see their video film and colour photo exhibition on cider making. It is open Monday to Saturday 9-1pm and 2-5.30pm. Closed on Sundays

Many people have found great pleasure in visiting QUINCE HONEY FARM in North Road, South Molton: acknowledged by experts to be the world's best Honeybee exhibition. It is an all weather attraction and is open daily from 9am-6pm from Easter-October.

A visit to ARLINGTON COURT should always be on your agenda when you are in this part of the country. Just 7 miles north east of Barnstaple, it will always give the visitor intense pleasure. It is by no means the most prepossessing of houses, quite severe in fact, and its exterior will certainly not prepare you for the amazing Victorian clutter inside; collections of all manner of articles, gathered together by the last occupant, Miss Rosalie Chichester, who lived here for 84 years before her death in 1949. Miss Chichester was an extraordinary woman who travelled the world. She struggled to keep Arlington going - her father had been a spendthrift and left her with debts which would have terrified most people and sent them scurrying to the Bankruptcy Courts. Not this courageous lady however. Her determination to hold on to Arlington never wavered; it meant that the estate was neglected however and when the National Trust took it over major restoration was needed and fortunately has been carried out splendidly. The grounds are a joy; there is an excellent exhibition of carriages. The house has been sorted out but not denuded of Miss Rosalie's treasures. I love the rather angry looking red amber elephant from China which stands in pride of place in the White Drawing Room. Her passionate devotion to all things living, whether plants or creatures, led her to allow her parrots to fly free in the house, causing irreparable damage to the curtains! On the first floor landing you can see a watercolour of her favourite parrot, Polly. The Jacob sheep and Shetland ponies in the park today are descendants of those she established as part of a wildlife refuge.

My time on Exmoor is over for this book. It is somewhere I never forget and somewhere to which I will always return for so many reasons, all of them pleasureable..

THE STAG HUNTERS HOTEL

Brendon, Lynton,
North Devon

Hotel & Public House

Tel: (05987) 222
Fax: (05987) 352

This wonderful part of North Devon, on the edge of the Exmoor National Park has inspired writers for generations. R.D. Blackmore with the immortal Lorna Doone and today a new book, Watersmeet, features the hotel.

The Stag Hunters Hotel is situated in the Doone Valley, the river flows past its doors. There are so many good reasons for visiting here whether it is just to enjoy the local ales including Staghunter's Real Ale, the excellence of the imaginative food, or to stay in one of the twelve en-suite bedrooms, giving one an opportunity to explore this spectacular area, sometimes gentle, more often awesome but always beautiful. Paul and Paddy Green, Gini Thomas and Glenn Phillips are the proprietors of this establishment which must surely please everyone who enters its portals. These four, experienced people, go out of their way to ensure that everyone is a welcome guest and that all their requirements are met.

Special diets present no problem, children are welcome, with highchairs and cots provided. Pets, including horses, are also welcomed in the scheme of things. The Bar provides a range of local dishes with specialities including venison and rabbit. The Restaurant is for residents only unless you have given twenty four hours notice - well worthwhile doing if you like good food and enjoy wines from all over the world. A simple pleasure like enjoying a beer in the garden by the river or strolling amongst the five acres of paddocks surrounded by wonderful countryside, is enough to make a visit here worthwhile.

USEFUL INFORMATION

OPEN: 11-11pm. Bar meals: 12-9.30pm
Closed winter 3-5pm
CHILDREN: Yes. Highchairs & cots
provided
CREDIT CARDS: Visa/Access/Diners/
Amex
LICENSED: Full On Licence
ACCOMMODATION: 12 en-suite
- 2 with four-posters

RESTAURANT: Residents only or
24 hour notice
BAR FOOD: Local dishes, venison &
rabbit
VEGETARIAN: Good selection
DISABLED ACCESS: Level entrance
GARDEN: Large lawn. Beer Garden by
river. 5 acres paddocks

THE CARNARVON ARMS HOTEL

Country House Hotel

Dulverton,
Somerset.

Tel: (0398) 23302
Fax: (0398) 24022

Just in Somerset, with Devon literally around the corner, one and a half miles from the picturesque village of Dulverton, the Carnarvon Arms stands guard at one of the approaches to Exmoor National Park. It is here that Mrs Toni Jones, with the support of her family and very loyal staff owns and runs one of the largest country hotels in this part of the world. It is definitely a sporting establishment with five and a half miles of fishing on the River Exe and River Barle. Shooting is available and very popular, stables are there for those wishing to bring their horses. The tennis courts are in excellent condition, and the outdoor heated swimming pool is wonderful in summer.

It is only a short drive to reach the wild beauty of Exmoor, a sudden transition from sheltered, wooded combs to springy clumps of heather, brilliant gorse, beautiful beech hedges, ferns, bracken and trees bent by the winds of centuries. Rare birds are to be seen; butterflies, flowers and plants, sheep and the endearing Exmoor ponies, even the elusive red deer. The lounges with open fires, are furnished with many fine antiques.

The 25 attractively decorated bedrooms, almost all with private bathrooms, include two rooms on the ground floor offering modest aids for the less able. The restaurant offers well balanced menus accompanied by fine wines. The less formal Buttery Bar is proud of its reputation. The Clock Tower complex has two large interconnecting rooms and an open-fronted barn which, with the attractive Clock Tower building forms an enclosed and sheltered courtyard. Ideal for conferences and wonderful for wedding receptions.

USEFUL INFORMATION

OPEN: All Year
CHILDREN: Welcome - and dogs
CREDIT CARDS: Access/Visa/Switch/ Connect
LICENSED: Full On Licence
ACCOMMODATION: 25 rooms, mainly with private bathrooms

RESTAURANT: Open to non-residents & a Buttery Bar
BAR FOOD: Wide range
VEGETARIAN: Always available in Restaurant and Bar
DISABLED ACCESS: Yes, also to accommodation
GARDEN: 50 acres, large gardens, outdoor heated swimming pool

TARR FARM

Tarr Steps, Dulverton,
Somerset.

Tel: (064) 385383

Tea Rooms, Restaurant, Gift Shop

Tarr Farm has withstood the elements for around 600 years. It is all slate and stone walls with slate mushrooms - the name James Harrison, the owner gives to the tables that stand outside on the grass! What a fascinating number of people it must have seen through the ages; some of whom will have sought shelter in the bleak winters from snow and flood. Today the visitors reach Tarr Farm far more readily, it stands on a hill overlooking the steps and down to the river, chortling away as it leaps and dances over the stones. The garden is a sun trap and a wonderful place in which to sample some of the farm's home-cooking.

Everything at Tarr Farm is home-cooked. It is traditional cooking with the delectable steak and kidney pie probably one of the favourite dishes on the menu. If you ask for a Ploughmans you will be presented with crisp bread, rich butter, pickles, a salad garnish and a huge hunk of cheese or slices of home-cooked ham. Locally made ice cream brings people from all over the place to savour its delicious and refreshing flavours. Lunch can be enriched with wine or a drink if you wish. The little gift shop is full of quite inexpensive gifts, there are books to tempt the browser and much information on Exmoor and Tarr Steps in particular.

Given 24 hours notice Tarr farm will cope with evening meals and also for parties who can select their own menu. Frequently people come to celebrate special occasions and groups also find it a good meeting place.

USEFUL INFORMATION

OPEN: 11am-5.30pm, 7 days a week. Evenings if reserved
CHILDREN: Welcome
CREDIT CARDS: None taken
LICENSED: Restaurant
ACCOMMODATION: Not applicable

RESTAURANT: From coffee to Licensed meals
BAR FOOD: Snacks available
VEGETARIAN: Always a selection
DISABLED ACCESS: Yes. Own car-park
GARDEN: Lovely grassed area with seating

THE TEA SHOPPE

Restaurant

High Street,
Dunster, Somerset.

Tel: (0643) 821304

Before you even reach this pretty building, emblazoned with hanging baskets and tubs during the summer, you will see passers-by stopping just to admire The Tea Shoppe. They should never pass by unless they want to miss a piece of old fashioned hospitality and delicious food. Rightly starred by Egon Ronay, recommended by Les Routiers and 'Out to Eat' plus an accolade from the Tea Council, Norman and Pam Goldsack, the proud owners, provide everything that one dreams of in a Tea Shoppe.

The Goldsacks have been here for six years and to her delight Pam found an Aga already installed. Since then she and the Aga have become well acquainted with each other and as she produces home-baked cakes, lunches and afternoon teas, she will tell you that some dishes would not be the same unless the Aga was used. Her Bramley Apple cake is just one instance. Every day a Specials board in the Shoppe tells you what the Specials of the day will be. If you are fortunate you will be there on a day when her Somerset Savoury Pudding is available. This is a recipe of her own which includes smoked sausage and bacon, bread, mushrooms and onions. It is fabulous. There is always a sumptuous selection of home-made cakes and puddings, including West Country Treacle Tart, another great favourite. You will not find a deep fryer here! Everything is produced on the premises, using local produce whenever possible and certainly nothing that is frozen. Please do not pass by The Tea Shoppe.

USEFUL INFORMATION

OPEN: Mar-Oct: 7 days a week 10-5pm
Nov & Dec: Weekends only
CHILDREN: Welcome
CREDIT CARDS: Access/Visa
LICENSED: Restaurant
ACCOMMODATION: Not applicable

RESTAURANT: Everything home-cooked
BAR FOOD: Not applicable
VEGETARIAN: Always available
DISABLED ACCESS: Level entrance
GARDEN: No

THE CORNER HOUSE

Riverside Road,
Lynmouth, North Devon.

Restaurant & Riverside Tea Gardens

Tel: (0598) 53300

This is an almost idyllic situation. The Corner House sits at the meeting of the East and West Lyn where Exmoor joins the sea and the Restaurant looks up into the Watersmeet Valley, the property of the National Trust. The house is charming and absolutely covered in Wisteria. One of the great pleasures is being able to sit on the terrace immediately alongside the river. There can hardly be a more tranquil place in Lynmouth on a sunny summer's day. The Corner House would be instantly recognisable by its distinctive black and white umbrellas! All along the outside wall flower beds, ablaze with colour, delight the eye.

It takes a very assured owner to run an open kitchen but Bob and Penny Whitwell are totally at ease with theirs. In fact the banter that goes back and forth between the kitchen and restaurant is part of the pleasure of being there. It is an immaculate kitchen and a delight to see how beautifully the food is prepared. The menu offers good food, with substantial portions at a very reasonable price. Steak is the speciality of the house using quality meat from the local butcher. Children are important people here and have their own menu. In the evening, when the busy day is calming down, the peaceful ambience of Lynmouth pervades the atmosphere in the restaurant, and one can relax and enjoy an intimate dinner for two.

The happy, overall atmosphere of the Corner House extends to those who stay a night or two in one of the three letting rooms. These spacious, light, tastefully furnished rooms overlooking the sea or the river, offer the traveller a quiet and comfortable respite. Appreciation from the guests can be seen in the Visitor's Book. The Corner House is a find.

USEFUL INFORMATION

OPEN: March until the end of Ocotber 8.30am until late

CHILDREN: Welcome, own menu

CREDIT CARDS: Yes

LICENSED: Restaurant

ACCOMMODATION: 3 rooms. en-suite available. AA recommended. Parking for residents

RESTAURANT: Good food, steaks a speciality

BAR FOOD: Snacks available from Coffee Shop

VEGETARIAN: Always 3 dishes

DISABLED ACCESS: Limited. Assistance available

GARDEN: Terrace seating overlooking river

THE SPINNING WHEEL

Restaurant

12 Lymouth Street,
Lynmouth, North Devon.

Tel: (0598) 53686

Everything about Lynton is picturesque and The Spinning Wheel is no exception. Whether you enter from the traffic free precinct at the pretty garden entrance, or from the riverside road, close to the harbour and Manor grounds you will find a friendly, family-run restaurant where the emphasis is on good meals at sensible prices, served throughout the day.

Here you can have coffee, lunches, cream teas, high teas and dine at night, all in the pleasant atmosphere of either the intimate 'Cottage' or the main dining room. The lovely courtyard seating area is a mecca for people in summer. Somewhere to sit, relax, enjoy the surroundings and relish the excellent food and drink. The menu offers something to please everyone from snack meals to succulent roast beef served on Sundays with a light Yorkshire pudding and a selection of fresh vegetables. In the afternoons the speciality is the cream tea with freshly baked scones, thick strawberry jam and clotted cream. Careful thought has been given to the needs of children who have their own menu. The service is always good but they do keep a watchful eye out for parents with small children making sure that they get fairly immediate attention - something for which mothers are always grateful.

At night the atmosphere changes. It is still as friendly but with the hustle and bustle of the day over The Spinning Wheel becomes somewhere in which you can enjoy a leisurely drink while you are waiting for your meal. It is essentially relaxed at this time.

USEFUL INFORMATION

OPEN: 10am - late in season. Closed Jan
CHILDREN: Welcome
CREDIT CARDS: Mastercard/Visa
LICENSED: Restaurant
ACCOMMODATION: Not applicable

RESTAURANT: Traditional, good value
BAR FOOD: Snack menu available
VEGETARIAN: Available on request
DISABLED ACCESS: Small step/step
Double doors riverside entrance
GARDEN: Courtyard with seating

HEWITTS COUNTRY HOUSE HOTEL

Country House Hotel & Restaurant

The Hoe, North Walk,
Lynton, North Devon.

Tel: (0598) 52293
Fax: (0598) 52489

Captivated by the view from North Walk, Sir Thomas Hewitt determined to please his much loved fiance by building themselves a country house there; the exact spot was chosen by tossing a stone over the edge. Work began in the 1860's and resulted in one of the West Country's loveliest homes where the Hewitt's spent many happy times. Indeed, together with George Newnes the publisher, Sir Thomas was involved in the construction of the world famous water driven cliff railway which connects Lynton with the picturesque harbour village of Lynmouth some 500 feet below.

These days the Hewitts' personal railway halt no longer operates but little else has changed and the house is still surrounded by private woodland which flanks the sea. It has nine, light, airy bedrooms with all the modern facilities expected of a highly rated hotel. However this is not at the expense of its traditional beauty, and the original wood panelled hall with its minstrels gallery and lovely stained glass windows remain to enchant each new visitor and although impressive, Hewitt's is not intimidating. Personally run, the resident owners soon persuade guests to unwind in front of one of the log fires or relax on the terrace and enjoy those same breathtaking views of the Bristol Channel that so enchanted Sir Thomas and his wife.

The cuisine at Hewitt's is excellent and the Hoe Restaurant is widely acclaimed as one of the best in the area and is featured in many relevant guides. Both table d'hote and a la carte menus are available and dishes are freshly prepared to order. Gourmet weekends are held during winter months. The hotel is open for coffees, teas and snacks during the day.

USEFUL INFORMATION

OPEN: All year. Open to non residents
CHILDREN: Yes. Special evening meal from 6-7pm
CREDIT CARDS: Visa/Access
LICENSED: Restaurant
ACCOMMODATION: 8 dbls, 2 sgls 4 twn. All private bathrooms. ETB 4 Crowns Highly Commended, AA** Red Rosette for Restaurant. Egon Ronay & Ashley Courtenay recommended

RESTAURANT: Continental in style, imaginative & varied
BAR FOOD: Tea, coffee, snacks daytime
VEGETARIAN: On request
DISABLED ACCESS: Not suitable
GARDEN: 150 ft Sun Terrace, 27 acres wooded hillside.

41

THE ROYAL OAK OF LUXBOROUGH

Inn & Restaurant

Luxborough,
Nr Dunster, Somerset.

Tel: (0984) 40319

The Royal Oak of Luxborough is set deep in the folds of the Brendon Hills, within the beautiful Exmoor National Park. To find it you will need to follow the winding lanes sign-posted from Dunster. Your journey will be rewarded by this truly rustic rural inn in which no piped music or fruit machines have been allowed to set foot. All rooms have flagstone, cobbled or boarded floors, low beams, old kitchen tables and hardly a pair of matching chairs. It is an undoubted gem.

Reputed to have been built in the 14th century, it has that wonderful smell of age, not of decay but of logs burning over the centuries and emitting that tantalising scent that lingers long after the logs have gone and only the ash remains. This is somewhere that it would be a joy to visit even if it did not have a great reputation for good food and beer. Robin and Helen Stamp have been here for six years during which time they have been almost overwhelmed by the accolades that have been thrust upon them by Egon Ronay, the Good Beer Guide to mention but a few.

Food is available 7 days a week and in amongst the traditional English fare you will find a lot of game, shot locally. Venison Casserole and Rabbit Pie are two favourite dishes. Everything is home-cooked and the week is brought to a triumphal end with the advent of a wonderful Sunday lunch. The garden at the rear of the pub is surrounded by wild flowers and an old rose bush which produces the huge, old fashioned and scented blooms. A walk in the garden before breakfast, if you are staying here in one of the two comfortable bedrooms, makes you feel that all is right with your world and The Royal Oak of Luxborough in particular.

USEFUL INFORMATION

OPEN: Mon-Sat: 11-2.30pm & 6-11pm
Sun: 12-3pm & 7-10.30pm
CHILDREN: Welcome
CREDIT CARDS: None taken
LICENSED: Full On Licence
ACCOMMODATION: 2 double not
en-suite

RESTAURANT: Traditional English fare including game plus more elaborate sauced dishes
BAR FOOD: Wide range, interesting dishes
VEGETARIAN: Dishes always available
DISABLED ACCESS: No
GARDEN: Lovely garden

PERITON PARK

Country House Hotel

Middlecombe,
Nr Minehead, West Somerset.

Tel: (0643) 706885
Fax: (0643) 706885

Periton Park is the family home of the owners whose love of the house and its surroundings is reflected in the care and hospitality they show to all who stay with them. Nestling in its own woodland and gardens, with colourful rhododendrons lining the drive and frequently the sight of rabbits and deer on the lawns in the morning, this house, built in 1875 as a handsome country residence, retains all the character and elegance of the Victorian era with spacious and light rooms. Although fully centrally heated, there is a log fire in the drawing room for the cooler months around which guests may relax with a book or an aperitif. The eight large bedrooms all have en-suite facilities, some are non-smoking rooms and there is one on the ground floor that has French windows leading directly to the garden. Each room is delightful and individual.

The panelled dining room looks over the garden and here you may take a leisurely breakfast or dine by candlelight at night - a perfect setting to enjoy the superb selection of original dishes created by the chef in the country house style that changes with the seasons. Fresh fish, meat, game and delicately cooked vegetables, as well as vegetarian dishes feature prominently on the menu. The wine list reflects a selection from around the world including specially selected wines from lesser known regions. The study on the ground floor can accommodate up to 14 in boardroom style for meetings, courses or for a private function. A wonderful base for the sports minded and for all those wanting to explore this truly special part of England.

USEFUL INFORMATION

OPEN: All year & to non-residents
CHILDREN: Welcome
CREDIT CARDS: Visa/Access/Amex
LICENSED: Residential & Restaurant
ACCOMMODATION: 8 large en-suite

RESTAURANT: Country house style, seasonal changes
BAR FOOD: Yes
VEGETARIAN: Several choices
DISABLED ACCESS: Yes
GARDEN: Woodland & gardens

AVILL HOUSE

Guest House

12 Townsend Road,
Minehead, Somerset.

Tel: (0643) 704370

Built at the turn of the century no one could miss Avill House with its stunning and colourful red and white display of hanging baskets. These baskets have become the trademark of this very pleasant guest house which is big enough to call itself a hotel. Quinton and Sandy Pooley run the house having taken over from Sandy's parents who came here in 1977. It has a great family atmosphere and is welcoming and relaxed from the moment you arrive. In the spacious lounge there is a bar where you can sit and enjoy a drink whilst the children play in a room of their own, well equipped with games of all kinds. This is a strictly non-smoking room.

Every bedroom has been prettily decorated with matching peach or rose white lampshades, bedspreads and curtains. There are nine altogether with three en-suite. Every room has colour TV and tea/coffee making facilities. One of the things that strikes one about Avill House is its air of well being and cleanliness; it sparkles. Big English breakfasts are served every morning for those who wish it and for those who prefer, a Continental breakfast is available.

In the evenings the dining room which is for residents only, serves good traditional food with very generous portions and an ever changing menu. You will never leave the table hungry at Avill house.

From Minehead there are so many places to visit. You will find the Pooleys more than willing to help you sort out where you want to go. Exmoor is close by and so are the many good beaches.

USEFUL INFORMATION

OPEN: All year
CHILDREN: Welcome and catered for
CREDIT CARDS: None taken
LICENSED: Residential
ACCOMMODATION: 9 rooms, 3 en-suite
   ETB: 2 Crowns, RAC: Acclaimed,
   AA: 3 Q's

RESTAURANT: Traditional meals.
   Residents only
BAR FOOD: Not applicable
VEGETARIAN: On request
DISABLED ACCESS: No, but welcome
GARDEN: No

THE OLD SHIP AGROUND

Quay Street, Minehead,
Somerset.

Tel: (0643) 702087

Public House, Hotel & Restaurant

The Old Ship Aground is one of the landmarks of Minehead and perhaps one of the few licensed premises in the country to have a church incorporated in the boundary of the pub - St Peters on the Quay. It has a super situation with extensive views across Minehead harbour and bay from the front garden, it is only 100 yards from the start of the 500 mile coastal path from Somerset to Dorset and only 5 minutes from the town centre and the West Somerset Steam Railway.

The pub is as wonderful as its situation. Tony and Sue Philips, the charming and lively owners, have an excellent staff and staying here is a refreshing experience. The five letting rooms, one of which is en-suite, are comfortably furnished; pets are allowed. There are three bars in operation during the summer months when the courtyard bar is very popular. In the winter it is the warmth and welcome in the inside two bars that act as a magnet to local people who come for the fun and conversation that abounds. The beer garden runs from the side to the front of The Old Ship Aground and overlooks the harbour. There is a full, wide ranging menu in the restaurant available 7 days a week, with a number of fresh fish dishes included as one might expect. The bar food is traditional but has something for everyone and like the restaurant provides a choice for Vegetarians.

You will always find a number of visitors from overseas here in the summer, thoroughly enjoying Minehead and the superb surrounding countryside including the majesty of Exmoor.

USEFUL INFORMATION

OPEN: April-Oct: 11-11pm,
   Nov-Mar: 11-3pm & 5-11pm
CHILDREN: Welcome if well behaved
CREDIT CARDS: None at present
LICENSED: Full On Licence
ACCOMMODATION: 5 rooms, 1 en-suite

RESTAURANT: Extensive choice
BAR FOOD: Wide range snacks,
   Roast lunches etc
VEGETARIAN: Always 5 dishes
DISABLED ACCESS: Level entrance
GARDEN: Beer Garden at side & front

COMBE SYDENHAM COUNTRY PARK

Historic Estate & Food Supplier

Monksilver,
Taunton, Somerset.

Tel: (0984) 56284

This is undoubtedly one of the most interesting attractions in Somerset. Combe Sydenham Country Park nestles in a hidden Exmoor valley, providing you with an opportunity to see history restored and nature revived. It was 40 years ago that the Theed family set out on their quest to restore the estate which is at last returning to self sufficiency through forestry, trout farming and estate produced delicacies. A day spent here is hardly enough to take everything in. There are 500 acres of beautiful Country Park teeming with flora and fauna, in which you may glimpse the shy fallow deer in the Deer Park. Hidden away you will find the deserted hamlet of Goodley, thought to have been decimated by the Black Death in 1348. You will be provided with a map which shows you all the woodland paths and you are requested to keep your dog on a lead. Children are always fascinated when they are introduced to the Magic Story Trails, which give a close view of nature while strolling through the 'Alice in Wonderland' and 'Ancient Trail of Trees' Story Trails.

You can learn Trout fishing on the beginners' lake, or fish the more advanced lake, all tackle supplied. You may also buy Somerset rainbow trout, oak smoked trout and pate made using a family recipe from Combe Sydenham. There is a remarkable Elizabethan courtroom, a restored medieval corn mill in production, milling their own stone ground flour which they use to produce additive-free bread in the on-site bakery.

Everywhere is magical from the fascinating connection between Sir Francis Drake and Combe Sydenham to the renowned home-produce from the shop and tea room which serves delicious lunches and teas. Combe Sydenham is an unforgettable experience.

USEFUL INFORMATION

OPEN: One week before Easter until end October: Sun-Fri: 10-5pm, Courtrooms & Gardens: Mon-Fri, 11-4pm
CHILDREN: Welcome - School parties by arrangement
CREDIT CARDS: None taken
LICENSED: Not applicable
ACCOMMODATION: Not applicable

RESTAURANT: Tea Rooms serving lunches and teas
BAR FOOD: Not applicable
VEGETARIAN: Always available
DISABLED ACCESS: Moderate access
GARDEN: Wonderful gardens & 500 acres of country park

THE NOTLEY ARMS
Inn

Monksilver,
Taunton, Somerset.

Tel: (0984) 56217

This is a country inn which has won deserved acclaim and has a star rating in the Good Food Guide and in Egon Ronay. Located in the small village of Monksilver, it is surrounded by fields of red sandstone soil. There is an interesting story told about Sir Francis Drake here. He married Elizabeth Sydenham in the church down the road at Stogumber but not before she had almost married another. Sir Francis had spent too long away from his beautiful heiress and she felt aggrieved. Agreeing to marry another, she arrived at the church for her wedding, and as she was about to enter a cannon ball came hurtling out of the sky and landed at her feet. Elizabeth realised it had come from Drake, she abandoned her fiance and ran home to await the arrival of the swashbuckling Sir Francis. You will certainly hear this story from the landlord Alastair Cade who with his wife Sarah runs this delightful hostelry.

It is the charming simplicity of The Notley Arms which makes it so special. The L-shaped bar is furnished with plain wooden furniture and there are twin wood-burning stoves. The walls are covered with the works of local artists, some of them quite exceptional. The Family room is cheery - not always the case at other establishments, and the tables are candlelit at night.

Notley Arms is renowned for its food, usually top notch traditional fare but always with just that something extra. This is why you will never see the pub empty; people come from long distances just to enjoy everything about it, the trim cottage garden with a stream, the general ambience, but probably most of all because of the genuine warmth of the welcome.

USEFUL INFORMATION

OPEN: Mon-Sat: 11.30-2.30pm & 6.30-11pm
    Sun: 12-2.30pm & 7-10.30pm
CHILDREN: Welcome. Family room
CREDIT CARDS: None taken
LICENSED: Full On Licence
ACCOMMODATION: Not applicable

RESTAURANT: Not applicable
BAR FOOD: Interesting, traditional,
    exotic, high standard
VEGETARIAN: Always available
DISABLED ACCESS: Level entrance
GARDEN: Exceptional, fenced stream
    secluded

THE COUNTRYMAN
Restaurant

High Street,
Porlock, Somerset.

Tel: (0643) 862241

It is the tantalising smell of freshly ground coffee that might be your first introduction to The Countryman, a busy restaurant and take away right in the centre of this pretty Exmoor coastal village. Glynn and Karen Bass, the owners, get their coffee from a well known local importer and there is nothing better than a cup after sampling the menu.

The food is traditional English with an emphasis on some West Country favourites such as Somerset Chicken, a dish of tender chicken cooked with apples in cider. Home-made pies are a speciality of the house as well as the original and delicious soups cooked by Glynn Bass. It is he who is responsible for all the cooking including the super home-made cakes and scones served in the afternoons. Service with a smile is something that Karen expects from her experienced waiting staff. Everyone is treated in a friendly manner, the orders are taken promptly and attention is paid immediately to families with young children. It is something that parents appreciate enormously; there is nothing more difficult than trying to keep children peaceful whilst they are waiting for their meal or a drink. Dinner is served every evening from 6.30-9.30pm and there is a well chosen wine list which includes five house wines at reasonable prices. The take-away service offers fish and chips, The Countryman's own burgers, local ice cream and drinks.

Originally built as a Methodist Chapel this restaurant has a lot of character. The interior is mainly wooden beams and panelling with a large wood burner next to the bar area. Certainly a different use for the chapel but a very inspired and happy one.

USEFUL INFORMATION

OPEN: Rest: 12-5pm, 6.30-9.30pm.
Take-away 10am-9pm
CHILDREN: High chairs, menu, baby
food, changing area
CREDIT CARDS: Access/Visa
LICENSED: Restaurant
ACCOMMODATION: Not applicable

RESTAURANT: Home-cooked English
food
BAR FOOD: Not applicable
VEGETARIAN: 4-5 dishes
DISABLED ACCESS: Level entrance
GARDEN: No

LOWERBOURNE HOUSE

High Street, Porlock,
Somerset.

Art & Bookshop with Tearoom

Tel: (0643) 862948
Fax: (0643) 862948

The Tea Room of Lowerbourne House is quite possible to miss even though it is in the High Street of the pretty village of Porlock. This is because from the outside you see a book and art shop - in fact once inside, you will find the Tea Room, a place of enchantment, tucked away behind all this, almost as a retreat.

The shop itself has an amazing assortment of art supplies, beautiful stationary, candles, chocolates, and much more, there are two rooms devoted to books, where in peace and quiet you may browse amongst a splendid collection including many excellent books on Exmoor. The second room is devoted to children's books; books to stimulate the young mind in a room in which they are encouraged to dip into the volumes small and large. The owners Pam and Mike Williams were both teachers and this is quite apparent in the manner in which they make young customers feel at home.

When you step into the Tea Room you see the open pine kitchen which lends an additional facet to the already excellent atmosphere. The owners stress that it is foremost a Tea Room, with light, wholesome lunches based simply on quiches, salads and cheese. They do not state that it is a vegetarian establishment, nonetheless you will not find meat on the menu. The delicious home-made cakes, cream teas or toasted muffins, served with locally blended tea or an excellent coffee are available all day. You are invited to sit at natural wood tables and it feels as though you have stepped into a friend's kitchen. If you have children at the table with you they will be offered crayons and paper with the object of letting their parents enjoy their meal in peace!

USEFUL INFORMATION

OPEN: Tea Rooms, Mon-Sat: 10-5pm, Sundays in season.Shop: 9am until sunset
CHILDREN: Particularly welcome
CREDIT CARDS: Visa/Master/Connect
LICENSED: Not licenced
ACCOMMODATION: Not applicable

RESTAURANT: Tea Rooms with wholesome food
BAR FOOD: Not applicable
VEGETARIAN: Yes, light lunches
DISABLED ACCESS: Not really but assistance given
GARDEN: No

PIGGY IN THE MIDDLE

*Restaurant with Seafood
as a Speciality*

High Street,
Porlock, Somerset.

Tel: (0643) 862647

Porlock is famous for being the gateway to Exmoor and also notorious for the dreaded, Porlock Hill. It is nonetheless a delightful and very quaint village. Right in the centre of the village is Piggy in the Middle. This enchanting restaurant carries out the name throughout the building. There are Piggy menus, bookends, teapots, ceramic pigs, cuddly toy pigs and even one that walks and oynks! The brainchild of Paul Barrs who runs it with Zoe, his wife, who have been here six years now. It was a boot and shoemakers about 100 years ago and since then has been a series of indifferent tearooms. All that has changed; now it is the place to be.

The restaurant has 32 covers which makes it possible for Paul and Zoe to do all the cooking themselves - something they excel at. It is also intimate, candlelit and friendly. The service is fast, efficient and frequently amusing because of the entertaining, quickwitted staff. During the season you can breakfast here from 9am, follow this with morning coffee, and a light lunch. Piggy's closes in the afternoon from 2-7pm reopening for the evening when Paul's gifted approach to his task becomes even more apparent. He specialises in fresh seafood and local game. You may well be offered Moules Mariniere, fresh lobster, dressed crab or venison steaks. The majority of the dishes are very reasonably priced. With your meal you may choose a good wine from the comprehensive list. Paul Barrs used to run a 15th century inn in Sussex with a reputation for fine food; he has certainly repeated that successful formula here.

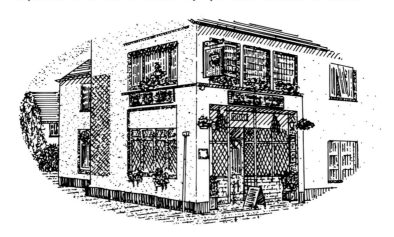

USEFUL INFORMATION

OPEN: In season 9-2pm & 7-11pm
  Winter: 12-2pm & 7-11pm.
  Closed all Jan & Feb
CHILDREN: Welcome with well
  behaved parents
CREDIT CARDS: Visa/Master/Euro
LICENSED: Restaurant Licence
ACCOMMODATION: Not applicable

RESTAURANT: Fine food, daily specials
BAR FOOD: Not applicable
VEGETARIAN: Interesting selection
DISABLED ACCESS: Small step,
  assistance given
GARDEN: No

THE SHIP INN

High Street, Porlock,
Somerset.

Inn

Tel: (0643) 862507

When you step through the door of The Ship Inn in Porlock you are entering a hostelry which has been providing sustenance since the 13th century, and is one of the oldest on Exmoor. Full of character, low ceilings, a warm atmosphere and good beer and food, it is a perfect place to stay. The moor and the sea are both within walking distance. The genuine old bar with up to four Real Ales is the haunt of locals as well as the many others who have sought this pub out over the years. Apart from adding modern necessities little has changed; the stone floors are uneven with age, the roaring log fires send out a welcoming warmth in winter and the sheer thickness of the old stone walls keeps the building cool in summer.

You will find no pipe music here. It is a place for fun and conversation. The eleven bedrooms, all centrally heated are mainly en-suite. All of them have colour television and tea making facilities. Children are welcome - half price accommodation is offered when sharing parents' bedroom. There is a games room with darts and pool, a beer garden and an area for children with swings and climbing frame. Dogs are most welcome and arrangements can be made for hunting with three local packs, pony trekking, sea and fly fishing, tennis and golf. There are good bar snacks with Specials of the day and an excellent dinner menu at a set price.

USEFUL INFORMATION

OPEN: Normal opening hours
CHILDREN: Welcome. Play area
CREDIT CARDS: Mastercard/Visa
LICENSED: Full On
ACCOMMODATION: 11 bedrooms,
   mainly en-suite

RESTAURANT: Traditional dishes
BAR FOOD: Wide range. Daily specials
VEGETARIAN: Always something
DISABLED ACCESS: No
GARDEN: Yes. Courtyard seating, play
   area

THE SIMONSBATH HOUSE HOTEL

Hotel & Boeveys Restaurant

Simonsbath,
Exmoor, Somerset.

Tel: (064383) 259

Inside the stout walls of this 300 years old house people have been waking up in the mornings knowing that it will be to the sounds of the real countryside. The first was James Boevey, a wily London merchant of Dutch Huguenot extraction, who as Warden of the Forest of Exmoor in 1654, chose a spot where all the tracks across the moor appeared to meet to build this fine house.

Many people famous, not so famous and sometimes infamous have enjoyed the hospitality of Simonsbath House in the ensuing years and there will be few who have not enjoyed the experience. Simonsbath means lots of things to lots of people. You can do everything, but you do not have to do anything. It is your holiday and the owners just want you to enjoy it. You can ride through the Forest to the top of Dunkery Beacon - Exmoor's highest point and if the day is clear see over a range of 150 miles to the Malvern Hills, Brown Willy on Bodmin Moor in Cornwall, from the Brecon Beacons in Wales to the rolling downs of Dorset. There are woodland walks, picturesque thatched inns, serious walking. This is the country of wild Red Deer, the last surviving herds in England, the game bird, the rainbow trout and the salmon.

When you have had your fill of so much beauty, Simonsbath House awaits you with an afternoon tea of home-made scones, strawberry jam and clotted cream. Boeveys restaurant, a barn conversion, is a completely separate building offering good food all day long. There are 3 self-catering apartments across from the restaurant. Simonsbath House offers so much that is to be enjoyed.

USEFUL INFORMATION

OPEN: Hotel closed Dec & Jan.
  Boeveys Restaurant is seasonal
CHILDREN: Welcome over 10 years
CREDIT CARDS: Access/Visa/Amex/
  Diners
LICENSED: Restaurant & Residential
ACCOMMODATION: 7 en-suite rooms

RESTAURANT: House residents only
BAR FOOD: Not in hotel. Boeveys has
  a wide range
VEGETARIAN: On request in hotel.
  Boeveys has vegetarian menu
DISABLED ACCESS: No
GARDEN: One acre

THE WEST SOMERSET HOTEL
Inn

Swain Street,
Watchet, Somerset.

Tel: (0984) 634434

Watchet with its small harbour attracts many visitors. It is a small friendly place and nowhere is more welcoming than The West Somerset Hotel in Swain Street. In recent years it has been beautifully refurbished and with its pretty courtyard, it is an ideal place for anyone wanting to stay or just have a meal and a drink. The hotel has 13 bedrooms which are quite large, very comfortable and although only some of them are en-suite, every one has TV and that boon, a teas-maid.

The pub is cricket mad! All the regulars, and there are many, are avid followers of local, county and English teams but they are equally welcoming to Australian cricketers who come and stay here on cricketing tours. You can imagine the cheerful ribbing and banter that goes on when they are in the bar. The Bar has a huge video/TV Screen which allows the enthusiasts to watch whilst they are enjoying their pints. The West Somerset Hotel is equally welcoming to people who do not have the same enthusiasm for sport.

Good food is another hallmark of the inn. The Steak menu offers excellent value and steaks cooked to your special taste. For those who like steak accompanied by a sauce, there are three choices. Starters and snacks are part of the menu as well as fish. You can enjoy ham and eggs, Cook's special curry or a roast of the day. There are several choices for vegetarians and a separate children's menu. Cliff and Vicky Barber are both down to earth, welcoming folk who will make sure you enjoy your visit.

USEFUL INFORMATION

OPEN: All year Mon-Sat: 11-11pm,
   Sun: 12-3pm & 7-10.30pm
CHILDREN: Welcome
CREDIT CARDS: Access/Visa
LICENSED: Full On
ACCOMMODATION: 13 rooms, mainly
   en-suite

RESTAURANT: Not applicable
BAR FOOD: Wide range, daily specials
VEGETARIAN: Always several dishes
DISABLED ACCESS: Level entrance.
   Not accommodation
GARDEN: Courtyard with flowers

53

WEST PORLOCK HOUSE

Country House Hotel

West Porlock,
Nr Minehead, Somerset.

Tel: (0643) 862880

Taking for granted that this excellent small country house hotel has attended to all your needs superbly during your stay, it is very possible that the memories of your visit will always be triggered by the outstanding beauty of the gardens and the silence, broken only by the call of the odd pheasant or two. All manner of unusual trees and plants abound in the garden which boasts perhaps the tallest Magnolia in England. The roses are superb and waft abroad that wonderful, unmistakable scent. Within the house there are flowers everywhere. The tables in the elegant dining room have small pretty vases filled with fragrant blooms.

West Porlock House belongs to Henry and Margery Dyer who, after years spent in Africa, bought the house and run it with their daughter Jane, much as they would a private residence and the result is a wonderfully friendly atmosphere. The house has many happy reminders of their years abroad and provides their guests with endless topics of conversation.

The four spacious bedrooms, one of which is en-suite, although the other three have their own private bathrooms close by, all have beautiful views. In addition there is one large family room. Delicious home-cooked meals using local produce are available for residents only every evening except Tuesday and Wednesday. Breakfast is a sumptuous repast with local free range eggs. It is a joy to stay here for anyone but it must be a special treat for someone who is a keen gardener. The Dyers, with the help of their daughter and their part time gardener Norman, do all the gardening themselves - no light task with two and a half acres to tend.

USEFUL INFORMATION

OPEN: All year except possibly Dec & Jan
CHILDREN: Older children welcome
CREDIT CARDS: None taken
LICENSED: Residential
ACCOMMODATION: 4 rooms, 1 en-suite
   1 family room

RESTAURANT: Dining for residents
BAR FOOD: Not applicable
VEGETARIAN: yes if notice if given
DISABLED ACCESS: No
GARDEN: Spectacular 5 acres

THE REST AND BE THANKFUL

Public House

Wheddon Cross,
Minehead, Somerset.

Tel: (0634) 841222

This interesting village pub acquired its name because in the days of coaching, horses had to pull the heavily laden coaches up the very steep hill on the Minehead to Tiverton Road. When they arrived at the crest of the hill the inn was there and coachman, passengers and horses could rest and be thankful that the summit had been achieved. The pub lives up to its name today although not for the same reason. Now it is because locals and visitors come here to a restful atmosphere and are thankful for the hospitality shown by the welcoming landlord, Mr Weaver.

This is a pub in which you can enjoy a well kept pint of traditional beer, conversation with local people and a good meal chosen from a menu which is a mixture of English recipes with a touch of International dishes. Every day there are different, appetising Specials from which to choose. The portions are generous and the prices realistic. During the winter months a very good Sunday lunch is available. In the bar, a wide range of all types of snacks and bar meals are popular. The service is efficient and fast. This is also a pub in which you are welcome to stay in one of the three en-suite double rooms, each with its own TV, direct telephone line, mini-bar, radio alarm and tea/coffee making facilities. It is ideal for holidaymakers or for business people. There is space for functions and meetings in a room that takes 45 people comfortably.

USEFUL INFORMATION

OPEN: 9.30-3p, & 6.30-11pm Oct-Mar. Evening opening from 7pm

CHILDREN: Childrens room, restaurant, dining room

CREDIT CARDS: Master/Visa/Access/ Switch

LICENSED: Full On

ACCOMMODATION: 3 dbls, en-suite

RESTAURANT: English & International dishes

BAR FOOD: Extensive menu. Daily specials

VEGETARIAN: 3 main courses approx

DISABLED ACCESS: Level

GARDEN: Patio, tables, chairs, playing field

THE ROYAL OAK INN

Inn

Winsford, Exmoor National Park, Somerset.

Tel: (064385) 455
Fax: (064385) 388

This lovely building which has a thatch as snug as a tea cosy must be the prettiest pub on Exmoor. The walls are cream washed, high on the thatch a peacock struts, the hanging baskets vie with each other for pride of place in their colourful array. Even the setting is right; next to the village green with its little ford and packhorse bridge, it could not be bettered. You may even see a horse or two tethered outside whilst their owners quench a thirst that has been acquired riding across the moor.

Inside the ceilings are low, the oak beams unmovable this side of time, log fires, an inglenook fireplace with a fine iron fire-back. Horse brasses keep company with some fine hunting prints on the walls. Hanging on a beam over the bar are well worn pewter tankards. It is a place of ease with big, cushioned window seats and Windsor armchairs. Pottery pet cats seem to have made themselves at home everywhere. Add to this picture the other ingredients, good food, good beer, wines, company, conversation, and service, you have a true picture of this wonderful establishment.

In the restaurant the tables are set with Wedgwood and fine glassware just to add to the pleasure of dining here. Only the freshest local produce is used to prepare the English traditional dishes to a consistently high standard. Everything, from hams and pies to pates and bread, is home-cooked. Eight of the bedrooms are situated in the inn and a further six have been created in the courtyard area. Dogs can be accommodated.

USEFUL INFORMATION

OPEN: All year
CHILDREN: Welcome
CREDIT CARDS: Visa/Amex/Diners/ Access/Euro
LICENSED: Full On
ACCOMMODATION: 14 en-suite rooms RAC 3 Star with two Merit Awards and ETB 4 Crown Highly Commended

RESTAURANT: Table d'hote traditional English. Sunday lunch
BAR FOOD: Traditional & Daily Specials
VEGETARIAN: A Vegitarian menu is available
DISABLED ACCESS: Level entrance. Ground floor accommodation
GARDEN: Small

THE ROYAL OAK INN

Withypool, Exmoor National
Park, Somerset.

Residential Inn

Tel: (064383) 506/7
Fax: (064383) 659

This small village in the heart of the Exmoor National Park, on the banks of the River Barle and surrounded by open moorland where wild Red Deer and Exmoor Ponies graze, is close to many historical sites and only 10 miles from the North Devon coast. Lovely in its own right it is enhanced by the presence of the award winning Royal Oak Inn, somewhere that can best be described as a 'Residential Inn and Restaurant'. No one is quite sure about its Royal connections but it was certainly a watering hole for wool traders in the 17th century and it has many fascinating historical connections. R.D. Blackmore stayed here while he was writing the immortal 'Lorna Doone' and less than 100 years later it played host to General Eisenhower whilst he was preparing for the D Day landings. Appropriately the inn was once owned by the head of MI5 who knew, no doubt, many of the plots that were hatched over a pint of ale.

    The aim here is to give guests a memorable stay. This is achieved - how could it not be - with delightfully furnished bedrooms, welcoming bars, superb food and a heartwarming, friendly welcome from the staff. Great emphasis is placed on the quality of the food; the head chef is a man of enormous experience and imaginative talent who controls an enthusiastic and committed team determined to excel. Sophistication there may be at this level and in the furnishings and accommodation but The Royal Oak maintains its role of Country Inn from which one can pursue riding, hunting, shooting and fishing, all arranged by Mike Bradley, the owner.

USEFUL INFORMATION

OPEN: 11-2.30pm & 6-11pm
CHILDREN: Over 10. Listening service, flexible meals
CREDIT CARDS: Amex/Diners/Access/ Visa
LICENSED: Full On
ACCOMMODATION: 8 doubles, private bathrooms

RESTAURANT: English cooking, Continental bias
BAR FOOD: Various ,from fish to cheese
VEGETARIAN: Yes with changing menu
DISABLED ACCESS: Not ideal, too many steps
GARDEN: Patio for limited numbers

WESTERCLOSE COUNTRY HOUSE
Hotel & Restaurant

Withypool,
Somerset.

Tel: (064383) 302

Five minutes walk from the village, set in its own fields, Westerclose Country House has stunning views over the surrounding countryside. It was built in 1928 as a hunting lodge for the Nicholson family, producers of the well known gin. It is a wonderful place to stay either to enjoy a break or to join in the organised walking weekends in the Spring and Autumn. Bird watching is another favourite pastime for the many experienced and amateur ornithologists who have discovered the hotel. Withypool nestles in a hollow in the heart of the Exmoor National Park.

Food is one of the pleasures of the walking weekends. The group has a splendid picnic lunch, returns to the hotel for tea and scones with clotted cream. Afterwards a bath, a change of clothes and perhaps a drink before a candlelit dinner. Riding is one of the principal pastimes on Exmoor and guests are able to use the facilities of the hotel's stables for their horses on request. The hotel is open to non-residents and what better place to lunch or dine. There is a choice of table d'hote or a la carte menus. The traditional English, West Country and vegetarian dishes are prepared with skill and imagination using locally produced fresh fish, meat and game. Most vegetables, herbs and flowers are grown in the hotel's kitchen garden. There is a comprehensive wine list with wines from around the world plus some local and organic ones. Catering for those on special diets is no problem. Packed lunches and light snacks are available on request. The conservatory bar is a delight; beautiful views across the fields to Withypool Hill, and doors leading to a flagstone patio and garden. This family run hotel should not be missed.

USEFUL INFORMATION

OPEN: All year. Rest Mon, residents only
   Lunch: 12.30-2.30pm, Tea: 3.30-5pm
   Dinner: 7.30-9.15pm
CHILDREN: Welcome. chairs, cots etc
CREDIT CARDS: Access/Visa/Amex
LICENSED: Full restaurant licence
ACCOMMODATION: 10 en-suite

RESTAURANT: English & West
   Country recipes
BAR FOOD: Upon request
VEGETARIAN: Always available
DISABLED ACCESS: No. Help
   available
GARDEN: Patio with tables & chairs

THE POLTIMORE ARMS
Inn

Yarde Down,
South Molton, Devon.

Tel: ((0598) 710381

In a wonderful situation, 1,000 ft up on Exmoor, way off the beaten track yet only seven miles north of South Molton and 12 miles from Barnstaple, The Politmore Arms is a delightful inn. On a clear day the views are stunning, you can see Hartland Point and Lundy beyond it. On a summer Sunday the village cricket pitch resounds to the sounds of bowlers and batsmen. It is the ideal venue for anyone wanting to get away from the stress of everyday living.

For over 300 years The Poltimore was a packhorse staging post, and served both Royalist and parliamentary forces in the Civil War of 1642-6. It has a ghost named Charlie who may well have been in occupation since then. He is a mischievous fellow who has been known to boil a kettle and regularly moves artefacts. Ten years ago a pixie was caught in the bar in the Exmoor Pixie Hunt! Apart from the fun and the welcoming hospitality, Mike and Mella Wright are ideal inn-keepers. The well being of their customers comes first.

Mella is the chef and produces delicious meals. Her home-made turkey pie is very popular and so are the various daily specials available. The bar and the restaurant menu are quite extensive and it would be very difficult not to find something to tempt the taste buds. There is a menu for children, one for vegetarians and even vegans are specially catered for. In summer there are Barbecues in the garden under cover. If there are more than 8 of you pre-bookings are preferred.

USEFUL INFORMATION

OPEN: 11.30-2.30pm & 6-11pm.
  Sun: 12-2pm & 7-10.30pm. Food until
  9.30pm all week
CHILDREN: Garden & games room
CREDIT CARDS: None taken
LICENSED: Cotleigh Tawney Bitter.
  Full wine list
ACCOMMODATION: Not applicable

RESTAURANT: Home-made country
  fare. A la carte evenings
BAR FOOD: Wide range. Home-made &
  take away
VEGETARIAN: 3 dishes & vegan
DISABLED ACCESS: Yes
GARDEN: Yes. BBQ in Summer

The Church of St Mary Magdelene, Taunton

NORTH WEST SOMERSET

INCLUDES

"Now spurs the lated traveller apace
To gain the timely inn."

William Shakespeare

NORTH WEST SOMERSET

 It was with reluctance that I left Exmoor but almost immediately I find myself conducting a love affair of another kind with the conflicting mixture of rural and urban life that is so much part of North West Somerset. The sea is never far away with Bridgwater Bay stretching out its encompassing arms to skirt the coast of Wales.

To start my journey I decided to take a ride on the WEST SOMERSET RAILWAY from Minehead to Bishops Lydeard. This delightful steam railway chugs along through some of the prettiest scenery in Somerset and has several stops at which you may alight. I wanted to go to **Williton** *and found the time-table allowed me to spend several hours there. The main road from Taunton and the A39 come from Bridgwater round the Quantocks and meet at Williton. This is by no means one of Somerset's most attractive villages. In fact it is large and a trifle ungainly but looks are not everything. On the outskirts en-route for Watchet you will find THE MASONS ARMS, a delightful thatched pub run by an equally delightful lady, Janet Stone. It is a warm-hearted place but beware of the low beams; they are lethal to anyone who is anything above average height. As you enter the restaurant you are advised to 'Duck or Grouse'!*

THE FORESTERS ARMS in Long Street, is another excellent establishment especially for those with a love of cricket or rugby. It is frequently the base for touring teams and you can imagine the lively conversation that ensues in the bars. On the quieter side there is a charming and intimate restaurant where you will be well fed in relaxed surroundings.

The 17th-century ORCHARD MILL is worth a visit. Here you have a large restored, overshot waterwheel. I marvelled at its size and the silence of the wooden gearings inside. The mill stones are still in place and help to illustrate the way in which the mill is operated. The Museum of Victorian and Edwardian by-gones, agricultural and domestic implements, including the earliest washing machine and vacuum cleaner, is housed in the Old Mill. There are altogether over 1000 items in the museum, covering all three storeys of the building and taking you back to earlier days when only the power of the horse worked the land. The craft and gift shop are full of things to tempt you to open your purse. Many items are made locally by Somerset craftspeople. Craft demonstrations are held from time to time. At the end of your visit the Mill House Restaurant will reward you with a light lunch or a meal. You can be sure of the best in wholesome home baking, using the freshest ingredients. The Mill House is open for morning coffee, lunches and afternoon teas. Cream teas are a speciality, served in the orchard garden on fine afternoons. It is open from March until the end of October from 10am-6pm. Closed on Mondays except Bank Holidays. Also closed Tuesdays during April and October.

*The end of my train journey was **Bishops Lydeard** where the church has been the example for many others in this area with fine sets of bench ends - always a source of interest and pleasure to me. The intricate carving and the sometimes comical creatures and people, make them fascinating.*

*Having returned to Minehead to pick up my car I drove slowly back southwards again, stopping this time at **Vellow** near Stogumber, where CURDON MILL is a fine country house at the foot of the Quantock Hills. It is the most wondefully peaceful spot where the stream gurgles away contentedly in tune with the restful attitude of the house. Stay here and you will be pampered. Not only you, if you have dogs or horses there are kennels and stables for them outside where they are royally looked after. No animals are allowed in the house. Twenty years ago Daphne and Richard Criddle converted an old barn and watermill and achieved this wonderful result. They do a lot of wedding receptions very successfully, frequently putting up an enormous marquee on the lawn.*

*If you were staying here you could take a look at YARD FARM, **Kingswood** where a local artist Barry Watkin, sells prints of his paintings, as well as displaying collections by other artists. He also caters for artists painting holidays. For further information ring (0984) 56568.*

Recently opened in Stogumber is THE BEE CENTRE. I know nothing about it nor have I been able to get details but I understand it is fascinating. More to my liking are the VELLOW TEA GARDENS where on a fine day you may wander in the beautiful gardens and then enjoy a delicious cream tea on the lawn. It is worthwhile just going for the gardens alone. Owned by Ann Bryant, the telephone number is (0984) 56411 if you want any more details.

*The Quantock Hills hide many picuresque villages and not a few country houses worth seeking out. For many **Crowcombe** is the jewel in* *the crown of the Quantocks. It nestles beneath the steep, well wooded Quantock slopes. Its church has some fourteenth century remains, but most of it is Perpendicular, with a finely finished south aisle and fan-vaulted southern porch. The bench ends, dated 1534 include such diverse subjects as a mermaid and two men spearing a dragon. They are splendidly opulent. Across the road is the historic CHURCH HOUSE built in the 15th century with a graceful, open timber roof. Open from the end of May until the end of September, Monday to Friday 2.30-4.30pm.*

Cothelstone House, situated between Cothelstone and East Bagborough in the Quantocks

*Not far away, north eastward, is the hamlet of **Halsway**, dominated by HALSWAY MANOR, a historic house with some fine decorated ceilings and panelling. The prime use of the house today is as a folk music and dance centre but if it is not being used for this or for a conference, it is open to the public.*

Slightly to the south west and off the B3224 is GAULDEN MANOR. Quite small and built in the local pink sandstone, it dates back to the 12th century. There was always a dwelling on this site and probably the oldest parts are now used as a workshop and cider house with a stone staircase connecting them to the rooms above.

In the main part of the house is the hall, which probably had a covered ceiling in Tudor times, which was later decorated with the magnificent plasterwork,in the early 1600s. Next to the hall is a small room known as the chapel which also has the original plaster decoration. On the left of the front door inside a Tudor porch, is the old kitchen (now the dining room) with open cooking fireplace and bread oven. On the staircase landing is an early window paned with the original hand-made glass. The main bedroom has more plasterwork, a large coat of arms over a stone fireplace. This is the arms of John Turberville and his wife Bridget Willoughby and dated 1642. All the furniture, pictures and china in the house come from families of the present owners. The furniture dates back to very early oak chests and a Dole cupboard right down to Victorian chairs and sofas.

Gaulden Manor

There are relics of former buildings at right angles to the house, now reduced to a rockery and smaller wood stores. There are two magnificent old thatched barns of great age still in use.   The gardens at Gaulden are of special interest to visitors as they were created bit by bit in the last 18 years out of a wilderness. A little is done each year and as visitors return they are always very interested in new additions or surprises. The garden is divided into different rooms such as the 'Rose Garden' with a small hedged corner for scented flowers and the Elizabethan herb garden, with a recently built camomile chair. There are a great variety of herbs for eating, medicine, cleaning, strewing, scenting, dyeing and all the uses that herbs were used for before modern drugs were concocted.

The 'Bog Garden' has many varieties of moisture-loving plants. There is also a 'Secret Garden' hidden away beyond the monk's fish pond, and coming round towards the back of the house is a bank of old fashioned shrub roses, leading into a small walled garden, known as the *'bishop's garden' with pots of lilies, geraniums and irises and surrounded by climbing roses and clematis. Cars and coaches containing disabled or elderly people may leave them at the entrance. Vehicles can then be parked in the allocated areas. There are no toilets for the disabled.*

Gaulden Manor is open from the beginning of May until mid-September in the afternoons from 2-6pm. Tuesday, Friday and Saturday it is for groups by appointment only. For further details ring (09847) 213.

At **West Bagborough** *you should take the opportunity of watching the QUANTOCK POTTERS create their unique ware. The large workshops are open all the year Monday to Friday 9am-6pm. You should also take a look at the fine 15th-century church, built out of the profits of the wool trade.*

Then there is THE QUANTOCK SHEEP MILKING CENTRE at **Nether Stowey** *where you have a fasincating chance to see life down at the farm. There is plenty to do, including sheep being milked. There is a children's play area, conservation and picnic areas, lots of farm animals and a farm walk. It is open lambing weekends from January to April and July to August plus Easter and summer holidays.*

The village of Nether Stowey has a lovely old manor house begun in the time of Henry VII and left unfinished until Queen Elizabeth I's time, because somebody had carelessly executed the builder on Tower Hill for joining the Cornish men who marched to London, protesting against taxation. Samuel Taylor Coleridge made Nether Stowey his home and was regularly visited by his friends William and Dorothy Wordsworth. Coleridge had taken refuge here when his periodical, The Watchman ran into financial difficulties. In the typical manner of a poet and a dreamer, he wrote to a friend that 'I hope to live here with a pig or two for I would rather be a self maintaining gardener than a Milton, if I could not be both.'

His home, COLERIDGE COTTAGE, is open from April to September, Tuesday to Thursday and Sunday from 2-5pm.

Close to Nether Stowey is the village of **Holford** *where, according to Dorothy Wordsworth 'there is everything here, sea and woods wild as fancy are painted'. That is not the only pretty vilage within easy reach.* **Combe Florey,** *must come high on the list. It is stunningly beautiful and* *once was the home of the Reverend Sydney Smith, and later the home of Evelyn Waugh.*

*Two miles away towards the coast is the village of **Stogursey**. Seeing this quiet place today, it is hard to imagine that in the 12th century the local lord, Fulke de Breaute, had around him, and under his command, a band of robbers who terrorised the surrounding countryside before he was brought to justice. If you fancy taking a look at the modern edifice of HINKLEY POINT NUCLEAR POWER STATION, there is a walk from Stogursey over the fields to Wick and then to **Stolford** on the coast. A left turn along the footpath will give you a good close view of the uninteresting buildings which stand on this featureless stretch of coast.*

*Field Marshall Viscount Montgomery grew up in the village of **Halse**. I wonder if his child's eyes ever appreciated the beauty of the abundance of thatched cottages. Probably not, they would have been less of a rarity in his childhood.*

***Milverton** is a village that dates back to the Doomsday study and boasts some glorious Georgian houses and a superb church. It was also the home of Thomas Young, whose work enabled the translation of Egyptian Hieroglyphics.*

*From here you are close to **Wiveliscombe**, not one of my favourite places but the church of St Andrew is outstandingly beautiful and has some fascinating catacombs. It was here that a safe haven was provided for many of the nation's treasures during World War II; a plaque inside the church records this.*

***Kingston Mary**, nestling at the southern end of the Quantocks is delightful. Its buildings are full of interest and it has a charming 18th-century church. It is also the home of the church farm weavers.*

*FYNE COURT at **Broomfield**, six miles north of Taunton belongs to the National Trust who acquired it under the will of a Mr Adams in 1967. There are 67 acres and it is the headquarters of the Somerset Trust for Nature Conservation. FYNE COURT GARDENS are the pleasure gardens that once were attached to the house, which was demolished following a disastrous fire in 1898. The grounds are now a nature reserve. There are pleasant woodland walks and a nature trail booklet is available. A lake, walled garden, two ponds and a small arboretum are among the attractions.*

*Mr Adams' generosity also allowed the National Trust to acquire GREAT & MARROW HILLS at **Triscombe**. This 141 acres of moor, grass and woodland on the south-west slope of the Quantocks has fine views over Taunton vale to the Brendon Hills and Exmoor. There is access by public footpaths. The public car park at the end of the road leading to **Cockercombe** is the best place to park.*

The Vale of Taunton

Triscombe should always be on your visiting list because it is a postcard village and has an enchanting pub, THE BLUE BALL INN, quite out of the usual run of village pubs. It is old, beamed with low ceilings, and full of nooks and crannies; you may well find yoursleves sitting in a corner which turns out to have been the former bread oven!

Without doubt the Quantocks are an unspoilt area of peace and quiet for anyone who loves the countryside. They are best explored on foot and always it is gentle hill walking, with quiet combes reaching from Taunton to the coast near Watchet.

*Another fine house with beautiful gardens is HESTERCOMBE HOUSE at **Cheriton Fitzpaine** just 4 miles east of Taunton. The appearance of the present house dates from the 1870's with a magnificent hallway and wooden staircase. It once belonged to Lord Portman but now is the headquarters of the Somerset County Council Fire Brigade. The main attraction is the historic multi-level garden laid out at the turn of the century by Sir Edwin Lutyens with planting by Gertrude Jekyll. Restoration by the County Council over the last ten years, to portray the* *garden in its original form, has been carried out perfectly. There is attractive stonework, a long pergola supported by stone pillars, and a magnificent Orangery on the east side of the garden. It is best seen in the months of June and July and early August. The views across the vale of Taunton Deane are stunnng. It is open all the year from Monday to Friday, in the afternoons from 12-5pm plus the last Sundays in June and July.*

I looked at one of the 'Official Guide Maps' for Taunton Deane and almost every bit of it from Taunton to Wellington, and to the coast at Watchet, was covered with little marks showing the places of interest to visit. There must be more in this part of Somerset than anywhere else. It is surrounded on three sides by gentle uplands. To the north are the Quantock Hills, much loved by the poets Wordsworth and Coleridge; today the home of deer and an area beloved of walkers and horseriders. Along the west side runs the famous West Somerset Steam Railway on its route from Minehead to Bishops Lydeard. Further west are the Brendon Hills which lead up to the wild expanse of Exmoor. To the south of the district are the Blackdown Hills with their majestic avenues of beech trees, recently acknowledged as an area of outstanding natural beauty.

Wellington *has never quite got over the surprise at the honour bestowed upon it when the hero of the Battle of Waterloo decided to take the name of this rural town for his Dukedom. The Duke of Wellington is believed only once to have visited the town but they have never forgotten. In his honour they built the monument standing high on the spur of the Blackdown Hills. This 175ft high construction looks not unlike Cleopatra's Needle when you see it, especially when it is floodlit at night. This compliment to the town brought them instant fame. The monument was meant to be crowned with a figure of the great man, and to be the centre of a group of cottages for Waterloo pensioners. Sadly, it was too expensive a scheme for the town which for years found the upkeep of the column, with its hundreds of steps, a big drain on the budget. There was great relief when it was taken over by the National Trust. Recently it has had a face lift and looks beautiful in the glow of the floodlighting. I must warn you though that the climb up to it is daunting and not for the feeble.*

The beautiful and timeless parish church in Wellington is descended mostly from the 13th and 14th century and the east window is about 700 years old. Sir John Popham lies here surrounded by his family. He was the man who sentenced Sir Walter Raleigh to death. I am amazed he had the temerity when his own character is not without stain. He was reputed to have acquired the manor of Littlecote in Wiltshire as payment for acquitting the owner, William Darell, after a sensational murder trial.

The town is a pleasant place in which to while away an hour or two. It dates from Saxon times and evolved as a market town with a cloth-making industry which was boosted first by the building of the Grand Western Canal, then by the building of the railway. Certainly worth visiting is THE CHECKERS RESTAURNT in the High Street. It is its unusual frontage which will attract you first of all. Checkers is a 16th century building owned by Liam Tinney, a talented chef, and his wife Christine. Liam is best known for his delicious, innovative food and you should always try and leave room for his exceptional 'Hot Sticky Toffee Pudding'.

*If you fancy a meal or a drink in a quiet pub in a pretty, unspoilt village, then on the border of Devon and Somerset, close to Wellington is **Holcombe Rogus**, easily accessible from junction 26 and 27 of the M5 and only two and a half miles from the A38. In its heart is THE PRINCE OF WALES. Douglas and Betty Whiteley are waiting there to welcome you. This likeable couple told me that they can genuinely say that, as they are known for the Real Ales in the bar, so they are known for bringing real family food to their restaurant.*

*Between Wellington and Taunton, SHEPPEYS FARMHOUSE CIDER at Three Bridges, **Bradford-on-Tone**, makes an interesting outing. They are the makers of high quality farmhouse cider on a 370 acre farm. You can see the cider making equipment, explore the excellent farm and cider museum or just wander through 30 acres of delightful orchards. If you want to picnic, there are special areas in the orchards, and finally before departing, you can visit the shop which not only sells cider but cheeses and cream, as well as other farm produce. The opening hours are Monday-Saturday from May 1st-September 30th, 8.30am-7pm. Monday-Saturday: October 1st-April 30th, 8.30am-6pm. Sunday from Easter to Christmas: 12 noon-2pm only.*

Cider making has been associated with the West Country for centuries and is as much a tradition as a craft. Somerset is deep in the heart of the true cider-producing area and no visit to the county is complete without learning a little bit about this ancient drink. At one time, many farms produced their own cider, not only to appear on the farm-house table with most meals, but also as an integral part of the farm labourer's wages. Indeed, it was not uncommon for a good worker to drink one or two gallons daily during the long hours of haymaking and harvest time!

Good cider is made from apples grown especially for this purpose with names like Kingston Black, Stoke Red, Dabinett and Yarlington Mill - evocative of the days when the apples were picked up from under the standard trees by local women for a few pence a sack. These days are gone, however. Todays orchard is likely to be the more intensive bush type, though some good standards remain, where the fruit is harvested by one of the mechanical pickers available. These machines vary from the sophisticated, tractor mounted type, conveying the fruit from ground to trailer, to the less expensive hand operated machines picking up into baskets. Picking usually begins in October.

There are still some farmer/cider makers among the small producers, where one is able to obtain a more traditional type of cider as we have seen at Sheppeys. If you are visiting in the Autumn, you may be able to see the milling of the apples, and the pressing out of the pulp, usually by hydraulic press. The juice is fermented out in oak barrels or vats, and after 'racking off' from the sediment or lees, is usually matured in these for some months before being sold. We have all heard of 'Scrumpy' but this is not really a cider maker's term at all. It is generally used to describe a rough unfiltered cider.

*Having made that statement I will probably get my knuckles rapped by TANPITS CIDER FARM at **Bathpool**, where Henry's Farmhouse Scrumpy is made. It is made from apples grown in Somerset and is naturally fermented. They have a small range of containers available for sale. You will find them approximately one and a half miles off junction 25 of the M5 along the A38. In addition to the cider making you can also see a goodly selection of farm birds and animals and a collection of old farm implements. They are open from 8.30am-8pm Mondays to Saturdays.*

***Taunton**, the county town of Somerset has many different facets.This is not as in most counties, an historic position, for Somerset's administration has only been totally concentrated here since 1936. Assizes however were held in the town from medieval times, and visits from the judges created, as in other assize towns, a 'season' when all the notability danced the night away at balls and visited the theatre, no doubt managing to dismiss the spectacle of felons hanging. Beside all this, the town has for even longer had an administrative function as a Saxon borough and as the vast centre of the estates of the medieval Bishops of Winchester.*

Taunton began as a military outpost built by King Ine before 722 and it seems likely that a missionary centre was soon established. This minster, which with its surrounding estates was bought from the Crown by Bishop Denewulf of Winchester in 904, may have stood within the outer precincts of the later castle. In the course of time it became a house of Augustinian Canons and in 1158 was given a new site outside the town's defences. Part of its huge graveyard was uncovered not so many years ago and one side of the precinct gate was, for long known as the Priory Barn, still stands by the County Cricket Ground and is used as a cricketing museum.

The removal of the old minster was achieved to extend the castle. Its site on low ground beside the Tone emphasises its non-military function, though the great, square keep, now the CASTLE HOTEL garden, is still imposing.

The subsequent history of the castle, includes minor repairs, alterations, damage and neglect by successive Bishops of Winchester and their officers, the siege of the town, when Robert Blake held out for Parliament in 1644-5, and the use of the Great Hall to hold the assizes, most notably by Chief Justice George Jeffreys, in his Bloody Assize after Monmouth's Rebellion in 1685. In 1873 the castle was saved by the Somerset Archaeological Society and has been their home ever since. Their fine collections, improved and extended under the care of Somerset County Council, instructively illustrate many aspects of the prehistory and history of the ancient county of Somerset. It now houses a Military Museum as well.

From behind the castle an attractive walk follows the banks of the River Tone, while in Vivary Park, beyond the High Street there are pleasant gardens with a jogging trail, a model railway and a model boating pond.

Taunton has two particularly fine churches. St Mary's is a sure reflection of the town's prosperity. It has a splendid tower seen at the best advantage from the train, and you cannot fail to enjoy the slender piers to the angels and the painted roof. This was the townsmen's church and between 1488 and 1514 they left money for the tower and the porch. Inside the nave has double aisles, the second arcade on the North being the earliest recognisable part, dating from the 13th century. St James's church seems a little more modest but its unquestioned magnificence is in its font, a little crude but as ornate as anything in the county.

At least three times in its history Taunton has supported the dissenter; in 1497 it proclaimed Perkin Warbeck king, and in the Civil War, Taunton backed Parliament and many of its population were killed or wounded in the Battle of Sedgemoor fighting for the Duke of Monmouth in 1685. It is a town of wide streets, a sprinkling of medieval buildings even in the centre of the town, notably the timber-framed and gabled houses in Fore Street. It is an excellent shopping centre, much of it pedestrianised. Surrounded by boutiques in the attractive, cobbled St James Courtyard, is FLOWERS, a restaurant and coffee shop where the tantalising smell of freshly brewed coffee will make you stop even if nothing else does. It is charming with tables and chairs outside for sunny days.

Tucked away in Bath Place, just off the High Street, is another thriving coffee house, ODD BODS, which has an attractive menu of simple and nourishing food at reasonable prices. I have always had a great affection for THE COUNTY HOTEL in East Street, now part of the Forte group. Originally a coaching inn, it has an impressive frontage on Taunton's main street. Carefully modernised it has lost none of its charm and still upholds the tradition of a County town hotel. It can justifiably boast of its reputation for serving good food, Somerset dishes in particular. Another hotel I have stayed in is the family run, CORNER HOUSE HOTEL in Park Street, which has the benefit of a large car park at the rear and a good restaurant within its doors.

If you have never tried a Travel Inn , you should. It is amazing value for money. A room is only £32.50 whether it is used as a single, a double or a family room. The room is complete with an en suite bathroom, colour TV and complimentary tea and coffee making facilities. Alongside, guests can breakfast, dine in the evening or enjoy delicious food from the bar in the WHITE LODGE BEEFEATER. You will find The White Lodge just five minutes from junction 25 of the M5. Take the A38 to Taunton after leaving J25 and the first exit off the 2nd roundabout. The White Lodge is 200 yards on the right hand side. For further information ring (0823) 321112. Forgive me if the price I have quoted is wrong, it may go up but it will not be by much.

The small team of professionals who run THE BREWHOUSE THEATRE will tell you that the theatre exists to present a wide range of arts and activities of the highest standard. The range is varied, drama, dance, opera, jazz and films make up the repetoire. It is recognised as one of the country's leading theatres and art centres. It provides hundreds of people with the opportunity to participate in the arts; either

73

through workshops and courses or by joining forces with the hundreds of volunteers who help out. If you want to learn more or to know what is playing write to the Brewhouse Theatre, Coal Orchard, Taunton, Somerset TA1 1JL.

Withies Drying at East Lyng

*There are two pubs that I enjoy whenever I am in this area. Just outside Taunton on the A361 Taunton to Glastonbury road at **East Lyng** is THE ROSE AND CROWN, a pub so popular with its regular clientele that the landlords, Pete Thyer and Derek Mason, can almost tell which day of the week it is by a visit from one of them. It is not the place for anyone who enjoys juke boxes, fruit machines or pool tables. For those who relish a good meal in comfortable surroundings in a splendid atmosphere it would be difficult to find somewhere better.*

*My second choice is THE MAYPOLE at **Thurloxton**, only a short distance from the M5. It is a pub that has an air of well being and of being cherished. The atmosphere is happy, and the food and drink superb, so it is an added bonus to find it standing in such glorious countryside on the edge of the Quantocks and Sedgemoor, with the Somerset Levels to the south.*

Somerset County Cricket Ground is in Taunton and the town is always alive to what is happening in the world of cricket. They always have players who are national names. This season has seen two of their number called up for England. It has a full programme of championship, Sunday League and cup matches which are staged from April- September amidst the beautiful surroundings of the county ground in the heart of the town. The club has a colourful history and has seen cricketing stars such as Ian Botham, Viv Richards, Martin Crowe, Steve Waugh and Jimmy Cook in the team. Somerset is renowned for being a team full of surprises and disappointments! The Club is open to members and the general public, with excellent refreshment and dining facilities available. An up to date fixture list is available upon request. It also has a cricket shop selling clothing, equipment and memorabilia which opens from 9.30am-4.30pm Tuesday to Saturday and home match days.

The Somerset Cricket Museum in The Priory Barn, which is an ancient monument, is adjacent to the cricket ground. It is an enthralling place and is open from 10-4pm every day except Sundays. From October-March it is advisable to ring to confirm that it is open. The number is (0823) 275893. It is also as well to note that during First Class cricket matches entrance is only available to cricket spectators. You reach it through the Priory Bridge Road entrance to the ground.

If I am staying in Taunton, another treat I give myself is a visit to POUNDISFORD PARK, three and a half miles south of the town on the by-road between **Trull** *and* **Pitminster**. *The Saxon deer park formed part of the estate granted to the Bishops of Winchester by King Ethelheard, around 730AD. It is still surrounded by the original bank or pale, hunted over by King John, and is the setting for this charming example of Tudor domestic architecture.*

It was built at the end of Henry VIII's reign by a merchant adventurer, and almost unaltered since. The cream walls, stone mullions and early glass give the house a comfortable and welcoming atmosphere. James I visited the house and his wife, Anne, stayed here. It was ransacked by the Royalists in the Civil War but otherwise it has been a peaceful family home, escaping implication in Monmouth's rebellion.

As you come up the short drive you will enter the House on the south side - once the rear - with its fascinating early lead work. The heavy studded door opens into the 'Screens Passage' and the 'Great Hall'. The interior has all the features of the great houses of this period, but scaled down to an intimate size. Beautiful plaster ceilings and intriguing architecture abound. Outside, the original detached kitchen, and surrounding buildings create a formal cobbled courtyard containing the 18th century pump house.

The very simple and peaceful garden of four acres with lawns, formal yew hedges and borders containing some unusual plants, complements the beautiful 17th century gazebo, and the symmetry of the North Front and the deliberate asymmetry of the west elevation of the house. A delightful woodland walk beyond the walled garden becomes the icing on this beautiful cake.

Poundisford Park is open from the beginning of May until the middle of September, Bank Holiday Mondays only from 11-5pm. Wednesday and Thursday also from 11-5pm and on Fridays at the same time in July and August. Groups can go at other times by appointment. The number to ring is (0823) 421244.

With the intention of spending some time in Bridgwater, I made my way up the A38 from Taunton stopping only to take a quick lunch in **Westonzoyland** *just to the south east of Bridgwater off the A39. THE SHOULDER OF MUTTON is a favourite watering hole for people working and living in Bridgwater, just three miles away. It is also ideal for those interested in history. The Battle of Sedgemoor took place here and the battlefield is a great tourist attraction; the site is only ten minutes from the pub. Diana Humphrey, the proprietor, will tell you that everyone is welcome and a liking for battlefields is not a condition of entry to the Shoulder of Mutton!*

It is quite difficult to imagine this battle. Whether you come to the battlefield from Bridgwater, or along from Middlezoy over what was once the Royal Air Force airfield at Westonzoyland, or down from the Poldens to Brandey, from where the rebel army crept stealthily onto the open moor, it is almost impossible to sense the feeling or recognise the key points of one of the strangest battles ever to take place on a July night. We would certainly not try to seek out the battlefield at night and yet this is what this odd army attempted. Neither side could have seen its enemy. The King's Sedgemoor drain, now the district's dominant water course, was not cut until 1790, and the Bussex Rhine, vital in the whole battle, has long been filled in; the rhine by the battlefield memorial did not exist in Feversham or Monmouth's time. It was in Westonzoyland that Lord Feversham had his headquarters and the open ground, north of the village, where the royal army encamped is now filled with houses, orchards, and gardens. Probably the only place that has not changed much is the village church, with its slender tower and late Gothic nave. This ancient church was so much a part of that ghastly night after the battle when Monmouth's rebels met their end. Looking at the beauty and peace of the 15th-century roofs with their traceried beams, rich pendants and lovely bosses, it is hard to imagine the awful scenes of suffering when 500 of Monmouth's men were locked up here, badly wounded. They would have lain on the 15th-century benches, crying in despair whilst their fitter comrades were forced to build gibbets outside for the hangings that took place in the morning.

In a chest, the church has a register with an entry describing the battle and another tells how much money the church spent on frankincense to rid it of the awful stench of death. You can read how the bells rang out when Monmouth was captured and for King James II when he rode from Bristol to see the battlefield.

I have found out more about this battle by the fine model in THE BLAKE MUSEUM at Bridgwater than anywhere else.

Westonzoyland is also known for its Pumping Station built in 1861 which is the earliest Steam Land Drainage Pumping Station on the Somerset Levels and is open to visitors. The Huntspill River nearby is a man made construction built during World War II to allow all manner of things to be ferried here and there, most of them top secret. Before its construction and that of the Westonzoyland Pumping Station the Somerset Levels were always under water during the wetter winter months frequently resulting in the slaughter of grazing stock.

Bridgwater, now an industrial centre, was a busy port until Bristol overshadowed it. The town grew up around what was the best crossing point of a river which could not be forded. At the Norman Conquest it was held by a Saxon, Merleswain who lost it to a Walter de Douai. At that time it was known as Brugie but became the Bridge of Walter, hence its present name. By the 26th June 1200, King John granted a Royal Charter giving borough status and permission to build a castle to protect the flourishing river port. The River Parrett has been used for commercial shipping since pre-Roman times and a relic of Phoenician ring money was discovered near the site of the old town bridge. In the 13th century the port was used as a victualling base for forays into Wales and Ireland, and by the 15th century had become a major port ranking 12th in the whole country. Woollen cloth was the principal export, the wool trade forming the basis of West Country wealth, and the main import was French wine.

It became the main point of entry and outlet for much of central and western Somerset. Taunton, Langport, Ilchester and even Yeovil sent, and received, goods through the estuary of the River Parret and by the canal to Taunton and beyond. Bridgwater is still a coasting port, but its riverside quay below the historic bridge is quiet, gone are the sailing brigantines and ketches, and the talk of seamen. Most of the ships that use the port of Bridgwater come no further than the wharf at Dunball, and the berths, a little higher upstream, where dredgers disgorge what they have sucked up from the Bristol Channel. A tidal bore comes up the River Parrett twice a day; the times are posted on the ancient bridge.

The Cornhill, Bridgwater

The town once had a great castle but that has almost disappeared. It is the 14th-century church of St Mary, with a graceful stone spire which is the town's best medieval survival. It is the contents of the church which are more notable than its architecture. They go back to the Stuart and Georgian periods of Bridgwater's prosperity, when the future Admiral Blake was but a boy. The screen, re-erected in a side chapel, is Jacobean and beautiful, and some of the opulent mural monuments are of about the same date.

In the chancel is a stunning painting, The Descent from the Cross, by an Italian painter of the Baroque period. It was a gift from the oddly named Lord Anne Poulet, of the well known county family from Hinton St George. He was a Member of Parliament for Bridgwater for many years and a godson of Queen Anne, from whom he got his name. It is thought to have been captured from a French ship.

From the tower of the church the rebel Duke of Monmouth is said to have surveyed the field before the Battle of Sedgemoor in 1685.

Robert Blake was born in Bridgwater in 1598. This is a man who came into the history books as Cromwell's greatest 'General at Sea'. Son of a local merchant, Blake was MP for Bridgwater and became a succesful army general during the Civil War before transforming Britain's infant navy into the world's most fearsome maritime force. Admiral Blake's victories over the Dutch and Spanish ensure his position, along with Drake and Nelson, as one of our greatest seamen.

THE ADMIRAL BLAKE MUSEUM, in Blake Street, off Dampiet Street occupies the house which was the Admiral's birthplace, and is somewhere every visitor should come. The main theme behind the exhibits displayed is the history of the town. With its varied and colourful history, it is a rewarding place to visit and not just a shelter for wet days! Subjects of the exhibitions include local archaeology, Robert Blake, the Battle of Sedgemoor, shipping and the brick and tile industry - once the mainstay of the town. The Alford Room displays the personal possessions of the Alfords, members of a prosperous family in the 19th century. The special exhibition room is now occupied by a large collection of paintings, the works of John Chubb (1746-1818). These are original works, mainly portraits.

The Museum is closed on Mondays but is open from Tuesday to Saturday 11am-4pm. Admission is free.

Bridgwater is proud of Blake and named the bridge built a short way upstream from the historic, medieval Bridgwater Bridge, after him. This freed the town centre from traffic congestion. Today you can wander aound the town in comparative peace enjoying the 'best Georgian Street in Somerset' according to Nicholas Pevsner, the eminent architectural historian. The street's early Georgian atmosphere is intact, and even if one allows strong competition from Bath, it still has to be quite perfect and the best in Somerset. Elsewhere in the town some of the good old buildings of the Greek revival proclaim the early 19th century when Bridgwater's prosperity was renewed.

It is always good to see a town go forward without losing its character. For those who come to live in the town it offers the best of the old and new in the choice of somewhere to live. Clever planning and architecture has given life to the old docks. The marine development surrounding them provides a full range of modern accommodation.

Two annual occasions are of major importance to the town. During the last week of September it hosts the four day St Matthew's Fair, one of the largest in the country. The fair originated in 1379 mainly for the sale of livestock, and this tradition continues to the present day, although now of less importance than the fun fair.

On the Thursday close to November 5th, Bridgwater stages its famous Guy Fawkes Carnival procession. The town has always celebrated the failure of the Gun Powder Plot and today's lavish presentation can be traced back to the 1800's. The lights, music, colour and a crowd of over 100,000 create an unforgettable night's entertainment.

For years I have found THE WHITE LION in the High Street to be one of the most welcoming hostelries in Bridgwater. It has a cheery landlady, Mrs Jones who genuinely likes people. From the old photographs on the walls you can piece together some of the pub's interesting history. The food is good, wholesome fare.

If you enjoy Indian food then try the ENGLISH RAJ TANDOORI in Claire Street. The policy is to follow traditional methods of Indian cooking and certainly whatever you choose from the extensive choice, is perfectly cooked and delicious.

THE OLD VICARGE RESTAURANT opposite St Mary's Church is a charming comfortable restaurant that is very much a part of Bridgwater's history. It is one of the three oldest buildings in the town. It is full of character, has a resident ghost and offers fine food based on English and French styles of cooking. In addition to the restaurant, excellent accommodation is provided for overnight guests. There are eleven rooms with bathrooms en suite. The pretty walled garden at the rear is an added attraction. It is advisable to ring first on(0278) 458891.

There are many places of interest on Bridgwater's doorstep. DURLEIGH MANOR at **West Bower** intrigues many. The central portion of the south front of the farmhouse contains imposing medieval walling with machiolation between semi-octagonal turrets. The building appears to be the remains of an elaborate gate house of the mid 15th century. The gateway was blocked, rather crudely at a fairly early date. One wonders whether the manor house itself, which should have stood beyond the gate house, was ever built. However the property belonged to the ill-fated Jane Seymour, Queen of Henry VIII, who was born here. Originally the house was approached from the south over a shallow valley. This was flooded in 1937 when the town needed a new reservoir. There is good trout fishing here.

At **Wembdon**, one mile north west of Bridgwater, there is an easy walk across the fields to Wembdon Common. Here you will find the church which was completely gutted by fire in 1867. In the churchyard is the base of a medieval cross which still retains part of its shaft. The village stocks are preserved in front of the south porch. From the church a footpath takes you up the hill, to the west, and you can look back over the *church to the Polden Hills. From the top of the hill there is an excellent view of the Bristol Channel and the Welsh coast, over a wide sweep of country. To the west lie the Quantock Hills and it is easy to recognise the hill called Danesborough.*

This is a good moment to tell you about POCOCKS RESTAURANT on Chilton Polden Hill. A major refurbishment has made this restaurant quite delightful. Over the years the name of the restaurant has been changed frequently. Its present owner, Leslie Johnstone, a former Savoy, London chef, decided to rename it Pococks after Tom Pocock, a notorious highwayman, said to have been the Robin Hood of the Polden Hills. The fame of this evil man vied with that of Exmoor highwayman Tom Faggus, who was immortalised by R.D. Blackmore in his novel, Lorna Doone. With excellent food, a choice wine list, attractive rooms in which to eat, and a welcoming host and hostess whose dream has always been to have a restaurant of their own, Pococks is a place to remember.

There is a very special pub close to Pococks on the Catcott Road at Burtle. This is a small village tucked away between the Mendips and Polden Hill, and in it YE OLD BURTLE INN offers a special brand of hospitality. It started off life as a cider house catering for drovers bringing their flocks and herds to market, which was held in what is now the car park. The food is excellent from the prime steaks to the morning cafetiere coffee and afternoon teas. Certainly a pub to be sought out.

Seven miles from Bridgwater and five miles from Glastonbury is MOORLYNCH VINEYARD at Moorlynch. There are signposts to the vineyard on both the A39 and the A361 roads as well as in the village of Moorlynch.

Centuries ago the monks of Glastonbury Abbey cultivated the vine. The tradition continues today at Moorlynch on the southern slopes of the Polden Hills. The vineyard was established in 1981 and now extends to 16 acres. The rest of the estate, 80 acres in all of rolling grassland, is there for you to stroll in or admire the magnificent sky-filled panorama of the Somerset levels.

Pasture management on the estate tries to be as conservation conscious as possible. Some of the land has had no spray or fertiliser for many years. They use a small flock of pedigree Welsh Black sheep as 'lawn mowers' though at certain times of the year these have to be helped out by stock from neighbouring farms, or just simple hay-making. Animal lovers will also find a few 'pets' to interest you - goats, ducks, chickens and geese. Signposted trails range from a few hundred yards to approaching a mile with a fairly steep climb.

81

Anne and Peter Farmer, the owners look forward to welcoming visitors and are delighted to show off the light, fresh, fragrant, Moorlynch award-winning wines which are estate-produced. The modern winery equipment is housed in a cool ancient barn, and can produce up to 35,000 bottles a year of blended and single grape varietal wines. A sparkling wine is also made. Tours and tastings help visitors understand the process and appreciate the product.

Spring Farm, the site of Moorlynch Vineyard, was one of two rest houses in the village for pilgrims journeying to Glastonbury Abbey, and the spring in the courtyard was a watering place for livestock. Today travellers will still find refreshment here. You can try a cool glass of Moorlynch wine, a light snack, or a delicious three-course meal in delightful surroundings. And you can still water your horse!

A stroll around the visitor centre and demonstration vineyard will give you an insight into the fascinating world of vine growing and wine making.

The Moorlynch shop allows you to make a leisurely choice of Moorlynch or other wines they sell, by the bottle or the case. They also stock bottled beers, lagers and soft drinks. For people looking for the perfect gift you should ask about the personalised label service which will turn a good bottle of wine into a gift to remember.

The facilities at Moorlynch Vineyard are available every day 10.30am-5pm except on Sundays when no wine sales are permitted before 12 noon. The restaurant is open for morning coffees, lunches and afternoon teas every day from the 27th March to the 31st December. It is open for evening meals during the same months every day except Sundays and Mondays. Tours cease at the end of September.

*You will want to visit NEW ROAD FARM at New Road, **East Huntspill**. Here you can discover that the natural world lives side by side with the domestic animals. All creatures great and small are welcome at the farm which is an open house to an astonishing range of wild and not-so-wild life. Over many years all sorts of creatures have passed through Derek and Pauline Kidner's home. Their work with orphaned and injured wildlife has increased alongside their own farm animals and pets. Hand rearing badgers and foxes, breeding tortoises, the unexpected can be seen - even axolotels!*

New Road Farm, with its listed buildings, is one of the oldest farms in the area, dating back to 1675. It is famiuly run with the help of the Kidner's two sons, Daniel and Simon. It demonstrates both modern and traditional methods of farming. Over sixty different breeds of animals can be found here, many unique to New Road Farm. Vistors are encouraged to enjoy the complete freedom of Derek and Pauline's home.

Somerset County Council's visitor centre, which offers unusual audio-visual effects and 'hands on' experiences for all ages, explains the farming on the Somerset Levels and moors. It is all part of your visit to this farm. Whatever the weather there is plenty to enjoy.

The children's play area is always popular and for the energetic an 'I Spy' farm trail taking approximately one hour - includes the River Brue. New Farm is open every day from 10am-6pm Mid-March to the beginning of November.

Visiting New Farm is a good excuse for popping into THE BASON BRIDGE INN closeby. This charming pub captures the heart of everyone who visits it. The food is freshly prepared, the ale well kept and the company great.

*Both East Huntspill and its nearby neighbour **West Huntspill** are part of the Somerset Levels. Divided only by the Polden Ridge, with its scattering of pretty villages, this is a mysterious place, home to heron, otter, swan and a host of other birds and insects. We know it was the setting for the Battle of Sedgemoor in 1685, and every year the Sealed Knot Society re-enact this battle over the fields of Sedgemoor, but we do not always realise that beneath the peat are relics of the distant past; trackways that are amongst the oldest in the world. Every year the harvesting of the Withies is still carried out and visitors can watch craftsmen continue the tradition of basket making. The willow grows everywhere and you can watch the colourful dragonflies hover over the wide ditches or 'rhynes' as they are called in this part of the world.*

West Huntspill is an area very popular with the angler, the walker and the birdwatcher. In the village there are a number of good places to stay, drink and eat that are sufficiently close to, but far away from the bustle of the coast. THE SCARLET PIMPERNEL for example on the main A38, attracts a wealth of visitors through its charming doors. Good, home-made food is available in the bar and the restaurant. Under 5's can eat free, Monday to Friday from the 'Junior Diners' menu, on a one adult, one child basis.

An extensive fish menu is one of the reasons for coming to THE SUNDOWNER HOTEL AND RESTAURANT. They serve Red Tallapia, a fresh water fish from the lakes of Africa which is unusual and delicious. Privately owned this is a hotel in which I can assure anyone they will be well cared for. My researchers stayed here while they were working on this book and they have nothing but praise for their treatment.

One of the great pleasures is to know of somewhere one can eat that is easily accessible from the motorway. THE WHITE COTTAGE in Old Pawlett Road, West Huntspill, answers this criteria. Dining here is an experience whether it is an ordinary evening or one of the special and very popular theme evenings. There are 'Brunch Jazz' mornings with live jazz bands, classical guitarists musical evenings. It is a remarkable and genuinely welcoming establishment.

A 19th-century curate built a lighthouse at **Burnham on Sea** *and exacted tolls from passing ships to finance two wells which were to establish the town as a spa. The venture failed but Burnham, with its 7 miles of sandy beach and its fine views across Bridgwater Bay, became popular with holiday-makers - and the wooden 'lighthouse on legs' is still a tourist attraction. The medieval church of St Andrew contains a 17th century marble reredos designed by Inigo Jones and carved by Grinling Gibbons; originally made for the chapel of Whitehall Palace, it passed to Hampton Court and Westminster Abbey before coming to rest here in the 19th century. The tower of the church tilts three feet from the vertical - the subsidence being due to its sandy foundations.*

Today Burnham is a busy place, full of visitors in summer and all the year round a home for people who have found that living here, and working in Bristol is having the best of both worlds. I enjoy the walk that one can take along the Esplanade and the riverside as far as the docks at **Highbridge**. *If you are a golfer you will enjoy Burnham's championship 18 hole course, right by the sea. The little town also has a very good indoor swimming pool.*

THE SOMERSET AND DORSET in the High Street is a pub I know of old. It is always welcoming no matter how busy it is. Real Ales are landlord Roy Hodges' great pleasure. A pint here is always in top condition.

Berrow *is popular as a camping and caravanning area, not surprisingly with its easy access to the beach. If you are not of the bucket and spade brigade you may well enjoy THE ANIMAL FARM COUNTRY PARK and LAND OF LEGENDS in Red Road, Berrow. There are all kinds of rare breeds, domestic farm animals and even a few surprises! You have the opportunity to feed and make friends with many of the animals. The static display of machinery and tools of yesteryear will take you back in time to when the horses were the power on the land. At various points round the park information is displayed which provides detailed material relating to the animals, local wildlife and conservation. The Land of Legends recreates scenes of the folklore of the West Country. It is quite spellbinding and the stories seem to enchant adults as much as the* *children. Animal farm is open from Easter until the end of October from 10-5pm every day.*

Brean Down Tropical Bird Garden

Along the seven miles of golden sands between Burnham and **Brean** *there are endless things and sights to delight your eyes. At the very end, a great hump which once was described to me as a submerging hippo, projects three-quarters of a mile into the sea. Man has probably lived here since the end of the IceAge 10,000 years ago. There are Bronze Age barrows and burial cairns, an Iron Age fort, Celtic field systems and on the second highest point of Brean Down, the foundations of a Roman temple. This small area provides hours of pleasure and the vegetation of the western-facing slope is almost unique in Britain. Nor must one forget the BREAN DOWN TROPICAL BIRD GARDEN.*

Close by this natural paradise is the lively BREAN LEISURE PARK which offers constant fun and entertainment. It has over 30 attractions for all the family including THE FARMERS TAVERN: one of Somerset's leading nightspots and is open all the year round, offering live cabaret, dining and dancing. The Farmers Den provides a family room facility and in the main season family entertainment is presented at which children are welcome.

If you would rather opt for something a little quieter I would suggest lunch at THE WHEATSHEAF INN in **Chapel Allerton***. It is set in a charming, rural area and is the epitome of a true country pub. The Wheatsheaf has the reputation for serving the most tender, succulent, rare beef. After lunch a visit to ASHTON WINDMILL would round off the day nicely. This unique 18th-century flour mill stands on the 'Isle of Wedmore',*

85

a ridge giving commanding views of the Cheddar Gorge, Somerset Levels and Brent Knoll, and is the only complete mill left in Somerset. Mention is made of a mill on this elevated site as far back as 1317. A straight sided construction, the windmill is girded by 3 iron hoops, which were added by the last miller, John Stevens, to ensure that the sails ran true.

Restored to working condition in 1958, with renovations carried out in 1979 by the Dorothea Restoration Engineers, it is now maintained by volunteers under the guidance of Sedgemoor District Council. Open 2.30-4.30pm every Sunday and Bank Holiday from Easter till the end of September. Admission is free, but naturally donations are appreciated.

Finally in this chapter I want to take you to the historic small town of **Axbridge** *which is totally charming. Its wonderful, old parish church of St John the Baptist has some good brasses and glass and a great sense of peace. People come here to see the National Trust Property, KING JOHN'S HUNTING LODGE. This medieval town house has retained its original timbered construction and it is a clear indication of Axbridge's position as a Royal Borough from the 9th to the 19th century. As well as being a fascinating building in its own right, the lodge also houses AXBRIDGE MUSEUM. This informative exhibition provides a keen insight to local Prehistoric Roman and medieval archaeology together with a numbr of changing displays. Open daily from 2-5pm April to September.*

Axbridge still contains a wealth of buildings from centuries past, one of which houses THE OLD OAK HOUSE, a licensed restaurant with accommodation, of great charm which has been tenanted since the 14th century. It is a wonderful place in which to stay or eat and especially for those who are sports minded. The Cook family can arrange fishing, golf, windsurfing and sailing, all within ten miles.

In the High Street THE AXBRIDGE LION is always worth visiting. It has been a pub for over 200 years and now has The Stable Restaurant as well. There is a little twist to this pub inasmuch as they have a 'Balti' menu as well as a traditional one. 'Balti' orginates from Pakistan and is very similar to Indian food. The chef, from Birmingham, has been taught the art of 'Balti' cooking under the watchful eye of Peter Pavan who owns a top restaurant in Birmingham.

THE AXBRIDGE LION

Pub & Restaurant

36 The High Street,
Axbridge, Somerset.

Tel: (0934) 733406

Just off the A38 the Medieval town of Axbridge is always worth visiting and any visit should include The Axbridge Lion with its friendly welcoming atmosphere. This likeable pub has been here for 200 years, and the charming Stable Restaurant still has the original stone floor. There is a skittle alley and also a function room, for hire, frequently in use for parties.

The owners Jenny and Steve Fox, before taking over the pub, were in outside catering in Worcestershire for 10 years. Steve, a chef for 25 years, has done most of the cooking himself. Jenny originates from Axbridge and is thoroughly pleased to be back in her home town.

There is a little twist to this pub and that is, they have a 'Balti' menu. Balti originates from Pakistan and is very similar to Indian food. The chef, from Birmingham has been taught the culinary art of Balti cooking under the watchful eye of Peter Pavan who owns a top restaurant in Birmingham.

There are two menus, one very traditional consisting of steaks, chicken, fish, grilled trout with almonds, and stuffed mushrooms with a delicious stuffing of Stilton, Danish Blue and walnuts, plus other tempting dishes. There is also a 3 course Sunday lunch available. The other menu is of course the very clever Balti menu, with some interesting ingredients. Try the keema aloo, keema channa or a chicken balti and if you are a vegan there is a suitable special dish. Children are welcome and they have their own menu. Whatever you try you can be sure of quality food at affordable prices.

USEFUL INFORMATION

OPEN: Mon-Thurs: 11-3pm & 6-11pm
All day Fri & Sat, Sun: 12-3pm - Sunday
lunch only, & 3-7pm - afternoon teas in
Summer, Sun: 7-10.30pm
CHILDREN: Welcome
CREDIT CARDS: No
LICENSED: Full
ACCOMMODATION: Not applicable

RESTAURANT: Balti & traditional
menus. Sunday lunch
BAR FOOD: Home-cooked. Daily
specials
VEGETARIAN: Always available
DISABLED ACCESS: Level access
GARDEN: Seating on small patio area

THE OAK HOUSE

Hotel with Restaurant

The Square, Axbridge, Somerset.

Tel: (0934) 732444
Fax: (0934) 733112

This is a welcoming establishment where sporting people will find everything they wish within ten miles. There is fishing, golf, wind-surfing and sailing. For those who are not so inclined, the countryside is lovely and Axbridge is within easy reach of so many interesting places. The Oak House is a family business run by Pat and Peter Cook ably supported by their sons, James and Jeremy. The whole family have a genuine desire to ensure every visitor, whether it is to stay or who comes for a meal and a drink, will enjoy themself so much that they will soon be beating a path to the door for another visit. People have been enjoying The Oak House for centuries and it is this tradition of good food and warm hospitality that the Cook family are continuing.

The hotel is charming and comfortable, its restaurant a recognised venue for local people as well as the many visitors who come to this medieval town of Axbridge. The combination of the culinary skills of the award winning chef, and the mouthwatering, local produce have made the restaurant renowned for its gourmet cooking. The dishes will surprise and delight you whatever the occasion. Staying here you will find the ten comfortable en-suite bedrooms delightful to retire to at the end of a busy day. The hotel is ideal for business people and is more than capable of hosting a conference or a product launch for up to forty people. Weddings are another facet of the hotel. The Cooks will be delighted to help organise the big day. Their experienced and practical help is invaluable and they fully understand the need to work to budgets.

USEFUL INFORMATION

OPEN: Rest: 12-3pm & 7-10pm
   Bistro/Lounge Bar: 11-3pm & 7-11pm
   Hotel: All year
CHILDREN: Yes. Cot facilities
CREDIT CARDS: Visa/Master/Euro
LICENSED: Full On
ACCOMMODATION: 10 en-suite rooms

RESTAURANT: Traditional English
   Specialising in fish and game
BAR FOOD: Fresh produce. Regularly
   changing menu
VEGETARIAN: 5-10 dishes
DISABLED ACCESS: Ground floor
GARDEN: Outdoor seating in The Square

THE WHITE LION

Public House

29 High Street,
Bridgwater, Somerset.

Tel: (0278) 429506

The White Lion is a lively attractive pub in Bridgwater town centre. It has been a hostelry for the last century during which time it has collected, within its four walls, an exciting atmosphere and it is obviously very popular with the locals. The original beams and stone walls add to the warm, friendly atmosphere. An almost L shaped bar leads up to a slightly raised section which is used for darts, and children can also use this part set back from the bar.

From old photographs which hang on the walls you can piece together some of the pubs interesting history, and if this fascinates you, the sociable landlady and landlord, Mr and Mrs Taylor, are always willing to spare time to tell you more.

Bridgwater is steeped in history and The White Lion has certainly had something to offer it over the years, as it still does today. Live music brings a wide range of young and old to the pub every Thursday and The White Lion's Real Ales are a real temptation. No other pub in Bridgwater has such a range. Visitors come from all over to sample them. John Smiths, Courage Best, Directors, Royal Oak and Old Speckled Hen all have their place.

The menu consists of fine quality, no nonsense fare served in generous portions. Amongst the favourite dishes is a first class chilli, a particularly good Sweet and Sour Chicken and jacket potatoes heaving with imaginative fillings. If you are looking for cold food, then the plentiful ploughman's with crispy bread or freshly made, well filled sandwiches are just right.

USEFUL INFORMATION

OPEN: 10.30am-11pm. Food 12-2pm
CHILDREN: Yes, no special facilities
CREDIT CARDS: None taken
LICENSED: Full
ACCOMMODATION: Not applicable

RESTAURANT: Not applicable
BAR FOOD: Good welcome
VEGETARIAN: By request
DISABLED ACCESS: Level entrance
GARDEN: No

YE OLDE BURTLE INN

Inn & Restaurant

Catcott Road,
Burtle, Somerset.

Tel: (0278) 722269

Burtle was an important Iron Age settlement and could only be visited by boat. Burtle actually means 'Sandbank'. There would not have been Ye Olde Burtle Inn there in the old days and even today this tucked away village is off the beaten track between the Mendips and Polden Hill. It is not shown on many maps but it is definitely worth seeking out.

People are fascinated when they see the pub for the first time. Having started life as a cider house catering for drovers bringing their flocks and herds to market, which was held in what is now the car park, it has developed over the years. Many of the original features are retained. Large, open log fires burn cheerfully, the ceilings are beamed and recently some of the old cob walling has been exposed in the lounge. Featured on the wall in the bar are the signatures of an old Somerset cricket team, from when they visited the inn for a game of skittles. A forge complete with bellow and tools is part of the restaurant and set in the wall is half a cart which was used in and around the village. The pub also boasts a ghost of a woman and two children.

The food is very special. You can choose a steak of whatever size you require cut from the whole joint, have it chargrilled exactly the way you like it, and help yourself from the salad table. The bread is freshly baked and on Sunday there is an excellent family Carvery lunch. There are 6-8 vegetarian dishes and a good choice of dishes in the bar. A patio and a large garden make Ye Olde Burtle Inn especially delightful in summer.

USEFUL INFORMATION

OPEN: All day, 7 days
CHILDREN: Menu, highchairs, drinks
CREDIT CARDS: Access/Visa/Barclay
LICENSED: Full + Supper Licence
ACCOMMODATION: Caravan &
  camping facilities

RESTAURANT: Fresh meat, steaks, fish
  & salads, Sunday carvery
BAR FOOD: Wide range, fresh produce
VEGETARIAN: 6-8 dishes
DISABLED ACCESS: Yes. No facilities
GARDEN: Large and patio, chairs

SOMERSET & DORSET

High Street, Burnham on Sea,
Somerset.

Inn

Tel: (0278) 783150

This is a pub I know of old, and in which I have spent many happy hours, including evenings when it has been host to crowds of people watching the famous carnival procession. Even on a busy night like that the landlord, Roy Hodge and his staff still find time to make customers welcome.

You will find The Somerset and Dorset in the busy High Street just a stroll away from the Promenade. It is a street full of interesting shops and the pub is an ideal venue after exploring this small but attractive Somerset town. The Somerset and Dorset acquired its name because it was adjacent to the old railway station of the Somerset and Dorset line; now no longer in existence. You will find the pub is full of old photographs reminding one of those great days of steam engines. In addition the collection of memorabilia is fascinating and the whole is capped by a stunning stained glass window depicting a train. One oddity is a shoe inside a box which is fixed to the wall. This is to ward off evil spirits - an ancient superstition which no one has been brave enough to disprove!

Real Ales are, Somerset born and bred Roy Hodge's, great pleasure. A pint here is always in top condition. The pub has won a Gold Award for the excellence of its service - well deserved. The food is good a la carte pub fare with a touch of a foreign influence brought to the dishes by the well travelled lady chef. This really is a fun place to be. There is a newly refurbished skittle alley clubroom and function room with a bar which will be available from September 1993. Live entertainment provides a good evening on Thursdays, every Monday is quiz night and in September a 'Victorian Week' will find everyone suitably clothed.

USEFUL INFORMATION

OPEN: Weekdays: 11-11pm,
  Sun: 12-3pm & 7-10.30pm
CHILDREN: Children's area & menu
CREDIT CARDS: Accss/Visa/Euro
LICENSED: Full On Licence
ACCOMMODATION: Not applicable

RESTAURANT: Fresh food, good value
BAR FOOD: Extensive range,
  traditional pub grub
VEGETARIAN: Always three dishes
DISABLED ACCESS: Yes. Wide doors
GARDEN: Cobbled courtyard & seating

THE WHEATSHEAF INN

Inn

Chapel Allerton,
Nr Axbridge, Somerset.

Tel: (0934) 712494

It is a great pleasure to come across a true country pub which is easily accessible from Bristol, Weston Super Mare and other seaside resorts like Burnham on Sea. The Wheatsheaf is set in a charming rural area and is one of those places in which one feels instantly at ease. Ian and John Wiggington the landlords, without doubt, contribute largely to the friendliness of this establishment. They have worked very hard to make The Wheatsheaf what it is today.

Inside there are two comfortable bars with a very small restaurant area at one end. Both bars in winter are encompassed in warmth from the roaring fires. Like any good pub it has devoted regulars, they welcome new faces with a warm smile.

In summer, the large garden leading from the verandah, from which hang an abundance of flowering baskets, is an ideal spot to sit at one of the rustic tables and enjoy a drink or a meal. Amongst the dishes on the menu is fresh salmon or crab during the summer months, perfectly cooked and served with crisp salads. During the winter Joan, who does the catering, makes her own special steak and kidney pies and they have a reputation all of their own. The Wheatsheaf also has a reputation for serving the most tender, succulent, rare beef. Of course there are specials every day on a good bar menu. No need to feel left out if you are a vegetarian, because there is always something delicious on the menu.

USEFUL INFORMATION

OPEN: 11.30-2.30pm & 6.30-11pm
(last food order at 9.30pm)
Winter: No food Sunday evenings
CHILDREN: Well behaved very welcome
CREDIT CARDS: None taken
LICENSED: Full
ACCOMMODATION: Not applicable

RESTAURANT: Traditional English
BAR FOOD: Wide range delicious food
VEGETARIAN: Yes, always available
DISABLED ACCESS: One small step
GARDEN: Lovely long garden with
tables

POCOCKS RESTAURANT

Chilton Polden Hill,
Nr Bridgwater, Somerset.

Tel: (0278) 722506

Restaurant & Cottage Accommodation

A major refurbishment has made Pococks quite delightful. Acquired recently by a former Savoy Hotel, London chef, Leslie Johnstone, the alterations have been brilliantly carried out. Over the years the name of the restaurant has changed frequently. At one time it was The Rumbling Tum and the last, Knight's Helm before Leslie Johnstone decided to christen it Pococks after Tom Pocock, a notorious highwaymen, said to have been the Robin Hood of the Poldens. The fame of this evil man vied with that of Exmoor highwayman Tom Faggus, who was immortalised by R.D. Blackmore in his novel, Lorna Doone. Les Johnstone has found him to be a fascinating study and you will find the highwayman logo is used throughout Pococks with letterheads, menus etc. The building is about 300 years old and is said to have been haunted by the figure of a lady in a long white dress. It is thought that the spirit may have been released when renovations were carried out some time ago and behind a baker's oven skeletal remains were found in a box. These were removed and placed in a museum and since that time the ghost has not been seen.

Traditional British style food is the hallmark of Pococks. Genuine old recipes are used with offerings from England. Wales, Ireland and Scotland. A superb steak, kidney and oyster pudding is rarely seen today but here at Pococks it has pride of place. On Sundays rib of beef is carved off the bone, just as it should be. The meat is the product of Somerset and the beautifully cooked vegetables are fresh local produce. With a choice wine list, attractive rooms in which to eat and a welcoming host and hostess, whose dream has always been to have a restaurant of their own, Pococks is a place to remember.

USEFUL INFORMATION

OPEN: Tues-Sat: 12-3pm & 7-11pm.
Sun: 12-3pm
CHILDREN: Welcome
CREDIT CARDS: All Major cards
LICENSED: Restaurant
ACCOMMODATION: Cottage at side of
Restaurant

RESTAURANT: Traditional British recipies
BAR FOOD: Lunchtime menu available
VEGETARIAN: Yes. Vegan on request
DISABLED ACCESS: Small step into
Restaurant
GARDEN: Outside seating

BASON BRIDGE INN

Public House

East Huntspill,
Highbridge, Somerset.

Tel: (0278) 782616

East Huntspill lies peacefully on the fringes of Sedgemoor between the Mendips and the Quantocks, and it is here that you will find The Bason Bridge Inn. It is hard to imagine that this magical haven for wild birds was the setting, in 1685, for one of England's most historical events, the Battle of Sedgemoor.

This charming pub is about 100 years old, and manages to capture the heart of every visitor with its warm and friendly atmosphere. Apart from the bar, there is a function room which caters for up to 75 people, making it the ideal venue for small weddings or other private parties. One of the main attractions to the Bason Bridge, is the double skittle alley that will bring hours of enjoyment for the whole family.

Food is freshly prepared using local, seasonal produce. A variety of home-made dishes are available and change daily. Choose from the specials of the day or enjoy a quick snack of beautifully presented sandwiches or a crusty filled roll. Vegetarians are not forgotten and imaginative dishes have been conjured up to suit every palette. The menu is carefully assembled to ensure everyone is accommodated for.

USEFUL INFORMATION

OPEN: Mon-Thu: 11.30-2.30pm & 7-11pm
    Fri-Sat: 11.30-3pm & 6.30-11pm
    Sun: 12-3pm & 7-10.30pm
CHILDREN: Yes. Children's room
    Double skittle alley
CREDIT CARDS: None
LICENSED: Full Licence
ACCOMMODATION: Not applicable

RESTAURANT: Home cooking
BAR FOOD: Yes, specials, steaks,
    sandwiches, rolls & seasonal produce
VEGETARIAN: Yes
DISABLED ACCESS: Level entrance
GARDEN: Large garden

THE ROSE AND CROWN

East Lyng,
Nr Taunton, Somerset.

Free House

Tel: (0823) 698235

This charming pub just outside Taunton, on the A361 Taunton/Glastonbury road is so well liked that the proprietors, Pete Thyer and Derek Mason, can almost tell which day of the week it is by a visit from their regular clientele who travel some distance to sample their hospitality. It is not the place for anyone who enjoys juke boxes, fruit machines or pool tables. For those who like to enjoy a good meal in comfortable surroundings in a splendid atmosphere it would be difficult to find somewhere better.

Pete has been in the business for years but Derek is a comparative newcomer having given up the sea in favour of this convivial lifestyle. These super hosts not only receive you with a warm welcome, but they ensure the farewell is equally friendly. For those who have travelled some distance and wish to stay the night, there are 2 en-suite bedrooms available and a delicious breakfast to complete your stay.

You have the choice of eating by reservation in the restaurant or electing to have a bar meal, available at lunch, and in the evening seven days a week, in the bar or little dining room where children are welcome. The restaurant has its own superb menu whilst the bar has an extensive choice including steaks and the lightest of omelettes not forgetting the blackboard specials, changed daily. For those among us with a sweet tooth, we can revel in the choice of home-made desserts. For a Sunday lunch outing it is hard to beat but make sure you book to avoid missing the extremely popular Roast Beef, piled high with trimmings. On a particularly balmy summer day, dining in the lovely well laid out garden is an added bonus.

USEFUL INFORMATION

OPEN: Mon-Sat: 11-2.30pm & 6.30-11pm
    Sun: 12-3pm & 7-10.30pm
CHILDREN: Welcome in dining room
CREDIT CARDS: Visa/Mastercard/Euro
LICENSED: Full licence
ACCOMMODATION: 2 dblen-suites, B&B

RESTAURANT: Steaks a speciality.
    Reservations please
BAR FOOD: Extensive choice. Daily
    specials, home-made sweets
VEGETARIAN: Dishes daily
DISABLED ACCESS: Easy access,
    welcome
GARDEN: Lovely, with tables

95

THE PRINCE OF WALES

Pubic House & Restaurant

Holcombe Rogus,
Nr Wellington, Somerset.

Tel: (0823) 672070

Holcombe Rogus is an unspoilt village on the border of Devon and Somerset, close to Wellington and easily accessible from junction 26 and 27 of the M5 and only two and a half miles from the A38. The only pub is the charming Prince of Wales Inn, originally four cottages, dating back to the late 16th and early 17th centuries.

Not so long ago it was acquired by Douglas Whiteley and his wife Betty, who with their son Stephen have developed it considerably. Their aim has been to give the pub a relaxing and happy atmosphere where customers can find a wide selection of real ales and delicious food at very competitive prices. Robert the chef de cuisine has won awards for his style and presentation and this is reflected in his imaginative and original menus which change frequently.

The restaurant is spaciously laid for 20 covers and provides a comfortable and intimate atmosphere with quality furniture and original oil paintings.

In addition to the traditional Sunday roast Robert provides a good old fashioned English breakfast at a very realistic price and this is proving very popular with those who prefer a brunch to a full Sunday lunch. So for a real treat make a date at the Prince of Wales and experience the rare joy of first class English cuisine.

USEFUL INFORMATION

OPEN: 12-3pm & 6.30-11pm (10.30 on Sun)
CHILDREN: Children's room
CREDIT CARDS: Not at present
LICENSED: Full On Licence
ACCOMMODATION: Not applicable

RESTAURANT: Varied & interesting
BAR FOOD: Traditional, home-cooked, plus Sunday brunch
VEGETARIAN: 4-6 dishes daily
DISABLED ACCESS: Yes
GARDEN: Spacious walled garden with lawn and flower beds & picnic tables

FLOWERS

Restaurant & Coffee Lounge

St James Courtyard,
Taunton, Somerset.

Tel: (0823) 324333

When you walk into the attractive St James Courtyard, still with its cobbles and now surrounded by little boutiques and Flowers Restaurant and Coffee Shop, it is almost impossible to believe that just over a decade ago the whole was a noisy, dirty factory. The conversion is quite brilliant and the consistently high standard of the shops has brought many customers, none more so than the lively Flowers, where the tantalising smell of freshly ground and brewed coffee assails your nostrils as you approach it.

Outside there are tables and chairs for use on sunny days and inside the friendly, relaxed atmosphere is just the thing for anyone wanting to get away from the bustle of the town centre of Taunton. Dawn Curtis is the owner and inspiration behind this venture. She has set about compiling a menu which is different, sensibly priced and totally acceptable to everyone. She will offer you a "Salad and Wine' - a deliciously crisp salad accompanied by a glass of house wine or that perennial favourite a Steamed Treacle Pudding - bad for the figure but what a temptation! Every day the blackboard displays a choice of hot dishes, all of them light and tasty. Throughout the day you can enjoy a whole range of coffees and teas from 'Flowers House Blend' to a mixed fruit teas. You will find the cake trolley hard to resist with its assortment of home-made cakes, or toasted teacakes, croissants and scones may suit you better. Flowers is licensed so you can enjoy a drink with your meal.

USEFUL INFORMATION

OPEN: Mon-Wed: 9-5pm, Thu-Sat: 9-10pm
   Closed Sundays
CHILDREN: Welcome
CREDIT CARDS: Master/Access/Visa
LICENSED: Table Licence
ACCOMMODATION: Not applicable

RESTAURANT: Wide choice
   Freshly prepared food
BAR FOOD: Not applicable
VEGETARIAN: 6 dishes approximately
DISABLED ACCESS: One step in,
   toilets upstairs
GARDEN: Patio with chairs & tables

ODD BODDS & TOP DRAWER

Restaurant, Coffee House & Top Drawer

Bath Place,
Taunton, Somerset.

Tel: (0823) 271034

Peter and Irene Nicol are the owners of Odd Bodds tucked away in Bath Place, a narrow street just off the busy High Street in Taunton. The Public Library backs onto Bath Place and the whole is a mixture of nice old buildings and houses. Odd Bodds was originally owned by a solicitor in the 17th century. It is a Listed building famous for its ceilings. In the 1970's it had some fairly radical alterations which extended it to its present size.

Upstairs, using a separate access, there is a large room, Top Drawer, which sells good quality ladies clothes on a fifty fifty basis, while downstairs Peter and Irene get on with their busy and thriving Coffee House. Odd Bodds has an attractive menu of simple and nourishing food at reasonable prices. The home-made soup with Garlic Bread and cheese is a meal in itself. It is the sort of place in which one can relax, not feel pressurised and simply enjoy the respite from the daily world. A lot of local people have discovered it use as an oasis after shopping and people working in the area certainly find it a godsend at lunchtime. It is certainly a find.

Taunton offers a lot to any visitor and for cricket lovers it is the home of the County side. A pleasant way to spend an afternoon particularly these days with players from the team playing for England - a fact of which Somerset is justly proud. Before you leave Bath Place however do take a look at Top Drawer; you are encouraged to browse and there really are some excellent bargains to be had.

USEFUL INFORMATION

OPEN: Mon-Sat: 9.30-5pm. Closed Bank Holidays
CHILDREN: Yes. Childs menu
CREDIT CARDS: Visa/Access
LICENSED: Restaurant
ACCOMMODATION: Not applicable

RESTAURANT: Home-cooked fare for all tastes
BAR FOOD: Daily specials
VEGETARIAN: 6-8 + daily specials
DISABLED ACCESS: Catered for
GARDEN: Outside tables

THE MAYPOLE INN

Thurloxton,
Taunton, Somerset.

Inn/Public House

Tel: (0823) 412286

The Maypole Inn in Thurloxton is attractive in its own right but the added benefit is the glorious countryside around it. Thurloxton is on the edge of the Quantocks and Sedgemoor with the Somerset Levels to the south. The pub stands at the edge of the village and close to main roads and only a short distance from the busy M5. It as an area for market gardening and there is also a Vineyard; in all truly rural and a delightful place to visit.

The pub was originally a farmhouse and then a Post Office before it took on the role of village hostelry and somewhere during that time it acquired a ghost; a maid who is harmless but seems to have no desire to leave the welcoming Maypole Inn - who can blame her! Tony and Julie Roost have been the landlords here for over thirteen years and they have built a superb reputation for the quality of the food and the condition of their four Real Ales. This pub has an air of well being and of being cherished.

The happy atmosphere obviously stems from the Roosts themselves but much of it comes from their regular clientele whose friendly chatter and sometimes leg pulling with each other is as enjoyable to people coming here for the first time as it is to themselves. The menu is full of good traditional dishes, beautifully presented and always freshly cooked using local produce wherever possible. Every day different Specials appear, sometimes time-honoured favourites and at others perhaps a little more adventurous. There are recipes from around the world but prepared in the kitchen of the inn. The portions are generous and the prices realistic. The Maypole Inn is a pub to remember.

USEFUL INFORMATION

OPEN: 11.30-2.30pm & 7-11pm,
  extended in summer
CHILDREN: Welcome
CREDIT CARDS: Visa/Master
LICENSED: Full On Licence
ACCOMMODATION: 3 rooms available
  and a caravan park from January 1994,
  ring for details

RESTAURANT: Wide choice
BAR FOOD: Traditional & daily specials
VEGETARIAN: Always available
DISABLED ACCESS: Yes & toilets
GARDEN: Yes with play area

CURDON MILL

Country House Hotel

Yellow, Stogumber,
Taunton, Somerset.

Tel: (0984) 56522

Open all the year round, Curdon Mill nestles in a beautiful and tranquil setting at the foot of the Quantocks. An ideal spot for the country-lover who wants to explore this picturesque and interesting part of Somerset but equally good for those who need peaceful surroundings in which to hold a small conference - thirty people can be catered for admirably.

For 20 years Richard and Daphne Criddle have been here, converting the house from an old barn and watermill and making it into the attractive place it is now. They have taken care to preserve and retain many of the bygone features including the waterwheel, mill stream water garden, exposed beams and log fires, along with the mill shaft which still hangs across the ceiling of the dining room. The comforts of the 20th century have not been omitted; the six en-suite bedrooms are all prettily decorated and have TV and that blessing, a hostess tray. When you look out in the morning, after a comfortable night's sleep, 200 acres of the Criddle's farmland stretches before you and on to some fine country views. The sitting room is adorned with chintzy chairs, fresh flowers and local information and adjoining it is the large, period dining room where a traditional English breakfast is served.

The menus are changing daily and fresh local produce is always used; frequently the Criddle's own home grown vegetables and fruits. The house is open to non-residents for meals. There are kennels and stables outside for dogs and horses but no animals are allowed in the house.

USEFUL INFORMATION

OPEN: All year. Reservations only
CHILDREN: Welcome over 8 years
CREDIT CARDS: Visa/Master/Euro
LICENSED: Restaurant
ACCOMMODATION: 6 en-suite rooms

RESTAURANT: Open to non-residents
BAR FOOD: Not applicable
VEGETARIAN: Always one available
DISABLED ACCESS: Welcome.
    No facilities
GARDEN: Huge gardens. 200 acres,
    farmland, streams

CHECKERS RESTAURANT

Restaurant

59 High Street,
Wellington, Somerset.

Tel: (0823) 662363

It is the unusual frontage to this attractive restaurant which will draw your attention at first. Once inside you will discover that it was more than worthwhile taking a greater interest in just the facade. Checkers is a 16th century building which once was an old drapers but today the pretty decor is fresh and charming enhanced by the mint green table covers and the flowers which adorn each one.

Situated in the centre of Wellington it is an ideal place to visit before or after exploring the area. You are close to the magic of the Blackdown hills and the Quantocks which team with deer. Equally close is the Wellington Monument which stands high on a hill and was built to honour the Iron Duke who took his title from the town although he had no known connection with it. It will certainly be beneficial to climb up to it after you have eaten a superb lunch and finished it off with a portion of Liam Tinney's exceptional 'Hot Sticky Toffee Pudding', for which he is well known.

Liam is a talented chef and runs Checkers with his wife, Christine. Apart from the generous portions - there is certainly no 'Nouvelle Cuisine' here - the food is delicious, innovative and the presentation is particularly good. The menus which provide a good choice, are changed regularly.

USEFUL INFORMATION

OPEN:. Lunch Tue-Sat: 12-2pm
  Dinner: Tues-Thurs: 7.30-9.30pm
  Fri-Sat: 7.30-10pm
CHILDREN: Well behaved welcome
CREDIT CARDS: Access/Visa
LICENSED: Restaurant Licence
ACCOMMODATION: Not applicable

RESTAURANT: Imaginative, generous
  portions
BAR FOOD: Not applicable
VEGETARIAN: Unusual selection on
  request
DISABLED ACCESS: Welcome
GARDEN: No

THE SCARLET PIMPERNEL

Public House & Restaurant

Main Road, West Huntspill,
Nr Highbridge, Somerset.

Tel: (0278) 783513

West Huntspill near Highbridge is on the main A38, set amongst north Somerset's delightful countryside. The Scarlet Pimpernel attracts a wealth of visitors through its charming doors. The bar is comfortable and quaint with its beamed ceilings adding a touch of romanticism to it. The Restaurant is light and airy and can seat 70 covers. It also boasts a Conservatory.

Paul and Barbara, the Managers have been publicans for eleven years but only moved here recently. Their lively, hospitable personalities have already endeared them to the locals.

Good home-made food is available in the Bar and Restaurant. The bar menu has a wide range of dishes, with Cottage Pie, steak and kidney pie, lasagna, fish platters and crisp salads are high on the popularity list, along with well-filled sandwiches freshly cut to order and jacket potatoes with a variety of fillings, a daily specials board also adds to the varied choice.

The Restaurant has a hot Carvery every Friday, Saturday & Sunday, which is very keenly priced, also specialising in grills, and can cater for functions, coach parties and weddings. You will rarely taste better Steak, Rainbow Trout, Garlic King Prawns or Beef Wellington. For sweet tooths there is always the large range of desserts to satisfy.' Children are not forgotten, under 5's can eat free, Monday to Friday from the 'Junior Diners' menu, on a one adult one child basis.

The wine list is extensive with some excellent bottles to choose from. Frequently at weekends dining is enlivened by live music in the bar.

USEFUL INFORMATION

OPEN: 11-2.30pm & 6-11pm
CHILDREN: Yes. Family room
CREDIT CARDS: Access/Visa/Amex
LICENSED: Full
ACCOMMODATION: Not applicable

RESTAURANT: 80 seats. No charge for children under 5. Hot & cold carvery, grills, a la carte
BAR FOOD: Traditional & home-cooked
VEGETARIAN: Small choice
DISABLED ACCESS: No
GARDEN: None

THE SUNDOWNER HOTEL
Hotel & Restaurant

74 The Main Road,
West Huntspill, Highbridge, Somerset.

Tel: (0278) 784766
Fax: (0278) 784766

If you are looking for a relaxing place to stay in warm friendly surroundings, in the picturesque Somerset countryside, The Sundowner Hotel and Restaurant, just off the A38 at West Huntspill is the place to head for. Ideally situated for travellers on business in the south west, or the weekend visitor it is relaxing and hospitable.

This privately owned hotel is owned by Don and Fiona Fisher. It has a deserved 2 star recommendations from the AA and the RAC. The hotel has cleverly combined modern facilities with an olde worlde charm. There are 8 beautifully decorated en-suite rooms, each with telephone, TV and tea and coffee making facilities. This attractive hotel has facilities for business conferences, dinners and any private function you may have in mind.

An extensive menu consists of fish dishes including Red Tallapia, a fresh water fish from the lakes of Africa, and from the grill there is anything from a succulent steak to a mixed grill. Try one of the chefs specials, a superlative Beef Wellington, or the honey-roast duckling served with an orange, sherry and red wine sauce. Follow any of these beautifully cooked meals with a home-made mouth watering sweet or choose from a selection of ice cream with a deliciously fattening dessert sauce. Vegetarians have their own interesting special menu.

USEFUL INFORMATION

OPEN: Non residents
CHILDREN: Welcome. Pets by arrangement
CREDIT CARDS: Visa/Access/Amex
LICENSED: Residential & Restaurant
ACCOMMODATION: 8 en-suite rooms.

RESTAURANT: Grills, fish, chicken. All home-cooked
BAR FOOD: Traditional home-cooked
VEGETARIAN: Special menu
DISABLED ACCESS: Yes to restaurant
GARDEN: Yes. Outside seating

THE WHITE COTTAGE

Restaurant

Old Pawlett Road (A38)
West Huntspill, Somerset.

Tel: (0278) 794692
Fax: (0278) 794309

One of the great pleasures is to know of somewhere where one can eat that is easily accessible from a Motorway. The White Cottage at West Huntspill answers this criteria. It is located midway between Bridgwater and Burnham-on-Sea on the A38 main road between Junction 22 and Junction 23 of the M5. Set in its own grounds, with a garden restaurant area, lounge and front area, with ample car parking, it is a great find.

Originally the restaurant was one cottage constructed in 1826. Since then it has been carefully and cleverly extended and improved by the owners, Gee Dawe and Martin Bargent, to provide a high level of cuisine and yet relaxing. It has been well known for years as the White Cottage but now is open for a la carte dinner, afternoon teas, morning coffee and party functions. It is doubtful whether one would find better quality anywhere in the county.

The restaurant seats 55 comfortably for dinner and for a buffet can accommodate up to 80 people. The kitchen is presided over by the master chef, Domenico Lamberti, who with 30 years experience can be relied on to produce outstanding dishes. His range is Modern European, everything is cooked to order, including the home-made pasta. The fresh fish menu includes Dover and Lemon Sole, Squid, Scallops and Sea Bass. The meat is of the highest quality and all the sauces are made on the premises as are the delectable desserts. Dining here is an experience whether it is on an ordinary evening or on one of the special and very popular Theme evenings. There are 'Brunch Jazz' Mornings with live Jazz Bands, Classical Guitarists Musical Evenings. It is a remarkable and genuinely welcoming establishment.

USEFUL INFORMATION

OPEN: Tue-Sat: 10.30-12 midnight.
  Sun: Roast Lunch: 12-3pm
CHILDREN: Well behaved
CREDIT CARDS: Access/Visa/Barclay
LICENSED: Restaurant, music & dancing
ACCOMMODATION: Not applicable

RESTAURANT: Modern European,
  Freshly cooked, home-prepared
BAR FOOD: Lite bites at lunchtime
VEGETARIAN: 3-4 dishes daily
DISABLED ACCESS: Level entrance
  No toilets
GARDEN: Front patio, countryside
  garden, seating, BBQ

THE SHOULDER OF MUTTON
Hotel

1 School Road, Westonzoyland, Nr Bridgwater, Somerset.

Tel: (0278) 691319

The Battle of Sedgmoor has always had a fascination for those interested in history and many people come to Westonzoyland to see the Battlefield. It is a great tourist attraction, and it is to be found just ten minutes away from The Shoulder of Mutton, a hostelry where everyone is very welcome; a liking for battlefields is not a condition of entry! Diana Humphrey the proprietor, who runs the pub with the help of her son Steven, and her daughter Joanne, is a lady who simply likes people and has worked hard to make this hotel so popular. It is large and spacious, modern in its decor, cheerful and a favourite with locals who regularly fill the bar with their lively chatter. There are seven, newly furnished and newly built en-suite bedrooms.

The fact that Westonzoyland is only three miles from Bridgwater means that they are often in use for business people coming to the town to carry out their tasks and enjoying the fact that this peaceful hotel awaits them after a busy day. At one time the pub was the favourite watering hole of the R.A.F from the nearby airfield from which they flew microlights. They came here to drink and be merry. Those days have gone but the drink is just as good and it is certainly a merry place. The huge function room is often in use for private parties and The Shoulder of Mutton specialises in wedding receptions. From the comprehensive a la carte menu there are some delicious pasta dishes, tender and beautifully cooked steaks and probably the best mixed grill for miles. The garden is large and has a splendid children's area as well as Barbecues on warm summer evenings.

USEFUL INFORMATION

OPEN: Mon-Fri: 11-3pm & 7-11pm.
  Sat: All day. Normal Sunday hours
CHILDREN: None taken
CREDIT CARDS: None taken
LICENSED: Full On Licence
ACCOMMODATION: 7 en-suite

RESTAURANT: A la carte.
  Comprehensive
BAR FOOD: Traditional
VEGETARIAN: 6 dishes approximately
DISABLED ACCESS: Ramps, gardens
  and Restaurant. Level to WC
GARDEN: Large. Childrens play area,
  Barbecue

THE FORESTERS ARMS
Hotel

55 Long Street,
Williton, Somerset.

Tel: (0984) 632508
Fax: (0984) 633692

If you enjoy a lively hotel which is frequently home to touring cricket and rugby teams, you will thoroughly enjoy the hospitality of The Foresters Arms in Long Street, Williton.

Comfortably, but unpretentiously furnished, it is a hotel that offers everyone who comes through its doors, a genuinely warm welcome, good conversation at the bar, where you can also get a snack or a meal and if you feel like it, dining in intimate, attractive surroundings.

The restaurant offers a selective menu of beautifully cooked and presented dishes. The Foresters Arms specialises in catering for groups of fisherman who come here to stay whilst they go sea fishing from Watchet harbour, just a mile or two away. The day's catch is quite frequently cooked for the fishermen either for dinner or for breakfast - nothing nicer than fish one has caught for oneself. This is a 17th-century building with all the nooks and crannies one might expect and is reputed to be haunted by a friendly female ghost.

The West Somerset Railway stops at Williton station on its scenic way from Minehead to Bishops Lydeard and passengers often break their journey to enjoy a drink or a meal at The Foresters, which is only a short walk away. Children are welcome,as are well behaved dogs. The Landlord is a Real Ale enthusiast and here you will usually find five Real Ales, of which two are Guest Bitters.

USEFUL INFORMATION

OPEN: Mon-Sat: 11-11pm, Sun: 12-3pm & 7.30-10.30pm
CHILDREN: Very welcome
CREDIT CARDS: Visa/Access
LICENSED: Full on & Supper Licence
ACCOMMODATION: Yes

RESTAURANT: Intimate, good choice
BAR FOOD: Wide choice throughout the day
VEGETARIAN: As required
DISABLED ACCESS: Level
GARDEN: Large, occasional barbecue

THE MASONS ARMS
Public House

2 North Road,
Williton, Somerset.

Tel: (0984) 632972

Williton is almost a small town rather than a village but it has lost none of its friendly attitude towards visitors. As you leave the village on the way to Watchett, just seconds off the main A39 you will see The Masons Arms, such a pretty pub with a thatched roof. Run by Janet Stone, a quiet spoken, delightful lady, it is an establishment full of interest. As you enter the restaurant you are advised to 'Duck or Grouse'! The low dark beams are lethal to anyone above average height.

On the bottom of the menus you will see a note addressed to 'The Connoisseur' which says 'You name it we can cook it. 24 hours notice please'. It is a pub where the needs of the customers is uppermost and with the help of her staff, Janet has achieved a great success. The restaurant which is separate from the bar, is a warm, intimate setting with burgundy velvet seating and soft pink walls. Fresh flowers adorn every table and it is the most relaxing place to sit and enjoy an aperitif whilst you are awaiting your meal. The menu is a simple one with a range of starters followed by a choice of fish, grills, and well tested favourites such as steak and kidney Pie, lasagne and chicken kiev. Special prices are available on weekdays for Senior Citizens lunches. The large bar which is almost hexagon in shape is supported in the middle with a real cut tree - most unusual. Bar snacks and basket meals are served here.

The Beer Garden is always popular and the play area for children has a climbing frame with sand covered ground for safety.

USEFUL INFORMATION

OPEN: Mon-Sat: 11am-11pm.
  Sun: Normal pub hours.
CHILDREN: Welcome
CREDIT CARDS: All major cards
LICENSED: Full On Licence
ACCOMMODATION: Not applicable

RESTAURANT: Traditional fare,
  emphasis on quality
BAR FOOD: Bar snacks & basket meals
VEGETARIAN: Selection of six dishes
DISABLED ACCESS: level entrance
GARDEN: Beer garden & play area

*A Bridge Over the Moat Leads to the Magic of the Walled
Formal Garden at Barrington Court*

SOUTH SOMERSET

INCLUDES

"When I demanded of my friend what viands he preferred,
he quoth 'A large cold bottle and a small hot bird'."

Eugene Field   109

SOUTH SOMERSET

 One leaflet I read said 'Come and share the secrets of South Somerset with us'. I did, and this is what I want to pass on to you. It is a part of the county that has just about everything. To the west the Somerset Levels and the Moors, to the south the Hamstone country, and to the east the mystical Camelot country. It is fabulous; filled with beauty, dignified monuments, stately homes and for those who love walking, it is paradise. For me paradise is a wander amongst the great diversity of garden styles to be enjoyed. Tucked away in the narrow lanes are eight wonderful gardens, representative of all that is beautiful, and where you can capture something of the essence of the classic English garden.

My route out of Taunton took me along the A358 towards Chard and Ilminster. I wanted to take a look at HATCH COURT at **Hatch Beauchamp**. *This fine Bath stone mansion in the Palladian style, is the home of Commander and Mrs Nation. It was designed in 1755 by Thomas Prowse of Axbridge. Curved wings, and a magnificent stone staircase strike one immediately. Much of the decoration was done about 1800. The house was bought by the present family in the late 19th century and restored by Brigadier A Hamilton Gault, M.P. for Taunton from 1924-1935. He also raised, equipped and ultimately commanded Princess Patricia's Canadian Light Infantry. One of the fascinating things about this house is the small museum containing regimental and other Canadian items.*

The house has a good collection of paintings, 17th and 18th century furniture and an unusual semi-circular China Room. The medieval parish church of St John the Baptist is situated nearby which contains some of my favourite pew ends. The church tower is a fine example of the fully developed west Somerset pinnacle plan. Under a memorial window lies a man who was one of the earliest VCs. As Lieutenant Chard, he was awarded the cross for gallantry at Rorke's Drift against the Zulus. His leadership had given the willpower to 100 men of the South Wales Borderers to withstand the onslaught of 3,000 Zulus for 12 hours, suffering less than 30 casualties. Hatch Court is surrounded by a small deer park containing a herd of fallow deer. The deer park has been in existence ever since the house was built in 1755 and is probably one of the smallest in the country.

The house is only open on Thursday afternoons from 2.30-5.30pm from July to September.

*Before I went to Hatch Court I stopped at THE FARMERS ARMS, in **West Hatch** just off the A358. This family run, happy establishment, was once a farmhouse, then a cider house and became a public house over a century ago. Everything here is freshly cooked and there is no better accompaniment to a meal than one of the pubs Real Ales, of which they have a large selection.*

*There are two small towns to which I have become attached over the years, that are just up the A378. **Langport**, a town of narrow streets and full of antique shops, lies on the River Parrett. The old warehouses standing by the riverside bear witness to the time when the town was busy with waterborne trade coming from Wales via Bridgwater. It was once a walled town but all that remains of the wall is THE HANGING CHAPEL - built over what was the East Gate. I used to think it had something to do with Judge Jeffreys but for once he is not responsible. Langport did play a decisive part in the Civil War though, in 1645 an important battle was fought on its outskirts, the site of which can still be seen if you follow the B3155 to Somerton. You will find a side road leading to **Wagg** and **Huish Episcopi** with the small waterway of the Wagg Rhyne alongside. The Royalists were well positioned on the Langport side where there was a very narrow ford across the rhyne. Only four horsemen could cross it abreast, but Fairfax ordered his cavalry to charge and after a fierce battle the day was won. The Royalists were defeated, their morale broken and the end of the Civil War was in sight.*

Go on to Huish Episcopi to see the historic church of St Marys with its wonderful perpendicular tower, niches and pinnacles. It is open in daylight hours. Afterwards go across to ELI's or to use its proper name, THE ROSE AND CROWN, a truly traditional inn. Its nickname comes from the family who have run it for 120 years.

***Somerton** claims to be the capital of ancient Wessex, and justifiably boasts much to entrance one for hours. The Church of St Michael has a roof that was created by the monks of Mulcheney from 7,000 fetter pieces. These monks obviously had a sense of humour; incorporated in the roof is a beer barrel playing on the name of Abbot Bere! If you wander down the leafy lane beside the church you will come into a delightful square of Georgian buildings, which has the misnomer of 'Cow Square', leading you into Broad Street which once was called Pig Lane. There has to be* *a reason for these names but I have found none. Somerton is graced with several good hostelries including THE RED LION which is still licensed to hire out post horses, and THE WHITE HART which stands on the site of Somerton's ancient castle.*

Market Cross, Somerton

*Once when I was in this neck of the woods about two years ago I started out exploring one day, and having had a good lunch in THE ROYAL OAK at **Stoke-St-Gregory**, the landlord was good enough to suggest several places that I might visit within easy reach. In Stoke-St-Gregory there are two traditional Somerset basket and hurdle makers. At THE WILLOW AND WETLAND VISITOR CENTRE not only can you view the process but there is also an extensive wetlands exhibition which reveals the unique landscape of the Somerset Levels. Add this to a basket museum and you will have good reason for visiting. Open: Monday to Friday 9am-5pm with guided tours from 10am-4pm at half hourly intervals. On Saturdays the times change to 10-5pm with just the showroom and the shop being open. Then there is THE ENGLISH BASKET CENTRE where not only can you see baskets and hurdles being made but you can walk through the adjoining growing willow beds. They are open from Monday-Friday 8am-5pm and on Saturday from 9am-1pm.*

*My next stop was **Curry Rivel** where the lovely 15th-century church looks over the village green. Take a look at the stone figures adorning the walls. There is one above the porch playing the bagpipes, and round the corner another playing the violin - they are known locally as the 'hunky punks'.*

MULCHENEY ABBEY is close by which was founded by the Benedictines in AD 950. Standing in beautiful grounds, you can see the excavated ground plan of the abbey church, preserved remains of the south cloister and the abbot's lodgings. It is open from Good Friday - 30th September daily from 10am-6pm. Also, in the village opposite the church, is the Priest's House, a thatched stone cottage built by the monks in 1308 to house the vicar of the parish. Although much has been altered inside, the exterior still displays a Gothic doorway, mullioned windows and the superb two-tiered window to the hall, with trefoil heads to the upper lights.

Just one mile south, the potter, John Leach, works from his thatched workshop. A selection of unique handthrown pots, including signed individual pieces is always available in the pottery shop. Open Monday to Friday 9-5pm and Saturdays 9-1pm

Life has been made much easier along the A358 with new roads. I found the journey from West Hatch to **Chard** *just flew by. Here is an old market town which you will either love or hate. I find it fascinating because of its history. Some used to think that a Saxon chieftain, Cerdic gave his name to the town, but it is more likely the name refers to a settlement on rough common. The town lies in a hollow between Windwhistle and the Blackdowns and is really more reminiscent of Devon and Cornwall than Somerset with its flint buildings and thatch.*

The Romans gave Chard its straight street but nature gave it something very different. A stream runs down each side of the main street, dividing at the bottom where one half sallies forth to pour itself into the English Channel, the other goes north to enter the Bristol Channel. It has always seemed to me that nature is telling us something. A little stream divides, gets stronger and meets again as part of the mighty Atlantic Ocean.

Fire destroyed much of Chard in 1577 but the perfectly proportioned 15th-century church survived, as well as the court house where Judge Jeffreys held trial after the Monmouth Rebellion. One of my favourite buildings is CHOUGH'S HOTEL built in 1644. A building of mystery and intrigue. Judge Jeffreys stayed here. You can still see his coat of arms in his bedroom. It is a hotel of hidden bedrooms, sealed cellars and what may have been an escape tunnel for priests fleeing from persecution. You will find a mummified bird kept in a coffin and superstition says it must always remain. Having taken all this in I suggest you go to the BELL AND CROWN just off the main street, for some refreshment. A friendly place, it has the benefit of a large car park. This is just one of several places I have

discovered in Chard, which are good. Just opposite the old Guildhall is
THE GEORGE HOTEL AND COPPER KETTLE RESTAURANT. They
are two separate establishments under the same ownership. The George
has been dispensing hospitality since the 1500's when it was a coaching
inn. It is a Listed building and part of its charm is the beautiful and
ornate ballroom upstairs, rich in red and golds, which reminds one of the
past when local society would have gathered to dance the night away.
Jewels, wonderful dresses, men in evening dress and probably several
in uniform would have made a wonderful picture.

The Copper Kettle Restaurant next door to The George, serves
simple, well cooked, home-made food and specialises in producing
imaginative meals for children. THE WELCOME BAP is a coffee shop
just a few steps from the centre in 9, Holyrood Street, and it is run by
members of the thriving Baptist church next door. It has an established
reputation for good food, reasonably priced and promptly served. The
ladies there told me about another piece of Chard's history. The town
has become known as the cradle of powered flight, because in a factory
here in 1848 John Stringfellow flew the first self-driven plane. Chard
now commemorates him by an attractive bronze sculpture in Fore Street.
Local Baptists themselves have a colourful history. Some stood
condemned in the Bloody Assizes after marching with Monmouth to
Sedgemoor in 1685. In the last century one of their lay-preachers, James
Gillingham, was the inventor and developer of artifical limbs. Much of
the history of Chard and many displays can be found in THE CHARD
MUSEUM in Godworthy House, in the High Street. It is open from early
May to Mid-October, Monday to Saturday 10.30am- 4.30pm. Plus
Sundays in July and August.

A superb place to stay is HORNSBURY MILL, just outside
Chard on the A358 to Ilminster. To come here is to experience a great
sense of history, to have one's imagination whetted, to eat in unusual and
delightful surroundings and if you decide to stay then the fully refurbished
living accommodation, set in its own grounds of five acres, is wonderful.
Mainly landscaped water garden, the Mill's resident family of ducks and
geese enchant people. There are level paths for the less mobile and
excellent disabled facilities. The Mill is a good example of an early 19th
century corn mill. Built of local flint stone with fine Hamstone mullion
windows, and with the majority of its timber parts made of elm wood, it
is essentially a Somerset mill.

Many efforts have been made to trace the exact age of the
building and it is believed that the present mill was built about 1835. It

is quite probable that there was a mill here before then but no proof has been found. The man-made leat bringing water to the mill is very long and leaves the River Isle some three quarters of a mile upstream. The water comes along the top of the bank into the back of the building, passes over the wheel and then joins the River Isle again just in front of the mill. There is a lot more about the people who owned the mill which you can discover for yourselves when you go there. There is a small museum of 'Bygones and Yesteryear' showing how our great grandfathers lived and worked.

FORDE ABBEY was founded by Cistercian monks 900 years ago. It remains a family home unaltered since the mid 17th century, but it is for its gardens that it is renowned. 30 acres are devoted to providing a graceful setting for the medieval abbey. The gardens which have a fine collection of mature trees and herbaceous borders were mostly laid out in the early 18th century, and have been cared for by three generations of the Roper family. A magnificent 'bog garden' was created in 1906 with statuesque plants and drifts of candelabra primulas in the summer, and a superb rock garden is being restored with the help of Alpine plantsman, Jack Drake. A walled kitchen garden supplies food for the household and the self-service restaurant which is open from April to October. The Abbey is open from Easter until the end of October on Sundays, Wednesdays and Bank Holidays from 1pm-4.30pm. The gardens are open daily throughout the year from 10am-4.30pm.

Penguins at Cricket St Thomas Wildlife Park

CRICKET ST THOMAS is midway between Chard and Crewkerne. It is one of the best wildlife and leisure parks in the country. The manor house was used for the TV series 'To The Manor Born' which many of us have enjoyed - even the repeats! It is set in a valley of outstanding natural beauty and provides a wonderful place for a happy family day out or as a member of an organised party. It is a working estate covering over a thousand acres. You can see anything from Asian elephants taking their daily walk to performing sea-lions disporting themselves. The Heavy Horse Centre is one of the few places in the country where these gentle giants are still bred and cared for. The miniature railway winds its way along the far side of the valley crossing a 40ft high bridge over the lake at one point. The adventure playground features a life-sized American fort, in addition to a large variety of 'assault course' challenges set along the woodland paths. Go there; it is excellent.

One tends to forget FERNE ANIMAL SANCTUARY, just three miles from Chard in the other direction. It started in 1939 when so many animals became homeless because their owners went off to war. The work of the sanctuary, which is a charity, continues today and they have some two hundred animals from horses to hamsters.

While I was staying in Chard this time I took the opportunity to have lunch with friends in the little village of **Dalwood**, over the Devon border and just off the A35. Easy to get to from Chard, it is not perhaps a place you have heard of. It is full of interest though, with the remarkable BURROW FARM GARDEN, a large bog garden in a Roman clay pit creating such fertile soil to produce a profuse display of azaleas, rhododendrons and roses. A wondrous sight at the right time of the year. Also the National Trust own LOUGHWOOD MEETING HOUSE. Nearby Kilmington was a stronghold of Baptists about 1653 and this simple, unadorned building was for their regular use until 1833. Surviving intact, it can now be seen throughout the year by one and all.

Where did I lunch? In the totally beautiful TUCKERS ARMS, the main part of which is 600 years old. It is a living example of change over the centuries with the original beams still in situ and a rare Jetted ceiling. I merely came to lunch but you can also stay here. There are a number of Real Ales, super malt whiskies and a few, carefully chosen wines including Dalwood wines from Australia, where the people who started the vineyard emigrated from Dalwood Vicarage.

WINDWHISTLE HILL beckons all who see it with its wonderful avenue of beech trees. Climb it and, on a clear day, you will be rewarded *with a view of the Bristol Channel on one side and the English Channel on the other, but always there is the enchanting sight of gentle Somerset beneath you. You will look down on **Crewkerne** from here. A town whose streets all converge on the market square. It has many old stone houses and four groups of almshouses but the church is the magnet. It is a grand 15th-century cruciform church with glorious windows. The west front is almost cathedral like. Inside it is a little disappointing but the width of the windows brings light to the lovely panelled roofs. Thirteen great stone angels stand holding up the enchanting nave roof.*

Crewkerne has always had the good fortune to be on the main road from London to Exeter making it a stoppng place for travellers. Catherine of Aragon stayed a night here on her way from Plymouth to marry Prince Arthur in 1501. By 1580 the town was a regular post stage and between 1619 and 1631. Thomas Hutchins, its postmaster, ran the first profitable postal system between London and Plymouth. Troops from both sides in the Civil War found it to their liking - at different times of course. They were entertained in the many inns and the officers could always find good accommodation.

At Crewkerne is one of Somerset's most interesting and beautiful gardens. CLAPTON COURT has over ten acres, with formal terraces, spacious lawns, rockery and water gardens. Recently designed is the gorgeous rose garden with arbors. There is a fascinating woodland garden with natural streams and glades alive with anemones, bluebells and primulas. Many plants and shrubs of botanical interest, include the biggest ash tree in Great Britain, which is over 230 years old and a fine Metasequoia, over 80 feet tall, planted in 1950 with seed collected in China by the Arnold Arboretum of Massachussets. This 'Garden for all Seasons' has a dazzling display of spring bulbs and glorious autumn colours. Many rare and unusual plants are for sale, also fuchsias and pelargoniums. Open March to October, Mondays to Fridays 10.30am-5pm and Sundays from 2-5pm, it has a licensed restaurant. Dogs are not allowed.

*Only a few miles up the A30 from Crewkerne is the little village of **Haselbury Plucknett**. This attractive hamstone village has many blessings but none better than the focal point of the village, THE HASELBURY INN. Here is a good, traditional country inn with great atmosphere. It is a warm-hearted place where everyone is welcome. James Pooley, the landlord will tell you that whilst children are welcome, he does keep a supply of six inch nails to nail them to the floor if they are troublesome! The pub is renowned for its food cooked by James' Czech* *born wife, Kathe who has an instinctive ability to get all the authentic flavours in her international menu.*

It is only a stone's throw from Crewkerne to **Hinton St George***, an estate village with a difference. Until recent years it was entirely owned by the Earls Poulett and fortunately has been left almost untouched by subsequent owners. Today restoration and protection are the name of the game. The church is a gem, showing Ham stone work at its very best. It was endowed with money in 1486 and a tower was built with a splendid crown and pinnacles. The body of the church belongs to the same period though the font is of the 13th century, recut to go with the building. There is a wealth of fascinating memorials most of them to members of the Poulett family.*

The Priory in the village is the oldest house in Hinton, which includes a 14th century window in the chapel at its east end although the house itself dates from the 16th century.

One of the favourite places in this village is THE POULETT ARMS which is full of a sense of the past and the comfort of the present. As you look round the walls you will spot some splendid old signs hanging below the original beams. One states 'Rooms 7/6d per night with attendant female staff.' Would that it were this price today.

The Minster Church, Ilminster

A choice of small country roads will take you from here to **Ilminster***, which as the name implies, was once a Saxon missionary centre, the minster on the River Ile, and said to have been founded by King*

Ine in 726. That is what the monks of Mulcheney Abbey claimed anyway, in a charter in their archives which subesequently was found to be forged but the facts true! Ilminster has a charming market place, Queen Victoria stayed here in The George Hotel, just before she became Queen. The Georgian houses in Court Barton demonstrate the prosperity of the 18th century which for over a hundred years had been an important cloth-making and gloving centre.

The superb crossing tower of the minster is reminiscent of the central tower at Wells Cathedral, with battlements and pinnacles. It is truly splendid. Behind the church in Court Barton is a 15th century chantry house, partly Georgianized and the former grammar school, founded by Humphrey Walrond in 1549, a successor to a school at least a century older.

No one coming to Ilminster should miss the opportunity of staying or calling in at the immaculately kept, SHRUBBERY HOTEL. For over thirty years Stuart and Liz Shepherd have owned this excellent hotel. One of the nicest things about it is its efficient informality; you may choose to eat where you will, whether it is in the sun lounge, the bar or the restaurant.

I discovered MINSTRELS in Silver Street, when I went there to buy a home-made cake. I had not realised that it was a traditional coffee shop as well. An ideal place to pop into for a coffee or a good lunch at reasonable prices.

*Two miles outside Ilminster is PERRY'S CIDER MILLS, a traditional Somerset cider farm set in **Dowlish Wake** a picturesque village with streams and a packhorse bridge. It is somewhere in which you can wander around, or take a look at the Museum of Farming with wagons and photographs of country life. In the autumn you can watch the cider making. Just the place for a peaceful afternoon. It is open throughout the year and there is a shop from which you can buy cider, scrumpy, Somerset cider brandy and all manner of gifts. The opening hours on weekdays are 9-1pm & 1.30-5.30pm. Saturdays 9.30-1pm & 1.30-4.30pm.Sundays 10am-1pm. Closed Sunday afternoons,*

*There is a good pub, THE ROYAL OAK at **Over Stratton**, just off the roundabout at the eastern end of the Ilminster by-pass. It is 400 year old, thatched and beautiful. It merges perfectly with the other buildings in the main street, so well that you have to be careful not to miss it. But for the sign above the door, the inn might well be a private house. Definitely a place to put on your visiting list.*

119

From Ilminster I always make my way to **Barrington**, *a village that is in the heart of the ham-stone country and carefully preserved. It has more than its fair share of beautiful thatched cottages and golden houses, several of them dating from the Middle Ages. It is delightful and made even more of a treat for me by the presence of BARRINGTON COURT. The magnificent ham-stone mansion, whose stones bear the signs of the Ham Hill masons, is an E shaped building with a central block of medieval plan with two long wings, one including a kitchen and a central porch. The third floor is formed into a long gallery. The mullioned and transomed windows and diagonal buttresses are remarkably plain but the roof line is a delight with its finials with ogee caps, twisted chimneys and octagonal buttress tops.*

Barrington Court

The superb garden was laid out in the 1920's to designs by architects Forbes and Tate who used basket weave brick paths and fine masonry in walls and outhouses to give the garden structure. The famous Gertrude Jekyll advised on the planting. The lily garden, where a central pool is surrounded with plants in reds and yellows, blending with mellow brick walls in the background, shows her sure touch. Christine Middleton, the present head gardener, has added a beautifully designed 'White' garden. In season, produce is sold from the acre of fruit and vegetables tended in the walled kitchen garden.

Barrington is open 12-5.30pm daily except Thursdays and Fridays from April 1st to October 1st. The Court House is open 1.30-5pm on Wednesdays for guided tours only from April 1st to October 1st.

Shepton Beauchamp *does not boast a VC like Hatch Beauchamp but it has a wonderful 15th-century church with a tower that is splendid inside and out, and not far away is a pub that is worthy of its name THE DUKE OF YORK. It is a happy place in which to drink or eat.*

Just up the winding road you will come to *Stembridge*, *a little hamlet quite near to* *Martock*. *I found it quite by chance when I was looking for East Lambrook Manor, another of Somerset's beautiful gardens. It was a happy find. THE RUSTY AXE with its thatched roof is welcoming and produces an excellent meal. Tanya Fitzgerald, the proprietor, is renowned for the standard of her food; not because it is exotic but because it is good, old fashioned country cooking.*

Stembridge Mill at High Ham

If you do not want to look at a garden then another option is BURROWHILL CIDER FARM where you can see cider being made at the right time of the year. For me it is a pilgrimage to EAST LAMBROOK MANOR where Margery Fish's great love for cottage gardens led her to create the listed garden at East Lambrook Manor during the 32 years that she lived there. Here planting almost dominates over design. With hardly a straight line in sight the garden has over 5,000 species and cultivars in tiny themed corners with down to earth names such as 'The Ditch', 'The Green Garden'', 'The Sundial Garden' and the 'Herb garden'. It is a plantsman's delight; a garden offering both lessons on the importance of siting plants, and the occasional surprise when you stumble across a rare plant.

East Lambrook is open from 10-5pm on Mondays to Saturdays from March 1st until the 31st October.

Many people drive straight through **South Petherton** which is a pity because it has a fine church, the second highest octagonal tower in the country. Today it houses the effigy of a curly headed knight dressed in chain mail. He is Sir Philip de Albini who died in 1292 but he was not buried with ceremony. His remains were unearthed by the side of the road where a pit was being dug for a petrol tank! If you were a National West customer in South Petherton you would constantly be reminded of the Monmouth rebellion; opposite the bank is Market House where three men were hanged in the courtyard from a beam by the order of the dreaded Judge Jeffreys.

The golden ham stone buildings of Martock make a good setting for an unusual enterprise. THE TOWN TREE NATURE RESERVE designed and landscaped by Chris Burnett has provided a variety of habitats to attract and support flora and fauna. Less than twenty years ago the land was a 100 acre farm but the difference was that no artificial fertiliser or pesticide had ever been used on it. Excavation has produced a large lake with several smaller ones, tapping water from the river Parrett. There are twenty acres providing a water habitat for many wading birds including snipes, sandpipers and red shanks, as well as swans, mallards, diving ducks, herons and kingfishers. Birds and animals have their own woodland habitat and it is not unusual to see goldcrests, tree creepers and woodpeckers. An old railway cuttng, once part of the Great Western Railway line from Yeovil to Taunton, forms a scrub area where there are grass snakes, slow-worms, butterflies and birds.

You need to set aside at least two hours to appreciate what the Town Tree Nature Reserve has to offer. A guided tour with an informative and entertaining commentary is provided by either Chris or his wife.

The farmhouse is constructed around a 17th century cob house and here you can get a good cup of tea and light refreshments. The final touch is a former cowshed, with original 16th century beams and cob walls, inside is an exhibition of the history of the farm.

Martock looks as though it has always been prosperous judging by the quality of even the small houses and this is continued in the surrounding hamlets of **Hurst, Bower Hinton, Coat, Stapleton,** and **Witcombe**. They all bear witness to the agricultural prosperity of the 17th and 18th centuries. Since the 19th century Martock has expanded *considerably. Its centre, with the market house of 1753, has something of an urban air which a carefully hidden modern shopping precinct has encouraged.*

The National Trust now owns the fabulous TREASURER'S HOUSE which comprises a medieval hall and cross wing; the wing has a window of the later 13th century and the hall was probably rebuilt about 1290. A kitchen wing was added beside the hall in the late 15th or early 16th century, when the whole was remodelled with a fireplace and new windows. The gateway belongs to this same period.

Opposite stands the church which may once have been a minster. It was certainly in existence in 1156 when it belonged to the Abbey of Mont St Michel. About 1190 it was acquired by Bishop Reginald of Bath and it was one of his successors, Bishop Jocelin, in 1226 who divided the income, giving half, and the patronage of the living to the treasurers of Wells Cathedral. Hence the Treasurer's House. A curiosity in the church on the north side is a buttress with footholds, cut in the 18th century to allow the recovery of five balls from the leads!

My journeying now is going to take me on a slightly circuitous route because I want to end up just over the Dorset border at Sherborne, where my daughter lives. To do this I am going to make my way steadily up the A303 to Wincanton and then Castle Cary before I drop back down to Sherborne and Yeovil.

*Modern road builders have been almost determined to make you miss **Ilchester**. Please do not do so. It may not appear to have much to see at first but when you start digging into its history you realise that here is a Roman town. It was founded where the great Fosse Way from Lincoln to Axmouth in Devon was joined by a road from the Bristol Channel to Dorchester at a ford. The Roman street pattern still remains but by the 4th century the town was walled, though buildings and graves are found well outside the line of the wall whenever new houses or roads are built.*

By 1086 the town had a market charter and was given a summer fair about 1183. By about 1250 it had at least six parish churches, a Dominican friary, a hospital and in 1298 it sent two representatives to parliament. It lost much of its importance and prosperity as time went on and of the six churches only the 13th century church of St Mary Major has survived. Well worth a visit though for its east window is a primitive form of tracery and its slightly later octagonal tower was the pattern for several neighbouring churches including Barrington and South Petherton.

123

Today Ilchester is quietly prosperous and has THE IVELCHESTER HOTEL AND RESTAURANT in The Square, a welcoming hotel and pub which feeds you well and ensures you have a good night's sleep.

*Closeby is the Naval Air Station at **Yeovilton**. One of the largest and busiest of the Fleet Air Arm bases. From the public's point of view it is better known for its famous FLEET AIR ARM MUSEUM. Here the story of the Fleet Air Arm is dramatically presented with over 50 historic aircraft, hundreds of models, photographs, paintings and exhibitions. To help you enjoy the breathtaking exhibits more simply, the museum is divided into sections and each display takes a piece of the Fleet Air Arm's history bringing it alive for you and your family.*

The Fleet Air Arm Museum offers you an adventure. You step into the world of aircraft and ships and sea-borne flight. You can relive the drama and excitement of bygone days - meet the heroes and heroines. The museum has a unique tale to tell all about the courage and daring - sometimes foolhardiness - needed to combat the hazards of the sea and air, the dangers of war and rescue.

You can see and hear World War I and World War II brought to life - the aircraft in the battlefields and the terrifying sounds of combat, with the men and women of the flying Navy - people very like you and I. You can find out about heroes like Rex Warneford VC - who brought down a German Zeppelin in 1915 but was forced to land behind enemy lines, and that is just the start of his story.

The spectacular displays make you a part of the Fleet Air Arm Adventure. just look if you like, but here you can actually touch the real thing - like 'Humphrey' the massive Wessex helicopter, a true veteran of the Falklands, bullet holes and all. If you would rather you can take a stroll through Concorde 002, one of the great achievments of 20th century engineering and built just up the road in Bristol.

There is a fine collection of uniforms, medals, letters and diaries, all belonging to a hero or heroine with a story to tell. If models fascinate you, you will find 250 examples of aircraft and ships, showing the skills of their makers and an astonishing eye for detail. An opportunity is there for you to pretend you are an ace pilot sitting in the cockpit of a Phantom or testing your skills in the Super X flight simulator.

The viewing galleries give you a chance to see the Harrier Jet in action. This amazing plane can fly vertically or horizontally. No child is ever disappointed with the 'Naval Aviation Adventure Playground'; hopefully they will be able to work off some surplus energy.

The Fleet Air Arm Museum is open every day of the year except Christmas Eve, Christmas Day and Boxing Day. From April- October 10am-5.30pm and November-March 10am-4.30pm

Just to the north of Ilchester is LYTES CARY. Once the home of medieval herbalist Henry Lyte, this late medieval manor house is surrounded by a garden which is an enchanting mixture of formality and simplicity. Hidden paths enclosed by high hedges of Yew topiary lead to surprise views - a pool with a fountain, a statue of a Greek goddess and occasional glimpses of the house - which have been skilfully used to evoke an Elizabethan atmosphere. At the foot of the garden an orchard of medlars, quinces, apples and pear trees is crossed by diagonal paths of mown grass. It is a wonderful experience.

Opening times are from 2-6pm, dusk if earlier, Monday, Wednesday and Saturdays from April until the end of October.

*Further along the A303 from Ilchester you will come to **Sparkford** where THE HANYES MOTOR MUSEUM must be one of the best in the country. The Haynes Motor Museum Trust was founded and endowed by John Haynes, chairman of the publishing group that bears his name, to form a permanent home for all the cars and bikes that as an enthusiastic motorist he has collected with great care and thought over the years. The Trust is now fully responsible for the upkeep management and development of what must now be ranked as one of the largest and best motor museums in the UK. The museum is well signposted and located just off the A 303 Sparkford bypass.*

The Haynes Motor Museum will interest and enthral you and your family and friends as you look over the unique and extraordinary range of over 200 veteran, vintage and classic cars, motorcycles, racing cars and bikes on display. All in as original and as new condition as possible.

Nearly every car and bike in the museum is driven at least every six months on the specially constructed 1 kilometre display and demonstration road round the museum. Something interesting like a 1930 four and a half litre Bentley or 400s Lamborghini Countach may be circulating when you visit.

125

Set in glorious countryside almost in the shadow of CADBURY CASTLE, the reputed Camelot of King Arthur and his court, the Museum has an ambience at one with the chivalrous ideals of the gallant King and his Knights of the Round Table. It is not a bad idea to bring a picnic and enjoy the view of the rolling hills and woodlands.

On display are vehicles ranging from a 1903 Olds mobile whose single cylinder 1900 cc engine is mounted under the rear facing passenger seat, through cars from the veteran, Edwardian, vintage and post vintage era to modern classics.

Also on display is the 'Red Collection' of sports cars from the 50's and 60's, such as the MG, TF, Midget, MGA and MGB, the Triumph TR3, 4A, 6 and 8, the Ginetta, G15, Jensen Healey, Alfa Romeo Spyder, Austn Healey 100/6, the 4.2 and V12'E' Types etc.

Other halls contain a fabulous collection of American cars including a Model 'T' Ford, Haynes V12, Cord and a supercharged Auburn Speedster, vintage cars such as Austins, Morris, Riley, Daimler, Lagonda, Bentley, Lanchester, and Rolls Royce are also on display, as are family cars from the 50s, 60s and 70s: Ford Popular, Standard Vanguard, and Vauxhall Cresta amongst many others, are all there.

The museum is also equipped with a 70 seat video cinema and the PIT STOP CAFE - much needed after so much sightseeing. For those who are camera happy you are invited to click away as much as you wish.

Haynes Motor Museum opens every day of the year except for Christmas Day and New Years Day from 9.30am - 5.30pm

*The pretty little village of **South Cadbury** and much of the surrounding countryside is dominated by one of the most famous archaelogical sites in the West Country. CADBURY CASTLE was known as early as Leland's time as the Camelot of Arthurian Legend. Between 1966 and 1970 this multi-vallateD hillfort was excavated on a large scale. It is somewhere which excites all those who revel in the stories of King Arthur and his Knights of the Round Table. At the foot of cadbury and in the Vale of Camelot is THE RED LION, a village pub of character offering Real Ales and a varied menu. Yours hosts, Alan and Dorothy Jefferys.*

In keeping with the legend of King Arthur there is said to be a ghost at The Red Lion. Alan Jefferys has seen doors open and a puff of smoke appear; it is said the king is buried in the hill!

126

What a bustling place **Castle Cary** is. Everything seems to be on a small scale. It has friendly shops, welcoming people and a great deal of charm although you would be hard put to find much in the way of outstanding architecture. It once had a castle with a motte and bailey structure but that has virtually gone, and its market hall was rebuilt in 1855 although there are some 17th century pillars. The church was largely rebuilt in 1855. There are some nice houses including the 18th century post office in Bailey Hill overlooking an intriguing lock-up of 1779. I am told it is frequently used as a threat of punishment to recalcitrant children! In the snug bar of the friendly WHITE HART in Fore Street you will find the walls lined with photographs showing what the old town was like in years gone by. For three hundred years this pub has served travellers and local people. Its character has grown in strength over the centuries and it is one of the nicest pubs for miles.

Whenever I think about **Wincanton** I think about horse racing. I have spent many happy hours on the course at various meetings. It is not a fashionable racecourse and is far less formal than its grander cousins but it is great fun - especially if you win! The town is frequently referred to as 'Queen of the Vale' referring, of course, to the Blackmore Vale. It is an interesting old town, abounding in hotels and inns to suit all tastes, many of them survivors of the coaching era, when about seventeen coaches a day stopped here on their journey from London to the cities of the west. In the town centre is THE BEAR INN which always fascinates me because of its amazing collection of Toby Jugs; over forty of them and all Royal Doulton. It has been an inn certainly since 1680 but probably much earlier.

In Market Street is DILLY'S an attractive coffee shop and licensed restaurant owned by Judy Lockley. It is somewhere where you can get food at sensible prices all day long starting with a splendid English Breakfast and finishing the day with a delicious, highly fattening cream tea.

Only half a mile out of Wincanton is a genuine English country house hotel, HOLBROOK HOUSE. It is a house that has every modern amenity but never has the 20th century been allowed to detract from its Georgian elegance. The fifteen acres of ground not only shield the house from the outside world, but allow guests to play squash and tennis and also swim in the heated pool during the summer. Staying here is sheer pleasure.

You should make your way to TOUT HILL while you are here. Once there must have been a manor house but is now known as 'The Dogs'. William of Orange spent a night here on his march to London in 1688 and it housed French prisoners of war during the Napoleonic wars. It is now in private ownership and appropriately guarded by a fearsome dog!

Within the town it is the fine Georgian buildings which are most memorable. Look carefully and you will see that there are many double sash wndows designed to give the most possible light for hand looms, producing serge, a cloth for which Wincanton was famous in the 18th century.

I am not enthusiastic about the church but the churchyard is full of fascinating epitaphs. In the porch is a medieval relief of St Eligius, patron Saint of metal workers and farriers, who later became a bishop. He is supposed to be shoeing a horse, but as neither the horse nor he has a head, and the horse is minus a leg, it is fair to suppose he was not very good at his job! If you have ever been to STOURHEAD HOUSE you will know the name of Nathaniel Ireson. This famous architect was one of Wincanton's notabilities, who died in 1769. He planned and designed his own monument as a memorial to himself and you can see him standing with a skull at his feet, with the names of other members of his family inscribed there on - the memorial, not the skull! His arrival in the town after a major fire resulted in a number of fine early 18th century buildings being built using brick, a rarity in South Somerset.

*There is a nice drive one can take in almost a cirular route from Wincanton. First of all to the east look for **Cucklington**. Climb a scarp to the village and there take the higer of two roads where there is a marvellous viewpoint with a wide expanse of BLACKMORE VALE extending before you, a landscape that obviously inspired Hardy. The Church of St Lawrence is mostly 13th century with a small side chapel dedicated to St Barbara, said to be the saint of the hills, whose very faded likeness appears in a window of the chapel, and whose well lies further down the street leading into the tiny village.*

*At the end of the village fork right downhill to drive along the flat bottom of the Vale to **Horsington.** In the village you will find its only pub, the attractive HALF MOON INN, built sometime in the 17th century, it was once a cider house. It is a good inn made even better by the addition of four chalets built around the pub making it possible for people to stay here.*

The way to the church lies beside a pond edged with yellow iris, the home of several ducks. Before you reach the church, a fine building although not of any great age, you will see on your left an ancient preaching cross of Ham Hill stone, centuries old, bearing a canopied figure with bones at its feet - possibly St Adhelm of Sherborne who is thought to have preached here about 705 AD before any church was built. The ground on which its stands was once the village market, and the Georgian building next to the church is now the HORSINGTON HOUSE HOTEL. The history of Horsington is well recorded with the cross on the green known to be a memorial of the grant given to the lord of the manor, William Russell in 1284 which allowed him to try, and hang a thief caught in the manor grounds.

*If you head back to the main road, turning left toward **Templecombe** you will find this ancient village still has its village stocks in place. Its name was taken from the medieval order of soldier monks, the Knights Templar, who were dedicated to the protection of pilgrims and religious treasures. The church, founded by the daughter of Alfred, houses one of the greatest treasures, a wooden panel painted with the face of Christ, about 700 years old. This was discovered in one of the cottages which once formed the Priest's house and was possibly copied from the Holy Shroud now in Turin, which the Knights Templar may once have held. It is a very remarkable painting, not to be missed. The village railway station won the first prize in British Rail's small station category, a tribute to the local people who fought to officially reopen the station in 1983.*

*Two miles south of Templecombe is the village of **Henstridge**. This is a busy place overlooking the Blackmore Vale and ideal for anyone wanting a base to tour the county. THE FOUNTAIN INN MOTEL provides the ideal accommodation. The inn is 17th century but the accommodation is modern and has everything one needs.*

At the only set of traffic lights on the main A30 at Henstridge you will discover THE VIRGINIA ASH a welcoming family pub with highchairs for little ones and an excellent play area in the attractive beer garden. Martin and Kris Shone, the landlords, work on the principle that a stranger is just a friend they have not yet met - something that makes them many friends. It is said that Sir Walter Raleigh smoked his first pipe of tobacco in this pub and his servant, thinking he was on fire, promptly doused him with a bucket of water - probably a founder member of the non-smoking brigade.

As you leave Henstridge turn right towards **Milborne Port** *where you have almost stepped into Dorset. As you enter Milborne Port look at the impressive facade of VENN HOUSE begun in 1698 and completed in 1731. Unusual because of its construction in brick. Formerly the third town in Somerset, a Royal Mint in Saxon times, and latterly an important gloving centre, Milborne Port is still a busy little place and it is well worth leaving the cafe to walk around. The old market house now the town hall has parking nearby and the ancient stone building with the Norman doorway is now the guildhall. But one of the most striking features of the little town must surely be the splendid Saxo-Norman church and the approach to it. This leads through to a beautiful 'Garden of Remembrance' to those who lost their lives in the two world wars, and adjoining this is the huge Fives Wall, built by the lord of the manor, Sir W.C. Medlycott in the year 1847 with the enjoinder: ' It is earnestly hoped that this Court which is meant for the health and amusement of the town will be protected from injury.' Up to now it certainly has been, and it is a splendid edifice.*

Take the Sherborne road and you will come to **Milborne Wick**, *a hamlet of about seven or eight dwellings beneath an enormous earthwork, it is a sheer delight. An old water-mill, its wheel still intact, dominates the place while the old millstream is the home of numerous ducks, and in the water meadows behind it you may see a flock of Canada geese which breed there. Free range poultry and Aylesbury ducks stroll the lanes at liberty and, of course, free-range eggs are on sale here. The tiny church, dominated by a soaring chestnut tree is the size of a large room with a piano in place of an organ! There is an air of quiet contentment about the place - possibly due to the blessed absence of traffic, although two roads meet here - one from Milborne Port and the other leading to* **Charlton Horethorne**, *two miles away.*

North Cheriton *is next where a long winding side road leads down a very steep hill to the vilage church. The corner on which the church stands makes a complete and perfect picture in itself - the fine old church, with the village stocks standing close at hand, the Manor House and manor farm, together with one of the finest war memorials to the eleven men of the village who fell in the great War. Close by are the remains of the Court and Five Wall where the Napoleonic officers imprisoned in 'The Dogs' at Wincanton could come and play Fives. You are almost back in Wincanton but there is one more stop at* **Lattiford** *where Commander and Mrs Aldrich have re-started the ancient craft of cider making in their 15th century thatched cottage, ROSE FARM. Using an 1850 cider press and many varieties of apple from orchards at Henstridge, North and South Cheriton, Horsington, Charlton Horethorne* *and many other surrounding villages, as well as their own crop, they are able to produce ciders with interesting variations of taste, according to where the apples come from and the variety used. Winners of the Bath and West Championship in 1987 and 1988 the Aldriches look upon their business as a conservation effort to preserve the cider apple tree. The acreage of cider apples has dwindled from over 20,000 acres to about 2,500 acres, which the Aldriches hope to increase again by encouraging the planting of more trees and buying the resulting crops.*

The Cider and Gift Shop open at 8.30am to 6.30pm every day except Sundays when it is noon to 3pm.

On the main road going toward Yeovil you will come to WORLDWIDE BUTTERFLIES and LULLINGSTONE SILK FARM at COMPTON HOUSE. In the setting of the house and its grounds, visitors can see butterflies alive and flying in exotic surroundings. You will see some wonderful displays and you wil be encouraged to learn to conserve. Worldwide Butterflies was founded by Robert Goodden over thirty years ago, creating a public awareness of butterflies that has spread enormously. The Lullingstone Silk Farm has supplied unique English silk for the last two coronations, for the Queen's wedding dress, and for many other royal occasions, including the wedding of the Prince and Princess of Wales. Here you can learn the ancient history of silk and see the silkworms producing English silk from the egg to the finished skein of soft, gleaming yarn. Open 10am-5pm daily from April 1st to 30th October (Good Friday if earlier).

*It was undoubtedly a tragedy that most of **Yeovil** was destroyed by fire some 500 years ago. It removed most of its historic past but did leave room for the new, and thankfully the 'Lantern of the West', the great church of St John, still stands. There it is in the heart of the town, an oasis of peace and a thing of splendour. It is no less than 146 feet long with a soaring tower 90ft high.*

There was once a mouse who made its home in the church, he loved the Harvest Festival and stuffed himself and then for the rest of the year was as poor as the proverbial church mouse. You will find him carved in four different places in the church, one of them under the base of the altar cross.

Yeovil became very familiar to us all over the Westlands affair and today this company still provides a large proportion of the employment. The Liberal Democrat Leader, Paddy Ashdown is the town's MP and often to be seen. He lives not far away in one of the pretty villages.

I was amused at the name of a pub I passed on the Ilchester Road, THE PICKETTY WITCH. There seems to be no particular reason for the name but it was enough to make me stop and pop in for a drink. I found a cheerful lady behind the bar who told me that she had been a barmaid here for 14 years. Her knowledge of the people and the area certainly reflected this. I was grateful for her help.

THE CORNER HOUSE in Union Street was a pleasant discovery. Here is a splendid Wholefood Restaurant and tearooms with some of the tastiest dishes one could ever wish for. Lunching here was a rare treat.

THE OCTAGON THEATRE is the Premier theatre of Somerset, presenting a full programme of drama, dance, concerts, musicals and pantomime, plus a restaurant, coffee shop and 3 licensed bars. All the facilities are fully accessible to the disabled and an induction loop system for the hard of hearing. There are performances throughout the year. For information and bookings ring (0935) 22884.

THE GOLDENSTONES POOLS & LEISURE CENTRE is a splendid place of which the town is suitably proud. It includes a 25m 6 Lane Main Pool, Teaching Pool, Hi Tec Gym, Sauna, Spa, Steam Room and Solariums. Open 7 days a week. Telephone (0935) 74166 for opening times.

*You should visit THE MUSEUM OF SOUTH SOMERSET, **Hendford**, Yeovil. Here you will discover the history of South Somerset among the splendid displays in this newly refurbished museum. From prehistoric and Roman occupation, through to agricultural and industrial revolutions, the museum shows, in an imaginative and exciting way, what rural life and times through the ages was really like. There are artefacts of a past and passing age set in scenes that recapture the atmosphere of their time. Housed in the former coach house of HENDFORD MANOR the Museum's modern displays draw upon many different collections brought together by Alderman W.R.E. Mitchelmore, Mayor of Yeovil from 1918-1921. Over the years benefactors have donated other important collections, including those of fossils, firearms, glassware and costume.*

The lo   r gallery of the coach house features South Somerset's association   leather and glove manufacturing, flax and hemp production,   neering, stone working and newspaper printing. Women outworkers   n be seen sewing gloves in the cramped conditions of their cottage, a reminder of a recently bygone era in South Somerset.

The impressive upper gallery features a reconstructed Roman dining room and kitchen complete with original mosaics recreated from

132

excavations of elegant villas found at Westland, Lufton and Ilchester. The opening hours are Tuesdays to Saturdays 10am-4pm and on Sundays 2-4pm.

*From Yeovil to **West Coker** is no distance. It has in its midst a super restaurant, SKITTLES, which is well worth trying. The building is over 400 years old, the atmosphere in the restaurant is delightful and the food is excellent. What more can you ask?*

Three wonderful places to visit within easy reach of Yeovil are, TINTINHULL, MONTACUTE HOUSE and BRYMPTON D'EVERCY.

TINTINHULL, designed by Phyllis Reiss and subsequently cared for by Penelope Hobhouse is a constant source of inspiration. An elegant and clearly defined structure divides the garden into a series of 'rooms' each with a different planting theme. In the pool garden yellow irises cluster in the corners of a small canal with two complementary borders: one filled with hot colours of red and yellow and the other with cool silvers and mauves. A path fringed with a soft haze of catmint leads through a kitchen garden to an orchard gate. Opening times 2-6pm on Wednesdays, Thursdays, Saturdays and Bank Holiday Mondays from 1st April to 30th September.

Montacute House Gardens

***Montacute**, three and a half miles from Yeovil is one of the finest Elizabethan Houses in the country. Montacute is complemented by suitably formal gardens. Smooth lawns, yew hedges and a sweeping drive provide an ideal setting for the architectural splendour of the house. A* *rich tapestry of greens highlights the mellow hamstone: strong colour is provided for much of the year by the mixed borders. Other features include a well-labelled rose border, an orangery, a fig walk, and a cedar lawn which was once called Pig's Wheatie's Orchard. Graham Stuart Thomas and Vita Sackville-West are among those who have contributed to the garden's appearance.*

You must make sure you visit, and preferably stay in the delightful KINGS ARMS INN in the village with its lovely mellowed ham-stone buildings.

BRYMPTON D'EVERCY is a house where time has stood still since the Duke of Monmouth stopped during his 'Progression ' to raise support for his 'Pitchfork Rebellion' in 1685. The warm, honey coloured stone buildings have escaped the embellishment of Victorian hands. The original Manor house stands alongside the 14th century parish church and now houses the Country Life Museum of old cider making equipment and agricultural bygones. It is said that great houses are noted for their architecture and remembered for their gardens. Brympton d'Evercy is no exception.

Alongside the house a vineyard has been established that now produces over 2000 bottles of English white wine. Opening times are from easter until the end of September from 2-6pm.

*Finally the icing on the cake in South Somerset has to be HAM HILL COUNTRY PARK. It looks down on Montacute, it sweeps out to touch the prety villages of **Norton-sub-Hamdon** and Stoke-sub-Hamdon. There are gentle strolls along the ramparts, a wide variety of wildlife and panoramic views to admire. The views are superb. In the west lies the Rampisham BBC World Service transmitter on the Dorset hills, the Windwhistle Ridge, above Cricket St Thomas, Exmoor, the Quantocks, and the willow-growing Somerset Moors.*

Burton Pynsent with the monument built by William Pitt the Elder and Burrow Hill of cider making fame, with its distinctive single tree, stand out to the north-west. Hinkley Point Nuclear Power Station beyond Bridgwater on the Bristol Channel can be seen on a good day and the Welsh hills beyond. To the north lies the sweep of the Mendip Hills behind Glastonbury Tor and the TV mast above Wells. Turning eastwards along the foothills of Salisbury Plain, Alfred's Tower can be seen on the Somerset/Wiltshire border. Also in the east lies the wooded hilltop of King Arthur's Camelot - South Cadbury Hillfort which leads the eye back into the woods of Hedgecock Hill which hides St Michael's Hill above Montacute with its climable tower.

THE WHITE HART

Fore Street,
Castle Cary, Somerset.

Public House

Tel: (0963) 50255

Castle Cary seems to change little. It is an ancient old market town which has maintained its original character and in the middle of the township standing where it has done for almost 300 years, is The White Hart. In the Snug Bar the walls are lined with photographs given by local people showing what the original town was like. Some are of the Market House and some of The White Hart. It is quite a fascinating collection. Quite recently original beams have been exposed in the bar bringing an even deeper character to this delightful old pub. However attractive a pub is it is nothing without good landlords and here Alan and Karen make sure everyone is welcome as their predecessors must have done all those hundreds of years ago.

The pub is open all day everyday except Sunday when normal hours apply. If you are sports minded there is a Skittle Alley or Table Skittles as well as Darts, Pool and that splendid old game of Shove Halfpenny for which you need a great deal of skill. If you decide to lunch you will be offered traditional home-cooked food which you may eat in the pub or if the day is kind, on the terrace. Just a stones throw away is the Round House on Bailey Hill, which was a temporary prison. Castle Cary also has a mill which still produces horse hair fabric; an interesting place to visit. If you have the energy after lunch, a stroll up Lodge Hill will give you a wonderful view right over the town and you can also see views over Somerset and Glastonbury Tor in its full glory, a longer walk along the Leyland Trail will also lead you here, and is an exhilarating experience. It is said that on a clear day you can see 32 church steeples up here!

USEFUL INFORMATION

OPEN: Mon-Sat: 10.30-11pm, normal
  Sunday Hours
CHILDREN: Welcome
CREDIT CARDS: Yes
LICENSED: Full On Licence
ACCOMMODATION: Cottage
  accommodation, ring for details

RESTAURANT: Not applicable
BAR FOOD: Home-cooked meals.
  Pasta, curries
VEGETARIAN: Always available
DISABLED ACCESS: Level at rear
GARDEN: Terraced area

THE BELL & CROWN
Inn

Coombe Street,
Chard, Somerset.

Tel: (0460) 62470

Tucked away behind the main street of Chard, is The Bell and Crown. One of its many virtues is the large car park which, in a town where parking is not the easiest thing to do, is a blessing. It is the sort of pub that is popular with the locals who regularly visit the long bar. The atmosphere is pleasantly welcoming with well polished oak tables on which stand small vases of freshly picked flowers. Visitors will find the Bell and Crown particularly convenient to have lunch and then take off for a wander around this old market town. Chard is only 20 minutes from the historic and delightful Lyme Regis, on the Dorset coast, just over the Somerset border.

There is a small beer garden at the rear where you can sit and enjoy a drink on a warm day and there is also a skittle alley in which to test your skills. You may inveigle one of the locals to have a game with you, but watch out - they are experts! Food is very important of course. You will find simple food here, well cooked and presented and, most importantly, extremely reasonably priced. The daily specials are very popular and in addition there are many pub grub favourites such as Scampi and chips, tender steaks, various chicken dishes and many snack items. The staff are a friendly crowd who offer service with a smile and have no objection to answering questions about the area. The Sunday roast with crisp potatoes and a selection of vegetables is incredible value.

USEFUL INFORMATION

OPEN: 11-2.30pm & 7-11pm
   Sun: 12-2.30pm & 7-10.30pm
CHILDREN: Welcome to eat
CREDIT CARDS: None taken
LICENSED: Full Licence
ACCOMMODATION: Not applicable

RESTAURANT: Not applicable
BAR FOOD: Wide choice, home-cooked
VEGETARIAN: 1-2 dishes daily
DISABLED ACCESS: Yes
GARDEN: Beer garden. Large car park

THE GEORGE HOTEL & COPPER KETTLE RESTAURANT

15 Fore Street,
Chard, Somerset.

Tel: (0460) 63413

Hotel & Restaurant

Chard is an excellent town in which to stay if you want a base for exploring this part of Somerset with its many and varied places of interest and history. Chard itself is a historic town and just opposite the old Guildhall you will find The George Hotel which has been dispensing hospitality since the 1500's when it was a coaching inn. Fire destroyed quite a lot of the building but some original parts still remain and it is a listed building now. The beautiful and ornate ballroom upstairs, rich in red and golds, reminds one of the past when local society would have gathered here to dance the night away.

Gordon and Natasha McDonald have made a splendid job of refurbishing the 12 bedrooms which are mostly en-suite. The newly decorated TV lounge, the large downstairs bar and restaurant area are friendly, welcoming places. The Hotel bar is open to the public and is frequently the venue for lively entertainment. The food is of a high standard and none better than the reasonably priced three course Sunday lunch.

Just next door, the McDonalds also own The Copper Kettle Restaurant which serves, simple, well cooked, home-made food and specialises in producing imaginative meals for children. Whether you pop in there for a super English breakfast, a good lunch - which is available from 11.30-2pm, or for afternoon tea you will come away contented. It is licensed.

USEFUL INFORMATION

OPEN: All year, 7 days a week
CHILDREN: Family rooms available children's menu, highchairs
CREDIT CARDS: None taken
LICENSED: Full licence
ACCOMMODATION: 12 rooms, mostly en-suite

RESTAURANT: Good home-cooked fare
BAR FOOD: Daily specials
VEGETARIAN: Wide variety
DISABLED ACCESS: Yes
GARDEN: No

HORNSBURY MILL

Hotel, Restaurant & Working Mill

Eleighwater,
Chard, Somerset.

Tel: (0460) 63317

Hornsbury Mill is signposted, and easy to find on the A358 between Ilminster and Chard. To come here is to experience a great sense of history, to have one's imagination whetted, to eat in unusual and delightful surroundings and if you decide to stay, then the fully refurbished luxury living accommodation, set in its own grounds of four acres, is wonderful.

The Mill is a good example of an early 19th century corn mill. Built of local flint stone with fine Ham stone mullion windows, and with the majority of its timber parts made of elm wood, it is essentially a Somerset mill. You will find more written about it in the beginning of this chapter.

Returning to the accommodation, all the rooms are en-suite, there is a television and a radio in each room and tea and coffee making facilities. Evening meals are available. For those visiting the Mill there is a bar and licensed restaurant with a view of the working waterwheel. It is open for coffees, light lunches and famous for its cream teas. Booking is advisable for Sunday lunches. Hornsbury Mill is open daily all the year round from 10am. Admission is free to the gardens and car park. There are ducks and wildfowl, leaping trout in the lake, a children's play area, the Watermill and Museum to see, and a gift shop in which you can browse before buying a memento of your visit. Hornsbury Mill is truly delightful and ideally situated as a 'stopover' en route to or from the West Country.

USEFUL INFORMATION

OPEN: All day, every day of the year
CHILDREN: Welcome
CREDIT CARDS: Access/Visa
LICENSED: Full On Licence
ACCOMMODATION: 4 rooms en-suite

RESTAURANT: Home-cooked, well presented food
BAR FOOD: Wide selection, unusual reasonable
VEGETARIAN: Always available
DISABLED ACCESS: Mobility room toilets
GARDEN: Wonderful grounds. Play area

THE WELCOME BAP

Coffee Shop

9 Holyrood Street,
Chard, Somerset.

Tel: (0460) 65904

Distinctive in its appearance and unusual in its style is The Welcome Bap, a new Coffee Shop just a few steps from the centre of Chard. Morning coffee and snack lunches are served daily by members of the thriving Baptist Church next door, and this shop-window to their work offers to all a cool quiet corner in a busy town. It has established a reputation for good food, reasonably priced and promptly served. Toasties and teacakes, salads and soups, jacket potatoes and of course baps are all served by volunteers, but to a professional standard. All cakes are home-made. Seating 32 and with easy street-level access, The Welcome Bap combines oak beams, part-flagstone floor and tasteful decor. This is a Coffee Shop with a difference.

Chard itself, flowing with water, is well worth a visit, especially the thatched Museum in the High Street with its quite remarkable collections. The town, its skyline still showing red-brick woollen (later lace) mills, is rich in historical achievements. Known as the cradle of powered flight, because in a factory here in 1848 John Stringfellow flew the first self-driven plane, Chard now commemorates him by an attractive bronze sculpture in Fore Street. St Mary's parish church is fifteenth century, whilst the opening of the Victorian Age brought improvements with the column-fronted Guildhall and a classical Baptist Church. Local Baptists themselves have a colourful history. Some stood condemned in the Bloody Assizes after marching with Monmouth to Sedgemoor in 1685. In the last century one of their lay-preachers, James Gillingham, was the inventor and developer of artificial limbs.

USEFUL INFORMATION

OPEN: Mon-Sat: 10-2pm (excluding Bank Holidays)
CHILDREN: Very welcome
CREDIT CARDS: None
LICENSED: Non-alcoholic, non-smoking
ACCOMMODATION: Not applicable

RESTAURANT: Good food, reasonably priced and promptly served
BAR FOOD: Not applicable
VEGETARIAN: Several choices
DISABLED ACCESS: Easy
GARDEN: Forecourt garden, seated in high summer

THE TUCKERS ARMS

Inn

Dalwood, Nr Axminster,
Somerset.

Tel: (0404) 88342

Dalwood is a small village, hidden away from the main road and not far from the busy market town of Axminster. It attracts many visitors because it is so full of history. Behind the village stands Dane's Hill where the workings of an old Danish Fort dominates the whole estuary of the River Axe.

However, most importantly Dalwood has a village pub, The totally beautiful Tuckers Arms, the main part of which is 600 years old. It is a living example of change over the centuries with the original beams still insitu and a rare Jetted ceiling. It was originally a Manor House and over the years has kept revealing its past secrets as careful restoration has taken place. For example the original thatch was found when the new one was blackened from the open fire.

You will seldom find a more attractive place in which to stop. There are five en-suite rooms and one family suite in which you will have a restful nights sleep and find an excellent English breakfast awaiting you in the morning. The high standard is carried on at lunchtime and in the evenings, when you will be invited to try Tuckers Specials or Tuckers Grills followed by a choice from The Tuck Shop, a range of delectable desserts including Tuckers Tiddies - a house speciality, Pillows of light Puff Pastry with a choice of home cooked Fillings. There are an array of dishes to suit everyone's taste and pocket. There are a number of Real Ales, super Malt Whiskies and a few, carefully chosen wines including Dalwood wines from Australia where the people who started the vineyard emigrated from Dalwood Vicarage.

USEFUL INFORMATION

OPEN: 11.30-3pm & 6.30-11pm
CHILDREN: Welcome. Family room
CREDIT CARDS: Access/Visa
LICENSED: Full On
ACCOMMODATION: 5 en-suite rooms,
  1 family suite

RESTAURANT: A range of high quality
  interesting food
BAR FOOD: Traditional & Specials
VEGETARIAN: Always available
DISABLED ACCESS: Level Access
GARDEN: Beautiful but seating only

HASELBURY INN

Haselbury Plucknett,
Nr Crewkerne, Somerset.

Public House

Tel: (0460) 72488

In close proximity to the attractive, hamstone village are many stately homes and it is also close to National Trust Land and the coast, so what better place to stop than the focal point of the village, The Haselbury Inn. Here is a good, traditional country inn with a great atmosphere. It is warm and comfortable with plenty of room for sofas and easy chairs to be pulled round the burning log fires in winter. No doubt that part of the atmosphere stems from its previous existence when it was used for making rope and sailcloth in the days of the old sailing ships.

You will find it quite difficult to decide what to have from the 19 starters and 22 main courses in addition to which there are no less than 15 puddings and anything up to 10 Daily Specials! I defy anyone not to find something that appeals to them. The wines also offer a great choice coming from countries all around the world. They are priced to fit in with anyone's budget.

James Pooley has for many years been associated with the licensed and catering business. His Czech born wife, Kathe does all the cooking and she has an instinctive ability to get the authentic flavours in her International menu. Children are welcome, but James will tell you that he keeps a supply of six inch nails to nail them to the floor if they are troublesome! This is a friendly and very informal, happy hostelry.

USEFUL INFORMATION

OPEN: 12-3pm & 7-10.30pm
CHILDREN: Well behaved welcome
CREDIT CARDS: Access/Visa/Master /Euro
LICENSED: Full On & Section 68
ACCOMMODATION: Not applicable

RESTAURANT: Superb, wholesome home-made
BAR FOOD: 63 dishes & specials of the day
VEGETARIAN: Nine dishes
DISABLED ACCESS: Yes
GARDEN: Yes, large. BBQ food

THE FOUNTAIN INN MOTEL

Inn, Motel

High Street, Henstridge,
Templecombe, Somerset.

Tel: (0963) 62722

Certain places lend themselves as ideal locations for those who want to tour a county, see its attractions and explore its history. The Fountain Inn Motel at Henstridge is just such a place. It stands in the centre of the village overlooking the Blackmore Vale and at the crossroads of the A30 and the A357, midway between Bournemouth and Bristol. The countryside is nothing short of beautiful and full of picturesque villages, historic towns and country houses.

Pat and Gerry Petts have been the proprietors here for over 14 years during which time they have brought this attractive establishment to a very high standard. Whilst much remains of the 17th century building, they have added an accommodation block which sits in harmony with the older building. There are 6 double bedded en-suite rooms with every facility including the key to their own front door. Inside the pub it is still a traditional locals' hostelry and an important part of the community with teams for skittles, darts, cribbage and pool. Apart from tourists, The Fountain is ideal for business people who want to stay away from a big town or city and enjoy a totally relaxed atmosphere.

A full menu is on offer 7 days a week midday and in the evenings. For residents there is also room service. Apart from the Petts family there is only one member of staff, Brenda, who is a gem; she is invaluable acting as a local dialect interpreter!

USEFUL INFORMATION

OPEN: Motel 24 hrs, 365 days
CHILDREN: Accommodation, yes
CREDIT CARDS: Access/Visa/Euro/
Master
LICENSED: Full On & Residential
ACCOMMODATION: 6 dbls, en-suite

RESTAURANT: Mid 1994
BAR FOOD: Sandwiches to full grills
VEGETARIAN: 5-6 dishes available
DISABLED ACCESS: Level, ramp
GARDEN: Patio area, tables, grass, play
area

VIRGINIA ASH

Henstridge, Templecombe,
Somerset.

Public House

Tel: (0963) 62267

At the only set of traffic lights on the main A30, midway between Shaftesbury and Sherborne, you will find the 17th century Virginia Ash. Originally it was a coaching inn but now has a large car park to deal with the traveller of this century. The pub has been designed internally to create an olde world atmosphere and to provide traditional homely comforts.

The Virginia Ash provides a welcome for all the family, with high chairs for the little ones and an excellent play area in the attractive Beer Garden. Because the rooms are so spacious children do not feel cooped up and their elders are able to relax and enjoy this very pleasant hostelry. There is also a great boon - a no smoking area. As a Free House they offer a wide selection of wines, spirits, continental lagers and beers including four traditional ales.

Martin and Kris Shone are the friendly landlords, who with their well trained staff revel in looking after their regulars and all the newcomers who find their way here. They always work on the principle that a stranger is just a friend they have not yet met! It works, for people do come back here again and again. The extensive menu provides succulent steaks, gammon, chicken, duck and fish dishes besides home-cooked casseroles, pies and flans - all served in generous portions to satisfy the largest appetite and sensibly small portions for the children. There are always home-made Specials every day and all the food is prepared and cooked by Kris Shone who delights in using her own well tried and very popular recipes.

USEFUL INFORMATION

OPEN: Mon-Sat: 11-2.30pm & 6.30-11pm
   Normal Sunday hours
CHILDREN: Welcome. Highchairs,
   play area
CREDIT CARDS: Visa/Master
LICENSED: Full On Licence
ACCOMMODATION: Not applicable

RESTAURANT: Extensive menu,
   generous portions
BAR FOOD: All home-cooked,
   interesting
VEGETARIAN: Always available
DISABLED ACCESS: Ramps & WC
GARDEN: Seating only

THE POULETT ARMS

Public House & Restaurant

High Street, Hinton St George,
Crewkerne, Somerset.

Tel: (0460) 73149

The immediate feeling you get as you walk into The Poulett Arms is a sense of the past and the comfort of the present. It is no more than one would expect because from the outside this thatched 17th-century pub is enchanting. Hinton St George itself is lovely and the pub is the focal point. As you look round the walls inside you will spot some superb old signs hanging below the original beams. One which will catch your eye says "Rooms 7/6d per night with attendant female staff"! It conjures up the past as do the many old pictures of uniformed men on horseback and those of old trains and cars which make one nostalgic.

In the garden at the rear is a Pelota Wall which is used for the Basque game in which a sort of basket is strapped to the arm in which one catches a hard ball. There are only five of these walls in the county.

The Poulett is a find for anyone who revels in a good wine cellar and equally for the Real Ale addicts. Food naturally is very important and this is produced in an immaculate kitchen run by Diane Chisnall who with her husband, Ray, owns this good pub. Diane is partnered in the kitchen by their talented chef son Andrew. Between them they prepare first class fare with a menu that has been designed and compiled to reflect a responsible and straight forward choice of dishes without being over ambitious. Both Diane and Andrew strive to use fresh and seasonal market produce. The results are delicious.

USEFUL INFORMATION

OPEN: 11.30-3pm & 7-11pm
Normal Sunday hours
CHILDREN: Welcome
CREDIT CARDS: Access/Visa
LICENSED: Full Licence
ACCOMMODATION: 1 room, en-suite

RESTAURANT: Wide choice
BAR FOOD: Snacks, specials, lite bites
VEGETARIAN: Always available
DISABLED ACCESS: Level access
at rear
GARDEN: Large, secluded. Not a
play area

Holbrook,
Nr Wincanton, Somerset.

Tel: (0963) 32377

HOLBROOK HOUSE HOTEL

Country House Hotel

A true Country House Hotel is somewhere that has a personal atmosphere, offers immediate comfort and hospitality and all of it without pretension. This you will find at Holbrook House. Mr Geoffrey Taylor came here with his late wife in 1946 when it was still a private house. It was then they started to create this delightful hotel, set in 15 acres of grounds. Modern amenities have been included but it has never lost that sense of being an elegant Georgian home. A hard court and croquet has been added to the original grass tennis court. The Stables that were in use for many years have given way to a Squash Court and near the Dovecote, in the old orchard area, is the beautiful setting for the outdoor heated swimming pool and club house in the summer.

It is a very private setting and entering the house one immediately feels at home with a warm welcome from Geoffrey Taylor and his second wife. Mrs Taylor may well introduce you to the doves whom she literally has feeding out of her hands. Taking a bowl of grain, she calls and they all fly out of the Dovecote across to the house. It is a spectacular sight. There are two comfortable lounges with log fires in winter, a charming Dining-Room in which the walls are covered with original 18th century prints of ladies in costumes for the different seasons. The room overlooks the walled garden and croquet lawn. The standard of food is very high and is complemented by a well stocked Cellar. Every bedroom is different, both in furnishing and size; each totally in keeping with the house. The Hotel is open to non-residents.

USEFUL INFORMATION

OPEN: Every day except New Year's Eve
CHILDREN: Welcome
CREDIT CARDS: Access/Visa/Master
LICENSED: Full On Licence
ACCOMMODATION: 4 fam, 5 dbl, 9 twn
6 sgl. Some en-suite

RESTAURANT: High standard, a la
Carte. Open to non residents
BAR FOOD: Lunchtime only except
Sunday
VEGETARIAN: Full menu
DISABLED ACCESS: No
GARDEN: 15 acres, tennis, croquet, pool

THE HALF MOON INN

Public House

Horsington,
Somerest.

Tel: (0963) 70140

At the heart of the village of Horsington is the attractive and only pub, The Half Moon Inn. When it was acquired some two years ago by Andrew and Philippa Tarling, it was a step into an entirely new life for them. They left the rat-race behind and rapidly settled into the life of innkeepers, much to the great pleasure of the local people. These two have a great love and enthusiasm for their new profession and a natural liking for the human race - all important!

The Half Moon was originally a Cider House built sometime in the 17th century although the cottage end is early Victorian. In those early days the orchards surrounding it produced enough apples for them to make their own cider. The orchards have been sold on but the pub is still surrounded by attractive gardens and there is nothing nicer than sitting outside on a summer's day enjoying a well-earned drink and perhaps a meal. The Tarlings have made some alterations and done many repairs but not in any instance has the original character or any of the original features been disturbed. The building is Grade II Listed and is said to have a well inside the pub although this is yet to be found.

The menu is simple, freshly cooked, pub fare with one or two exotic dishes thrown in for good measure. Every day a selection of 'Specials' are featured on the Blackboard in the Bar. Three Real Ales are always available and usually two or three Guest Beers as well. The Wine list has been carefully chosen and the House Wine is both palatable and affordable. Four chalets around the pub are available for letting. They are well appointed, children are welcome but pets are not allowed.

USEFUL INFORMATION

OPEN: 11.30-2.30pm & 6-11pm, Sat: 12.00
  Sun: Normal hours
CHILDREN: Welcome
CREDIT CARDS: None taken
LICENSED: Full On
ACCOMMODATION: 4 self-contained
  chalets

RESTAURANT: Not applicable
BAR FOOD: Traditional fare plus
  Blackboard specials
VEGETARIAN: Always available
DISABLED ACCESS: Limited. No WC
GARDEN: Outside seating back and
  front

THE IVELCHESTER HOTEL & RESTAURANT

Hotel & Restaurant

The Square, Ilchester,
Somerset.

Tel: (0935) 840220

This fine, gracious Georgian building dominates the approach into Ilchester. The years have only added to its stature and today part of the building is covered with the rich, deep green ivy which clings lovingly to its walls. The Ivelchester is gaining a very good reputation for food and is an excellent place to stay if you have business in the area or if you wish to explore the delights of this beautiful part of Somerset.

The hotel acquired new owners about twelve months ago. Tony Pedroni and Carl O'Donaghue, both trained by the Forte group, have brought their expertise to running this business. The experience of the mighty Forte hotels has given them a keen knowledge of the industry but to run a village hostelry and hotel demands much more. It is a 'people' business and these two men have become popular with the locals and the many visitors who come this way. They have managed to combine their efficiency with a delightful informality which makes this such a pleasurable place to be.

The food, created by Carl is innovative and delicious and whilst he works caringly in the kitchen, Tony looks after the front of the house. It is an admirable combination. There are eight en-suite bedrooms, tastefully decorated. Ilchester is so near to a number of stately homes and National Trust properties and the splendid Fleet Air Arms Museum at Yeovilton is always worth a visit.

USEFUL INFORMATION

OPEN: All day
CHILDREN: Welcome
CREDIT CARDS: Master/Visa/Access/ Amex
LICENSED: Full Restaurant
ACCOMMODATION: 8 en-suite rooms

RESTAURANT: Small but delicious menu
BAR FOOD: Blackboard of daily specials
VEGETARIAN: Always available
DISABLED ACCESS: None
GARDEN: Seating area only

MINSTRELS
Coffee Shop

14 Silver Street,
Ilminster, Somerset.

Tel: (0460) 57050

The historical interest in the Minster has brought visitors to Ilminster for many years and many people have discovered that Minstrels, the small, attractive Coffee Shop and Restaurant next door is ideal after walking around and trying to digest all that there is to learn about in the church. Minstrels is owned by two enterprising men, Steve Smith and Michael Gaskell who, since they arrived here in 1992, have set about refurbishing the Coffee Shop in a manner which they feel befits its standing in the town. The building dates back to 1899 and was once a shoe shop - hard to imagine when you see it today. The frontage of Minstrels is now Listed and is really very attractive. Inside the atmosphere is that of an old world, traditional coffee shop.

You may pop in for morning coffee and a scone perhaps or enjoy a light lunch. Everything is freshly made on the premises and this includes some delicious home-made cakes, and pies with pastry that melts in your mouth. As an added bonus you can buy the cakes and pies to take-away if you wish.

As from Ocotber 1993 the opening hours will be extended from Thursday to Saturday to include evening meals offering a full a la carte menu; Minstrels already has a licence. Steve and Michael are very happy to cater for private parties and receptions on the premises, by arrangement, at any time. Children are very welcome here and there are always a number of dishes for Vegetarians. From Minstrels it is very easy to set out to see the Fleet Air Arm Museum at Yeovilton, Montacute House, and many more fascinating places.

USEFUL INFORMATION

OPEN: Mon-Sat: 9-5pm except Thurs: 9-2.30pm Eves: Thurs-Sat: 7-11pm
CHILDREN: Welcome. Highchairs
CREDIT CARDS: None taken
LICENSED: Restaurant
ACCOMMODATION: Not applicable

RESTAURANT: Home-made food at affordable prices
BAR FOOD: Not applicable
VEGETARIAN: Always available
DISABLED ACCESS: Small step into premises
GARDEN: None

THE SHRUBBERY HOTEL

Hotel

Ilminster, Somerset.

Tel: (0460) 52108
Fax: (0460) 53660

The Shrubbery at Ilminster has been considered one of the foremost hotels in Somerset for some years. The situation is unrivalled, being ten minutes from junction 25 of the M5, and central to the West Country. For leisure within 60 minutes one can be in Lyme Regis, Dorchester, Weston-Super-Mare, Exmoor, Dartmoor, Quantocks, Hardy Country and many National Trust properties.

Owned and run by Stuart and Liz Shepherd for over thirty years, The Shrubbery is a well loved and cared for establishment which can be described as being at once both relaxing and vital. The three star hotel has fourteen individual style rooms, all fully en-suite. They are both comfortable and charming. The house contains many interesting features including fireplaces carved by the original owner who strangely enough was also called Shepherd but no relation of the present owners. There are marble carvings by Italian Carvers shipwrecked in Lyme Bay and a complete set of Bruce Bairnfaters 1st World War 'Old Bill' prints. The public rooms are delightful and include Shepherd's Restaurant in which one can have a delicious full meal or 'Just a Bite'.

One of the nice things about The Shrubbery is its efficient informality; you may choose to eat where you want, whether it is in the Sun Lounge, the Bar or the Restaurant. In the suntrap of two and a half acres of terraced lawns is the hotel's own 25 metre heated pool. In addition to all this The Shrubbery offers the largest function, banqueting and conference facilities in the district; a wonderful place in which to have a wedding reception.

USEFUL INFORMATION

OPEN: All year
CHILDREN: Welcome
CREDIT CARDS: All major cards
LICENSED: Full On
ACCOMMODATION: 14 en-suite

RESTAURANT: High standard, excellent choice
BAR FOOD: Wide range, sensible prices
VEGETARIAN: Always available
DISABLED ACCESS: Limited
GARDEN: 2.5 acres of terraced lawns

THE KINGS ARMS INN

Public House, Hotel & Restaurant

Bishopston, Montacute, Somerset.

Tel: (0935) 822513
Fax: (0935) 826549

Most people will have heard of the fine, National Property, Montacute House, a short distance from Yeovil but not so many will have discovered the pretty village with its lovely mellowed ham-stone buildings. Situated on the edge of Ham Hill Country Park it is truly beautiful and worth visiting. You should not miss The Kings Arms Inn, a 16th century ham-stone property with lovely mullioned windows and exposed stonework.

Originally it was a Staging Post between Plymouth and London; the Inn, Hotel and Restaurant provide unique charm and comfort. This is somewhere that is ideal for touring the West Country, being a focal point between Bath, Bristol, Exeter and Bournemouth, all of which can be reached in under an hour. It would be very rewarding to spend a great day exploring the wonders of Bath, perhaps the Cathedral at Exeter or even more closely Montacute House and then return to The Kings Arms knowing that a delightful en-suite bedroom with a four-poster was awaiting you and before retiring to bed you could sample one of the best dinners in this part of Somerset accompanied by wine from a well chosen list.

The menu has a wide choice of classical English food using fresh local produce whilst in the Bars, traditional fare is available including some delicious Daily Specials. You do not need to stay here to enjoy some of the benefits of The Kings Arms because you are equally welcome to drink or lunch, enjoy the large and beautifully kept garden and orchard. Michael and Vicki Harrison own and personally manage the business with the assistance of a first class staff and a superb chef.

USEFUL INFORMATION

OPEN: All year, every day until midnight
CHILDREN: Welcome
CREDIT CARDS: Access/Visa/Amex/ Diners
LICENSED: Full On
ACCOMMODATION: 11 en-suite rooms including four-posters

RESTAURANT: Classical English using fresh, local produce
BAR FOOD: Traditional fare plus many Chef's Specials
VEGETARIAN: 2 dishes daily
DISABLED ACCESS: No
GARDEN: Large, beautifully kept with an orchard

THE ROYAL OAK

Public House & Restaurant

Over Stratton,
Nr Ilminster, Somerset.

Tel: (0460) 40906

This 400 year old thatched country inn merges so well with the other buildings in the main street that you might well pass it without realising it is a delightful hostelry. All that announces its presence is a sign above the door. It is certainly not a place to be missed. The moment you enter its doors you realise that this is no ordinary establishment. It has a genuine olde-worlde atmosphere which is wonderful. Original features like old beams, ham-stone and flag floors, combine successfully with dark rag-rolled walls, scrubbed wooden tables, a polished granite bar counter and extensive displays of dried flowers, hops and strings of garlic. The candlelit dining room adorned with colourful dried flowers is intimate and cosy.

Lyn Holland is the landlady who combines a keen wit, charm, and enthusiasm with an instinctive feeling for what her customers are going to enjoy. A la carte dishes include a wide selection of dishes from all over the world. Anything from Hawaiian pineapple and prawns to Polynesian lamb kebabs. Everything is home-cooked including the Royal Oak's own char-grilled burgers. Amongst Lyn's good ideas is the Booty Box on the children's menu, full of goodies including a wholemeal sandwich, cheese, fruit, crisps and a crunchy bar in a special box the children can take away with them. The grown up version of this is a Barbecue pack containing lamb cutlets, sausage, gammon steak and a chicken drumstick as well as salad and a jacket potato. Wonderful stuff on a fine day when the children can play on the swings, the junior assault course and no less than three trampolines.

USEFUL INFORMATION

OPEN: 12-2.30pm & 7-11pm
CHILDREN: Yes. Garden & dining room
CREDIT CARDS: Visa/Master/Switch
LICENSED: Full On
ACCOMMODATION: Not applicable

RESTAURANT: Winter & Summer menus. A little different
BAR FOOD: Comprehensive & interesting
VEGETARIAN: 6 with 2 total Vegan
DISABLED ACCESS: Small step. Level into WC
GARDEN: Huge play area

151

THE RUSTY AXE

Public House

Stembridge, Nr
Martock, Somerset.

Tel: (0460) 40109

The 16th century, thatched Rusty Axe, is the focal point in the little hamlet of Stembridge, near Martock. An unusual name for a pub one might think. The reason is that a tree was chopped down and a rusty axe was found embedded in the trunk - the axe is now on the outside wall of the pub.

The Rusty Axe is just half a mile away from a Cider farm known Nationally for making Cider brandy. For those who have yet to walk through its welcoming doors, it is an experience which you will want to repeat.

Apart from its friendly atmosphere and well kept beers, Tanya Fitzgerald, the proprietor is renowned for the standard of her food; not because it is exotic but because it is good, old fashioned country cooking. Daily Specials are available at sensible prices from Monday to Friday and on Sunday the traditional Sunday roast is served. This would be a good place to lunch before setting off to visit Burrowhill Cider Farm where you can see the cider being made or a little further away to take a look at the fantastic Fleet Air Arm Museum. Children are welcome and there is a Children's room. A word of warning - The Rusty Axe dabbles in Cocktails, some you will know but they have some concoctions of their own -delicious but dangerous!

USEFUL INFORMATION

OPEN: 11.30-2.40pm & 5.30-11pm
  All day Saturday
CHILDREN: Families welcome.
  Children's room
CREDIT CARDS: None
LICENSED: Full On Licence
ACCOMMODATION: Not applicable

RESTAURANT: Country home-cooking
  all fresh produce
BAR FOOD: In a Bun
VEGETARIAN: 6-8 dishes
DISABLED ACCESS: Level entrance
GARDEN: Large, lovely. Tables, swings
  BBQ

THE RED LION

South Cadbury,
Yeovil, Somerset.

Public House

Tel: (0963) 40448

The romantic story of King Arthur and his Knights, is enhanced here by the presence of Cadbury Castle at the foot of which, in the lovely Vale of Camelot, is South Cadbury. A pretty village in its own right, it is enhanced by the presence of The Red Lion, a pub that brims over with character.

It is essentially a village pub and the centre for much of the village's activity. It is a welcoming hostelry for all those who enjoy a good atmosphere, well kept Real Ales and a comprehensive menu which includes exciting dishes such as Lemon and whole cracked pepper marinated chicken breasts or Salmon in an Asparagus sauce. The landlords are Alan and Dorothy Jefferys. Alan is the sort of man one would not expect to fantasise, so when he tells you that he has seen the ghost which haunts The Red Lion, he is to be believed. Apparently a door opens mysteriously and a puff of smoke appears. The locals will tell you it is the spirit of King Arthur who is said to be buried on the hill.

Dorothy does all the cooking, as she has done for the last thirty years. She uses as much local produce as is available and frequently her own home grown fruit and vegetables. Her Daily Specials are popular with people who come from quite a distance to sample her food. You do not have to have a full meal, she is more than happy to produce freshly baked baguettes made to order or a massive, beautifully garnished Ploughmans. In the summer many people take to the pretty Beer Garden where one can both eat and drink.

USEFUL INFORMATION

OPEN: Mon-Sat: 12.3pm & 7-11pm.
  Normal Sunday hours
CHILDREN: Very welcome
CREDIT CARDS: None taken
LICENSED: Full On Licence
ACCOMMODATION: Not applicable

RESTAURANT: Not applicable
BAR FOOD: Mainly home-made
VEGETARIAN: Always available
DISABLED ACCESS: Limited access
GARDEN: Very pretty Beer Garden

SKITTLES RESTAURANT

Restaurant

West Coker Square, West Coker,
Nr Yeovil, Somerset.

Tel: (0935) 863986

For over four hundred years this delightful building was the welcoming, resting place of weary travellers, passengers on the coaches from Exeter to London. Now a restaurant highly regarded and mentioned many times in newspapers and food guides, Skittles has a wonderful old world atmosphere. It is decorated and furnished in keeping with the tradition and age of the establishment and no one who comes here should miss the pleasure of walking round the old walled garden and courtyards - a splendid aperitif before enjoying the delicious choice of food from the International menu.

The dishes are imaginative and different. A Seafood Spaghetti delights the tastebuds and so do the generous Smoked Fish Platters, Pigeon Breast Salad, Breast of Duck Stir Fry and many others. You have to come here several times to even begin to savour all that is on offer. For those who do not want to be adventurous the menu also has many well tried and popular local favourites. Dave Prosser and Ross Aitken own Skittles and it has always been their policy to ensure that everything served is of the highest standard. In addition they have acquired a great following for the skill and understanding that they bring to wedding receptions and private parties of any kind, for which a large private dining room is available. You can enjoy a drink in the Stable Bar and if you wish a game of skittles - a remnant no doubt from the days of the old coaching inn.

USEFUL INFORMATION

OPEN: 12-3pm & 7-10pm. Closed Sunday evening
CHILDREN: Welcome
CREDIT CARDS: Access/Visa
LICENSED: Restaurant
ACCOMMODATION: Not applicable

RESTAURANT: International & Local favourites
BAR FOOD: Not applicable
VEGETARIAN: Always 6-8 dishes
DISABLED ACCESS: Yes
GARDEN: Delightful walled garden and courtyard

FARMERS ARMS
Public House

Slough Hill, West Hatch,
Taunton, Somerset.

Tel: (0823) 480480

Just off the A358 Ilminster to Chard road is the Farmers Arms. This rather quaint village pub is surrounded by beautiful countryside and started life as a farmhouse. The main building is 16th century, once a cider house it became a public house over a century ago. It is the sole surviving pub in this tiny village of West Hatch.

The Farmers Arms is family run, friendly and welcoming. Robin and Sue Appleby, mine hosts, will cater to your every need. There is a skittle alley, a large beer garden, a children's play area and games room. A large self-contained function room with disco facilities and bar, makes it the ideal venue for a special occasion.

In the bar, traditional snacks and grills are available. The restaurant serves modern English dishes with a slightly continental flare making it that little bit special. Everything is freshly home-cooked and there are always daily specials available. If you are vegetarian then dishes are prepared on request. There is no better accompaniment to a meal than one of the Real Ales from The Farmers Arms' large selection. Your choice grows steadily wider as new ales are tried and introduced to this charming little Somerset pub.

USEFUL INFORMATION

OPEN: 11-3pm & 6-11pm
CHILDREN: Welcome
CREDIT CARDS: Access/Visa/Master
LICENSED: Full On
ACCOMMODATION: Not applicable

RESTAURANT: Modern English fare
   with a continental touch
BAR FOOD: Snacks and grills
VEGETARIAN: On request
DISABLED ACCESS: No
GARDEN: Garden & play area

THE BEAR INN

Inn

12 Market Place,
Wincanton, Somerset.

Tel: (0963) 32581

The Bear Inn is a town centre pub in Wincanton, a town probably best known today for its Racecourse. The town came to prominence in the 17th and 18th centuries, as a busy staging post; it is halfway between London and Plymouth, both are 111 miles distant. If anyone asked you what you remembered about a visit to The Bear, apart from the warmth of the welcome, you would probably say the fantastic collection of approximately 40 Royal Doulton Toby Jugs. They are full of interest. It is a little difficult to tell how long The Bear has been an inn but documents show it was dispensing hospitality as far back as 1680.

The inn is famous in the area for its range of Real Ales and also for the excellence of its quick serve bar meals and delicious home-made pies. It is difficult to choose between Steak and Kidney or Chicken and Mushroom. It is a favourite pub with the locals and has a 'Happy Hour' each evening which they enjoy and so do the visitors who have been wise enough to make The Bear a port of call. Separate Function rooms are available. Joe and Jan Arnell are the landlords. Ask Joe to tell you the legend of Jack White - a hair raising story of murder and trial by ordeal. Joe has a newspaper dated 1880 which reports the gruesome event.

USEFUL INFORMATION

OPEN: Mon-Fri: 11-2.30pm & 5.30-11pm
 Sat: 11-11pm. Sun: Normal hours
CHILDREN: Welcome
CREDIT CARDS: None taken
LICENSED: Full On
ACCOMMODATION: Not applicable

RESTAURANT: Not applicable
BAR FOOD: Wide range, daily specials
VEGETARIAN: Yes
DISABLED ACCESS: No
GARDEN: No

DILLY'S RESTAURANT

Restaurant & Bistro

4 Market Place,
Wincanton, Somerset.

Tel: (0963) 33216

In the Market Place of the old and historic Somerset town of Wincanton, is the pretty Dilly's Restaurant and Bistro, conveniently situated near car parks and the very attractive General Post Office. Six years ago the property was used as a saddlery and forge but when it was bought by Judy Lockley, she wrought a transformation, created a warm and welcoming atmosphere and brought to Wincanton a restaurant that has become one of the places to be. It took a little market research before Judy opened the doors of Dilly's to discover what it was that would bring local people and visitors through her doors. She added to this research her own innate ability to produce interesting dishes at realistic prices and her success was assured.

You can start your day here, if you wish, with Breakfast from 8.30am. Everything is cooked to order; scrambled eggs are light and fluffy, the bacon crisp. All day long Dilly's sandwiches are available. These massive three tiered toasted sandwiches are filled either with prawns in mayonnaise, egg and cress, bacon and egg or turkey Salad, all served with salad and crisps. Lunch is always generous in its portions with several good starters including a Salad Nicoise. The main courses can be anything from a 10oz steak cooked to your preference or a home-made Steak and Kidney Pie with pastry that melts in your mouth. There are salads, ploughmans, omelettes and pasta dishes - something for everyone including children. Later in the afternoon Dilly's devotes itself to afternoon teas with home-made cakes and pastries. The restaurant is licensed and has a very good value house wine.

USEFUL INFORMATION

OPEN: Mon-Sat: 8-5.30pm. Closed Sundays
CHILDREN: Welcome. Children's menu
CREDIT CARDS: None taken
LICENSED: Restaurant Licence
ACCOMMODATION: Not applicable

RESTAURANT: Interesting, home-made
BAR FOOD: Not applicable
VEGETARIAN: 5-6 dishes daily
DISABLED ACCESS: Level. Large doorway
GARDEN: None

THE CORNER HOUSE

Wholefood Restaurant & Tearooms

Union Street, Yeovil, Somerset.

Tel: (0935) 73722

Yeovil is a busy Somerset town in which much has been done to make it easier for residents and visitors. There is an attractive pedestrianised shopping area and located not very far away is one of those unusual and interesting restaurants which also boasts tearooms. The Corner House is situated on the corner of Union Street. From the outside it is a neat and tidy building with the entrance flanked by hanging baskets and two neat conifers in pots. The two blackboards on the walls tell you what the soup and special of the day are. It is a Wholefood Restaurant and everything is totally fresh.

Whatever you choose from the fairly extensive menu is prepared and cooked to order served at your table by friendly and welcoming staff. Many people perhaps who have viewed wholefood restaurants as a place of bland and uninteresting food, are in for a shock. The dishes on offer are some of the tastiest you will find anywhere and those who have discovered the Corner House have rapidly become converts with such an enthusiasm that they return with great regularity if they live locally, and as often as possible if they are visitors. Apart from the main course meals there are delicious home-made cakes and scones. A salad bar which has all sorts of variations. Vegetarians will find The Corner House very good with never less than seven dishes available every day. Children are very welcome. High chairs are available and sensibly small portions are given to small ones. The Corner House is a rare treat.

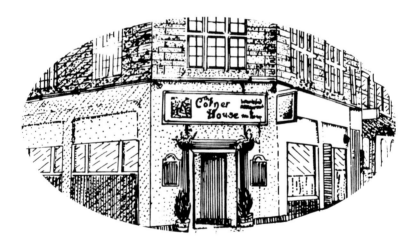

USEFUL INFORMATION

OPEN: Mon-Sat: 9.30-5pm
CHILDREN: Welcome. Highchairs, small portions
CREDIT CARDS: Not applicable
LICENSED: Wines & beers
ACCOMMODATION: Not applicable

RESTAURANT: All fresh Wholefood
BAR FOOD: Not applilcable
VEGETARIAN: 7 plus fish dishes
DISABLED ACCESS: One small step
GARDEN: No

PICKETTY WITCH

147 Ilchester Road,
Yeovil, Somerset.

Public House

Tel: (0935) 23770

This is a traditional Somerset pub to be found on the main Ilchester road out of Yeovil. Only one mile from the town centre it is nonetheless only two minutes from some very attractive countryside. The sort of pub that one would be happy to visit after a morning taking a look at Yeovil's shops, many of which are now in the pedestrianised area. Not far away are several interesting places to visit. For example, tucked away in a small valley not far from Yeovil is Barwick village and a group of strange and wonderful follies which once marked the edge of Barwick Park. The follies are on private property but can be seen from 'Two Tower Lane'. Each folly has a name; Jack the Treacle Eater, The Fish Tower and Messiters' Cone.

Inside The Picketty Witch you will find the welcoming landlords, Len and Sheilagh Quigley who came from Guernsey to run this friendly pub. They have no regrets and are rapidly learning from their regular customers all there is to know about this part of Somerset. They were lucky enough also to inherit a barmaid, Elsie Castle, who has worked at the Picketty Witch for 14 years and is always willing to talk to visitors. This is a Real Ale pub, and well known for it, and is one of the reasons it is so popular. The other is the good, if basic bar food, which is served every day. It is not in the least pretentious but everything is freshly prepared and there are always Daily Specials, most of which are tried and tested favourites. Children have their own menu and Vegetarians are not forgotten.

USEFUL INFORMATION

OPEN: 12 noon
CHILDREN: For meals only or in Beer Garden
CREDIT CARDS: None taken
LICENSED: Full On
ACCOMMODATION: Not applicable

RESTAURANT: Not applicable
BAR FOOD: Basic bar meals, daily specials
VEGETARIAN: Always 5 dishes
DISABLED ACCESS: Yes
GARDEN: Sunken garden at rear

Vicar's Close, Wells
The Most Complete Medieval Street in Europe

NORTH EAST SOMERSET

INCLUDES

'Did you ever taste beer?' 'I had a sip of it once',
said a small servant. 'Here's a state of things!'
cried Mr Swiveller ... 'She never tasted it,
it can't be tasted in a sip!'

Charles Dickens

NORTH EAST SOMERSET

 The District of Mendip is situated in north-east Somerset, and has borders with the counties of Avon and Wiltshire. Mendip covers an area of 285 square miles or 184,700 acres. It encompasses some of Somerset's most attractive and varied landscapes, from the summits of the Mendip Hills to the broad expanse of the Somerset Levels and includes many of the region's best known tourist attractions such as Wells Cathedral, Wookey Hole Caves and Glastonbury Abbey.

Each of Mendip's five towns, Frome, Glastonbury, Shepton Mallet, Street and the Cathedral city of Wells, has its own distinctive character and range of facilities, and all are well connected by a network of good main roads and scenic country lanes, with convenient links to neighbouring centres such as Bath, Bristol, Bridgwater, Taunton, Yeovil and the M5 Motorway. Interspersed around the five towns are all sorts of attractive villages, full of charm and history.

***Frome** is enchanting, it runs up and down and in and out with its narrow streets full of quaint old houses and with a river from which it takes its name. From here you are almost into Wiltshire and everywhere around you there are some of Somerset's loveliest villages. If there is anything that disappoints me about Frome, it is the parish church which has been there for centuries. It still has a knotwork carving of the Saxon mason and a lion with his tail between his legs. The next oldest thing is the 14th century Lady Chapel. It has an 18th century bell with a wonderful inscription,*

' God made Cockey and Cockey made me,
In the year of our Lord 1743.'

Yes, it does have a lot of beautiful things but it does not have the charm of so many of Somerset's churches. Somehow it is overdone, there is too much decoration, every quatrefoil has a rose in it, every bit of wood is painted. Inside and out it is ornate. You have to climb up steps from the street to reach it and even these are lined with scupltured groups. There are figures carved on the guttering and somebody told me that if you count you will find no less than 300 stone figures of all sorts and that is before you look at a monument

Via Crucis, St James Church, Frome

Frome became prosperous as one of the ancient woollen towns of the West Country and in subsequent centuries the town has grown until it is the biggest in the Mendips yet it still only has about 24,000 residents. Wander around the town and you will discover it is a friendly place with some interesting shops and I found two entirely different but equally delightful restaurants. The first, strictly in alphabetical order and not preference, is CROFTS at 21, Fromefield on the main Bath-Frome road. It is a venue not to be missed and is situated in one of the many Listed buildings, in this case dating back to 1690. Two small, and very individual rooms make up the dining area. Each has a welcoming fireplace, which in winter throws out a wall of warmth. While you are looking at the fixed price menu and sipping your aperitif, you will be offered tiny little nibbles, a mouthful of crumbly pastry flavoured with anchovy, just enough to alert the tastebuds for the treat to come. Wonderful.

My second find was LA BISALTA, an Italian Restaurant named after the mountain in the home town of Luigi Violino, the proprietor, who comes from Boves in north west Italy. At lunchtime there is a bistro menu and at night it is deliciously Italian. A great experience.

I love visiting THE ANGEL INN in King Street. This ancient pub is still obliged to take horses and travellers by a law that has been on the statute books since the 17th century. It seems quite right and proper to have this fine hostelry which has been a public house since the 13th century, in the centre of a conservation area, with medieval streets, which still have water running down the middle.

*There are several delightful places within easy distance, **Mells** is just 2 miles to the west. What a delightful village it is and is connected, albeit on flimsy ground, with the nursery rhyme 'Little Jack Horner'. Why, you may ask? The answer is simple; the Elizabethan manor house once belonged to the Horner family. Jack, the Abbot of Glastonbury's steward was sent to placate Thomas Cromwell with a bribe - the deeds of several of the Abbey's manors. According to the well-known story, somehow the deeds have become the pie filling and Jack is supposed to have stolen the 'plum' from this pie - namely the deeds to Mells Manor. The stone cottages are of grey and yellow stone, wreathed by trees and lawns. The church of St Andrew has a splendid 15th-century tower with triple windows. Every three hours one of four tunes is chimed. The church is open daily during daylight hours.*

*South of Mells, just off the A361, is **Nunney**, with its ruined 14th century castle, surrounded by a moat still filled with water. Originally built by the Montfort family, the castle was damaged by Oliver Cromwell's troops during the English Civil War. English Heritage have the care of the castle and it is open to the public daily.*

Between Mells and Nunney is WHATLEY VINEYARD and HERB GARDEN, a very pleasant place in which to spend an hour or two. It is peaceful and beautiful with a vineyard that extends to four acres and includes five grape varieties: Seyval Blanc, Reichensteiner, Huxelrebe, Schonburger, and Madeline Angevine. All the varieties have been chosen for their suitability to the local soils and climate.

The Herb Garden design is based around the shape of a cross, traditionally used in monastic times to ward off evil spirits. The paved cross divides the garden into medicinal aromatic, culinary and cosmetic plants. The garden is completely enclosed by a high wall which protects the herbs and creates a peaceful, scented atmosphere. Many of the plants seen in the herb garden can be purchased from their nursery stock.

A conducted tour can be arranged. This will include the herb garden, the vineyard and a wine-tasting in the cellars. Together with a light meal this makes an entertaining and interesting evening. The minimum number is 20, the maximum 45. For further details ring 037384 467.

*Three miles north of Shepton Mallet is **Oakhill**, once famed for its large brewery. Today that brewery is closed but there is still one in the village, once again serving Mendip pubs with its refreshing beers. Nearby* runs the Roman Fosse Way, so Oakhill may well have been known to them; certainly Beacon Hill above the village would have been a landmark then as it is today.

To the west, towards Wells is **Croscombe**, with its many fine and interesting buildings, including its church, which unusually for Somerset has a spire rather than a tower and dates from the 13th century although much of it was rebuilt somewhere in the 15th century. Behind the church is the medieval manor house which has been beautifully restored by the Landmark Trust. The village also has one of the best pubs in Somerset, THE BULL TERRIER. The main building of the pub follows the traditional pattern of a medieval house and was built in the last part of the 15th century. The Inglenook Bar - once the main hall - had a fireplace and ceiling added in the 16th century and the fine beams are the original. It was originally called The Rose and Crown and was first granted a licence to sell ale in 1612 so it can truly claim to be one of Somerset's oldest pubs. In 1976 the name was changed to The Bull Terrier by a previous owner and this unique name has made it a regular calling place for Bull Terrier breeders and owners from all over the world. Today it is an unspoiled village inn and good to visit.

You should also take a look at **Pilton**, a large village just off the main Glastonbury road which has a manor that was a residence of the Abbots of Glastonbury and is now the centre of a flourishing vineyard. Also belonging to the abbey was the Tithe Barn which is still there today. The church is odd inasmuch as it has a clerestory but no aisles and its oldest feature is the Norman south doorway with its zigzag carving.

On the banks of the river Frome, close to the Wiltshire border, stands FARLEIGH HUNGERFORD CASTLE, built in the 14th century but now in ruins. Within the castle grounds is the Chapel of St Leonard originally a parish church but now a museum housing relics of the Civil War period. The Manor at one time belonged to the Hungerford family, one of whom became the first Speaker of the House of Commons.

Holcombe is another lovely village with a wonderful pub, THE RING OF ROSES, to which I always return having spent just a little while thinking about the past when Captain Scott of Antartic fame, came to bury his father in the churchyard of the old church. His brother, sister and mother are also buried here. His mother must have had great courage. She died in Hampton Court Palace at the age of 84 but she did not want to be buried there. It was her wish to be brought to Holcombe, and be carried across the fields to be laid to rest in this peaceful place, so far from her son who died in Antartica.

Six miles to the north of the town is **Rode** *where THE TROPICAL BIRD GARDENS are laid out in 17 acres of beautiful grounds, terraced and planted many years ago with ornamental trees and shrubs now in full maturity which give shade and shelter. There are flower gardens, a Clematis collection, a wood inhabited with exquisitely coloured ornamental pheasants who wander round at liberty. There is a chain of lakes fed by a stream and a waterfall where you will see all kinds of water birds swimming and diving, including flamingoes and penguins; macaws fly free among the trees.*

The aviaries, which are all outdoors are designed to blend with the surroundings. They are naturally planted and so extensive that visitors can enjoy watching the birds in full flight and admire their brilliant colours as they flash in the sunshine. The collection which is constantly being added to, now numbers over 1,000 rare birds of approximately 230 different species. The gardens are open every day except Christmas Day. The times in summer are 10am-6.30pm and in winter from 10am until dusk.

One of the Famous Lions of Longleat

LONGLEAT is in close proximity to Frome and surely must offer one of the best days out, whatever your age. It is a magnificent 16th-century house set in rolling parkland. It has priceless family heirlooms spanning four centuries. A safari park with lions, white tigers, monkeys, rhinos, wolves, zebras, giraffes, camels, buffalo and elephants. Fascinating exhibitions including the 'Doctor Who' exhibition. There are rides, amusements and the world's largest maze. Adventure Castle is a two acre playpark which is a child's paradise. Spend a day here and you will be in good company. Queen Elizabeth I visited Sir John Thynne, the builder of the house in 1574, and in 1980 Queen Elizabeth II honoured the father of the present Marquess of Bath, a direct descendant of Sir John's by joining him in the celebration of the four hundredth anniversary of the completion of his home. Longleat is an architectural masterpiece in its own right. It is also home to one of the finest private book collections in the world. Longleat is open every day except Christmas Day from 10am-6pm Easter-September and 10am-4pm during the rest of the year.

***Beckington**, north east of Frome, has a church which can claim to have the largest and most ornate Norman tower in Somerset. The village itself is largely stone-built, with interesting buildings such as The Cedars, an early Georgian house, and the Abbey, the finest house in Beckington. It was probably built as the Hospital for the Augustinian Canons who were founded here in 1502. Seymours Court is another of Beckington's fine buildings; a farmhouse once owned by Sir Thomas Seymour, who married Catherine Parr, the widow of Henry VIII.*

*To the north lies the charming village of **Norton St Philip** with its famous inn, THE GEORGE, built by the monks of Hinton priory in the 15th century and once used as a cloth hall. The village also has several attractive 17th century houses with mullioned windows and stone roofs. Close to the village, on the Bath road, is NORWOOD FARM RARE BREEDS CENTRE where many types of animals can be seen.*

*If you wander the lanes to the west you will come to the sleepy hollow that envelops the village of **Litton**. It is an old place with streets that are steep and winding. On the walls of the old church are four hideous gargoyles and two angels interspersed with about 30 stone heads amongst which are laughing men, some with beards and women wearing wimples. Inside there are ancient benches, a Jacobean pulpit and a 15th-century font. Appropriately the excellent village pub is called YE OLDE KINGS ARMS.*

***Stratton on the Fosse** is an old place with a village street that is part of the long paved road the Romans made to the south coast from Lincolnshire. If you take a look you will see wide flat bricks in the church walls which would have been made by the Romans and used again when the church was rebuilt in Norman days. One oddity in the church is the organ which was made for Brighton Pavilion and was listened to there by thousands in the great Regency days. Apparently it was given to Stratton as a present from Brighton.*

Shepton Mallet *is a wonderful mixture of old and new; a combination of ancient market town and modern industrial community nestling in a fold towards the western edge of the Mendip escarpment. Historically, Shepton Mallet has always been strategically well placed; the Roman Fosse Way passes close by; the town's position on the river Sheppey led to its growth during the Middle Ages as a centre for the wool trade, and enabled the brewing industry to be established. Today this location makes Shepton Mallet ideal for anyone wanting to explore the region's many and varied attractions. It was probably at its most affluent as a market and wool-trading centre in the 15th century. Cloth weaving rose to importance in the 17th century. Several wealthy cloth merchants built themselves some fine houses in the town many of which are still there.*

The town is not proud of one episode in its history. It happened in 1685 when the Market Cross was the scene for several executions of the unfortunate men of the Duke of Monmouth's 'Pitchfork Army' who were sentenced to death by that dreadful man, Judge Jeffreys.

The parish church of St Peter and St Paul has a fine 14th century tower and the nave roof provides one of the best examples of wagon-roof in England, with 350 panels and 300 bosses, each of a different design. The 50ft high Market Cross dates from 1500, and nearby is a remnant of The Shambles, a 15th century covered market stall. You should also visit Collett Park, which has an attractive lake and an aviary.

During the Second World War, the Domesday Book was held in the prison of Shepton Mallet for safe keeping - not a place for visitors and in any case the book is now back in its rightful home.

If you want to learn more of the history of Shepton Mallet, the local History Museum tells the story of the town from pre-Roman times to the present day. You will find it at the top of the High Street. Ring (0749) 345258 for opening times.

Two of the most respected agricultural shows are held at Shepton Mallet. The most famous is the ROYAL BATH AND WEST, held a few miles outside the town on its permanent site. It occurs every May and stretches over four days. Later in the year, on a Saturday in August, the Mid-Somerset Show is held in the town itself. Not so grand as the Bath and West but a great deal of fun. There is also a busy weekly market, every Friday, in the centre of the town around the Market Cross.

For anyone looking for a good hostelry, I can whole-heartedly recommend THE CANNARDS WELL INN. It is an inn steeped in local history, at one end of the bar is a toft well, which is said to be of Roman origin. Certainly a Roman fortress was found about 500 yards from the pub. At the other end of the bar is the grave of Tom Giles, the last person in Shepton to be hung for sheep stealing. He has been seen walking the corridors and bedrooms of the pub ever since!

In Charlton Road there is a comparatively modern inn which has enormous charm. THE THATCHED COTTAGE has a delightful, intimate atmosphere and eight beautifully furnished and decorated bedrooms with enormous bathrooms. Great place to stay or to eat.

*Due east of Shepton Mallet are two villages worth looking at. The first is **Doulting** with its wonderful church and 17th century manor house. There is a 15th century Tithe Barn which once belonged to the Abbots of Glastonbury.*

All Aboard for the East Somerset Railway

*Further to the east is Cranmore or to be more accurate **West Cranmore**, the home of THE EAST SOMERSET RAILWAY opened in 1858. Known as The Strawberry Line, the railway of today was founded by its chairman, wildlife artist David Shepherd, and was officially opened in 1975 by Prince Bernhard of the Netherlands. It runs along a pretty route from Cranmore to Mendip Vale and gives many visitors a great deal of pleasure. The fine replica Victorian engine shed and workshops now house many interesting steam locomotives, from David Shepherd's 140* ton steam giant *Black Prince* to the diminutive, *Lord Fisher,* always popular with the children. There is a fine collection of tank engines, including a rare crane locomotive built by Dubs in Glasgow in 1901. The E1 class locomotive, built in 1877 by the LBSCR, is the only one of its type now in existence. Among the interesting items of rolling stock, the line has the only coach built by BR with an all fibreglass body. The railway is one of only two 100% steam railways in the country.

A wide selection of David Shepherd's wildlife, steam railway and landscape fine art prints is always available. Railway Prints by Don Breckon and a selection of David Shepherd wildlife videos are also available in the Art Gallery at Cranmore Station.

There are various attractions held here through the year including the Vintage Vehicle rally, a Jazz Night and a Steam Festival.

Talking to the volunteers who operate this line and care for the locomotives you take on board the enthusiasm they all have for their tasks. They will tell you that the opportunities to test their skils are endless, from coach and loco restoration, to selling prints in the Art Gallery. If you would like to join them, you will make a lot of new friends and will be helping to preserve part of Britain's great steam railway heritage, so why not join then and help run the railway? Membership application forms can be obtained from Cranmore station.

It is not possible for me to lay out the timetable of train times for you so I suggest you apply to Cranmore Railway Station, Shepton Mallet, Somerset for a timetable. If you would rather telephone, the number is (0749) 880417.

The most southerly of the towns in the Mendip District is **Street** which stands just over a mile beyond Glastonbury, across the River Brue. It is right to call it the 'newest' town both in history and appearance. It first gained fame as a tanning centre and for the manufacture of sheepskin rugs but Street has now gained worldwide recognition as the home base of the huge footwear making organisation of C and J Clark Ltd, whose headquarters border on the High Street and has long been one of the town's principal employers. There is a very interesting shoe museum portraying the history of footwear which is also located on the premises. You can see shoes from Roman times to the present day, also, a remarkable collection of snuff boxes, advertising posters, fashion plates, buckles and shoe making machinery of the 19th century. It is certainly different.

The Morlands who dealt in sheep skins, and still do, were the other family who played a large part in the growth of Street. In 1870 Morlands established a working tannery producing first quality skins and by 1906 with the revolutionary growth of the motor car, Morlands were manufacturing coats, rugs, and footwarmers for the discerning motorist. As technology advanced so did the need for more practical ways of keeping warm. In 1919, Morlands started to make boots and slippers. Thirty years on, the company were supplying boots and jackets to the Air Force and, indeed, to the famous Sir Edmund Hilary, who made the first perilous ascent of Mount Everest. You can look for yourselves in Morland's factory shop to see what they do today. There is ample parking and it is open from Monday-Saturday from 9.30am-5pm. Many shops in the High Street specialise in shoe sales and bargain hunting is popular with residents and visitors. The shopping centre altogether is a pleasant place.

Of the town's older buildings probably the Parish Church of Holy Trinity is the finest. Although it was rebuilt in the 19th century, it still has a 14th century tower and chancel. The Friends' Meeting House, a dignified building of 1850 is a reminder of the vital role the Quakers played in the industrial wealth of this part of Somerset. The origins of the Clark factory lay in the farming community but it was their strict Quaker upbringing which led them not only to build the factory, but to concern themselves with education, housing and the welfare of their workers. And, even allow a little recreation and fun within the strict confines of Quaker traditions!

Looking at sedate Street it is a little hard to envisage a time when creatures before civilisation itself, roamed the fields before they became extinct a million years ago. There are ten of these historic monsters, a plesiousaurus and nine ichthyosauris which were found in the quarries of blue lias from which the village was made. They are preserved in the small museum. Will Street enjoy Jurassic Park or will it give them nightmares? I wonder.

*Glastonbury beckons but I cannot leave out magical **Bruton**. This little town is one of the loveliest in Somerset. It has two parts, divided by the River Brue which meanders gently over stones and under a packhorse bridge. The part to the south which runs beneath and beyond the church, is oldest Bruton, a Saxon religious centre which once had two churches, one founded by St Aldhelm. There was a mint here in the 10th century which opened up the way for the growth of a small town by the 11th century growing beyond the river around a market place near the present Patwell*

171

and Quaperlake streets. What attracts me so much about this pretty place is the way in which the red roofed houses cling to each other in the winding and narrow streets. Standing on the little pack horse bridge sights of the past evoke all sorts of memories and the bonus is the entrancing peeps across the valleys.

The Romans passed this way to the Mendip lead mines, and Bruton's first church is recorded at the dawn of Saxon England. From that time only the town plan remains, with many narrow alleys - here called bartons - connecting the High Street houses to rear lanes. Bruton grew rich on wool after 1330, when cloth weavers came to Somerset. The pre-Reformation Priory, later an Abbey, was replaced by a great house which was abandoned in the 18th century, leaving a unique dovecot, now in the care of the National Trust, in its park, overlooking the town.

The parish church of St Mary is no earlier than the 14th century but it is remarkable for its two towers, one over the North porch of the later 14th century, the other at the west end which is late 15th century. The magnificent 16th century screening wall of Berkeley House also survives to puzzle us. The architecture of the town shows a rare continuity, through six centuries, of styles and techniques used where stone meets timber in Wessex. Many houses survived a fire in 1647.

The regular form of the High Street is medieval town planning at its best. The street has much of interest. It includes the former Abbey Court House of the mid 15th century and Sexey's Hospital. Believe it or not this was established by a local stable lad who made his name and fortune and returned to Bruton to found this fine school. The school stands in a suburb called Lusty! Education is now the biggest business in Bruton.

THE BLUE BALL HOTEL in Coombe Street, called The Unicorn in the 17th century and reckoned one of the best in Somerset, still has its Georgian Assembly Rooms; Rooms that were much in demand for occasions in Bruton which was something of a social centre. There are many more tales about Bruton that you will hear if you visit The Blue Ball. It stands on the site of an earlier hostelry which was destroyed by fire in the mid 18th century which devastated the whole town. In the hospitable Forge Bar, John Steinbeck is reputed to have written 'The Grapes of Wrath'.

I doubt if there is a better place to eat than THE CLAIRE DE LUNE in High Street. Run by Thomas and Kate Stewart, they also have two en-suite double rooms. The Stewarts are innovative, producing beautiful and delicious modern English food every day in the restaurant and simpler but equally good food in the bistro/bar. Visitors to Bruton should always enquire the dates of their special evenings which they hold twice a month. Sometimes Italian, Spanish or Oriental it can equally well be Lobster Gourmet, Roux Brothers, Classic Cuisine or even a Casino evening.

The Ruins of Glastonbury Abbey

The ruined abbey is the central attraction of the market town of **Glastonbury**. *It is also thought of as the cradle of English christianity. but for me it is a place of legend, history, mystery and an overworked imagination. It may well have been the earliest christian shrine but it is certainly the site of the richest monastery, and to this day still a place of pilgrimage. The Glastonbury legends are told again and again, and over the centuries have no doubt been embellished, but I never fail to feel excited by the thought of a visit here.*

Towering over the town is GLASTONBURY TOR, some 521 feet above sea level, and a landmark visible for miles around. St Michael's Tower on the summit is the remains of a 15th century church, the effort of climbing to which is rewarded by wonderful views. First the home of primitive man, then a place of Christian pilgrimage, the Tor is still visited by thousands every year. I would advise you to walk up the Tor if it is possible because of the restricted availability of car parking nearby.

One of the legends told is of Christ coming here as a child with his merchant uncle, Joseph of Arimathea. Another is of Joseph coming here with the Holy Grail and yet another of the Apostle Philip sending missionaries from Gaul to establish a church, and of those missionaries finding a church already here, dedicated by Christ Himself. The undoubted Irish influence here is traced back to St Patrick who came first as an Abbot and to whom the lower church in Glastonbury is dedicated. Then there is the story of St Bridget from Kildare, Ireland, who left her bell and wallet behind at Beckery just one mile south west.

It is true that the Tor was occupied in the Dark Ages by someone of taste and wealth who imported wine and oil from the Mediterranean and who also had a liking for meat. How all these things are worked out is always amazing to me. The tradition is that it was the stronghold of Melwas, King of Somerset, who abducted Queen Guinevere and kept King Arthur at bay. That is certainly borne out by traces on the Tor.

All sorts of churches have been built here over the centuries. By 1184, there was more than just a church of wattles. Tradition has it that St David had come with seven bishops but found that the church had already been consecrated by Christ himself; so he built another church and consecrated that. The Welsh seem to have put in an appearance as well with Saint Gilda being prominent. King Ine who died in 726 built a new church which he dedicated to the Apostles Peter and Paul. This church, at the east end of the Lady Chapel was replaced by another built by Abbot Herlwin before 1125.

It was St Dunstan who laid the foundation of Glastonbury's spiritual and economic power. Conventual buildings, a cloister and a chapel are representative of his desire to create a religious community. Three English Kings, Edmund, Edgar, and Edmund Ironside were buried here although Edgar was later moved to the east end of the Abbey church to a magnificent fan-vaulted chapel built by the last two Abbots, Richard Bere and Richard Whiting.

By the time of Domesday, Glastonbury owned an eighth of the county of Somerset covering much of The Somerset Levels, large parts of which were almost immediately drained to bring gain to the Abbot. Norman Abbots continued to add to the building but it was the powerful, rich, Henry of Blois, Bishop of Winchester who built himself lodgings on such a scale that they would have made Buckinbgham Palace look small. The huge foundations of this building were uncovered not so many years ago. He also built a bell-tower, chapter house and cloister, a great gatehouse and other buildings for the monks. It was also Henry who invited William of Malmesbury to write the history of the house which has helped us develop the legends of Glastonbury over the centuries. However this magnificent group of buildings was destroyed by fire in 1184 apart from the bell-tower, a chamber and a chapel. Those were not the days of insurance but the wealth was such that building started again immediately, beginning with the Lady Chapel on the site of the old church, and now the most complete part of the Abbey church. Hard times came to the monks in 1189 when Royal support dried up and the monks were thrown back on their own resources but the good Lord was smiling down upon then and legend says that whilst they were digging a grave for a monk, they found, between the shafts of two ancient crosses, 16ft down in a wooden sarcophagus, the bones of a large man and a woman who must have been very beautiful; she certainly had long golden tresses - the story said these locks were totally preserved until one monk with straying hands touched them and they fell to dust. The monks were in no doubt that here were the remains of King Arthur and Queen Guinevere. Strangely however, William of Malmesbury had never mentioned Arthur in his 'History of Glastonbury' but the monks were adamant, and for them their acute need for money was immediately alleviated by this lovely, romantic idea. They never looked back.

By 1278 Edward I and his Queen came to the ceremony in which Arthur was finally placed in a great tomb in the choir, and the main part of the Abbey was complete. It must have been wonderful but today only a part of this magnificence survives in the Abbey Museum. At the Dissolution in 1539 the monastery was still thriving, with over 50 monks. After the mock trial and shocking execution of Abbot Whiting and two monks on the Tor, the buildings were soon used as a quarry. The original Glastonbury Thorn remained until a Puritan fanatic decided it was wrong and cut it down in the 17th century but a piece rescued was planted, and today is to be seen in the Abbots kitchen. I think the Abbots of the past would have been horrified if they had known that the Abbot's Kitchen was used in the 16th century by weavers and in the 17th century as a Quaker meeting house.

Between the Abbey precinct and the Tor is the Abbey Barn, originally one of the Abbey's Tithe Barns, but now houses THE SOMERSET RURAL LIFE MUSEUM. It is full of relics from Somerset's past, and depicts the history and development of a whole range of trades and industries; agriculture, cider-making, peat digging, thatching and other rural crafts, imaginatively laid out and described.

Another specific attraction for visitors is THE CHALICE WELL, at the foot of the Tor. Set in attractive gardens,the waters of the well are claimed to have curative powers, and legend has it that Joseph of Arimathea hid the Chalice of the Holy Grail here.

Another interesting Museum is the LAKE VILLAGE MUSEUM in the High Street which displays many of the artefacts from an Iron-Age settlement near Glastonbury, discovered by Dr. Arthur Bulleid in 1892. Also in the High Street is the Glastonbury Tourist Information Centre housed in the fine Tribunal building. They are not the only interesting buildings. Further along is the Parish Church of St John the Baptist. THE GEORGE AND PILGRIMS HOTEL, a 14th century inn which still offers accommodation to pilgrims and tourists.

The Church of St John the Baptist is where, Joseph of Arimathea thrust his staff into the ground in what is now the churchyard and it immediately bloomed - the Glastonbury Thorn. The church is wonderful, its 134ft 15th-century tower is the second tallest in the county. It is a church full of light, created by the tall nave arcades and clerestory, with shafts on angel corbels supporting the timber roof. The 15th-century stained glass in the chancel is exquisite. You can go into the church anyday between 8am-8pm except in winter when the church shuts at 6pm.

You are bound to be hungry and thirsty after exploring. I have two favourite watering holes here, the Victorian MARKET HOUSE INN situated directly opposite the ruins of Glastonbury Abbey. This is an establishment much loved by sports touring sides throughout the year. Golf, fishing, shooting and some hunting trips are arranged for guests. It is the suntrap of a garden which I like especially. Here the spreading arms of a 130 year old wysteria are being trained to provide some shade. It is such a restful spot.

In a quiet street just off Market Cross is THE MITRE INN. Originally a coaching house, this 300 year old building is said to have the ghost of a highwayman. Take a close look at the tables - they are the antique bases of Singer and Jones sewing machines.

Thousands of years ago Glastonbury lay among lakes and marshland, and this gave rise to the rich black peat formed from vegetation of centuries ago. On the Levels to the east of Glastonbury the remains of several trackways have been found, built by early man to cross the marshes.

At **Westhay** is the PEAT MOORS VISITOR CENTRE, where you can learn about the extraordinary history and natural history of the Somerset Levels, plus a reconstruction of a wooden trackway dating from 4,000 BC, and a description of the peat-digging industry, all aptly portrayed.

If you travel the short distance to the village of **Meare** you can see the ABBOT'S FISH HOUSE dating back to the 14th century. This is where fish caught in the former Meare pool was dried, salted and stored by the monks of Glastonbury Abbey.

To the east of Glastonbury lies the village of **Baltonsborough**, the birthplace of St Dunstan. It is said that it was he who diverted the River Brue, sending it along the course of the little southward stream so that the village might have more power for its mill. The mill is still here and the straight bit of the Brue above Catsham is still called St Dunstan's Dyke. The river flows past the church of St Dunstans, it has been altered but much remains. A bench end near the pulpit holds the hourglass stand, another has one of the old flap seats sometimes added by an owner for a servant. Much to that servant's embarassment, I may say, finding himself stuck out on view in the aisle.

The cottage gardens of Baltonsborough are full of flowers and in the summer Sweet Williams grow in profusion, a flower I love and which always reminds me of my father whom I used to call, irreverently, Sweet William. In the church tower there is a tomb in which lies a Sweet William of Baltonsborough and his epitaph says:

> Would you know whom this tombe covers
> Tis the nonparell of lovers?
> Its a Sweet William, sweeter far
> Than the flowers that so stiled are.

About three miles south of Glastonbury is **Butleigh**, a village set amid beautiful countryside. The magnificent Butleigh Court was built in 1845 for the local squire, but was later damaged by fire. The building is now divided into several houses, but still beautiful, it can be seen to the left of the road as you enter the village from the direction of Street.

This is a village that stands on the top of the world surrounded by its high woodland, rich in almost every type of tree. It is on a knoll here *on Windmill Hill that the great column to Samuel Hood stands. From one side of the column one looks down on a typical Somerset scene with its hills and troughs and then on the other side the beeches have been cut to frame a view of Glastonbury Tor. A wonderful place to sit and gaze. The Hood Column catches the eye of everyone who comes into this beautiful setting.*

In the mainly 14th century church are memorials to Samuel Hood and his two sailor brothers with a lengthy epitaph written by Robert Southey, whose younger brother was killed with Alexander Hood. Hood will never be forgotten by this country, from the time he first showed his mettle when as a young commander he captured the French gunship Belliquex and the Bellona frigate until he was almost 70 in 1793 when he went to the Mediterranean, beseiged Toulon, captured Corsica and so fired the enthusiasm of his men that Nelson wrote of him 'the best officer, take him altogether, that England has to boast of; great in all situations which an admiral can be placed in.'

***Godney** to the north-west of Glastonbury is somewhere the old monks used to call the Island of God; one of their seals has been found among the ruins of Glastonbury Abbey. It is older than any monk, older than christianity and in a field is Lake Village dating back to 250 BC. There have been counted 80 or 90 mounds so a few hundred people must have lived here. Their village was surrounded by a palisade as an attempt at security. We know that they had a good knowledge of agriculture, spinning and weaving, and they loved beautiful things because Glastonbury Museum has a bronze bowl found here decorated with bosses, ornaments of amber, glass and jet, and many other treasures found under their clay floors. It was over a hundred years ago that these remains were discovered but little remains on site today, most of it is either at Glastonbury or the County Museum at Taunton.*

*The very word Camelot conjures up the romanticism of the Arthurian legend. Over the centuries historians and experts have sited the seat of King Arthur's Court in different parts of England even Wales. But since 1967, when three years of excavation began which revealed some amazing discoveries, CADBURY CASTLE at South Cadbury, near Glastonbury, has emerged the clear favourite. This is reason enough for THE CAMELOT Inn at **Polsham**, on the A39 midway between Wells and Glastonbury, to be called by this evocative name. It really is a good pub and from time to time when you stand at the bar or listen to the chatter* *around you as you eat, you may well think it is a mini United Nations, with all sorts of languages in use.*

*I have left **Wells** until last because it is so very special and outstandingly beautiful. A place which delights the eye and makes the heart beat faster. It is the smallest city in England with a population of just 9,400 but it is its Cathedral which gives it city standing. It is, in fact, Somerset's only city. It lies sheltered beneath the southern slopes of the Mendip Hills, and combines a wealth of historic interest and beautiful architecture with its role as a thriving market centre.*

The site of Wells was occupied by the Romans but did not become significant until the west Saxon King Ine founded a church by the wells; these springs near the Bishop's Palace gave the city its name.

The Bishops Palace, Wells

From a distance you see its three towers standing out against the green foothills of the Mendips. As you come closer approaching through one of the medieval gateways, you are faced with the superb West front, twice as wide as it is high, still carrying 293 pieces of medieval sculpture extending across the whole facade. Such an array of sculptured figures is unique in Europe.

Inside, the nave presents one of the earliest completely Gothic designs, its austerity relieved by the elaborate sculpture of capitals, corbels and head stops. If I take someone with me to the cathedral who

179

has not been before I always set them a task in the south transept - to find the man with toothache, the woman with the thorn in her foot, the farmer and the fruit stealer, the pedlar with his bag and a string of beads and finally a queer monster with his hands on his knees. It is an exciting hunt and very rewarding; there is so much beauty. In the north transept the clock of 1390 is to be seen. Every quarter of an hour horsemen make their tournament and the same knight is knocked off his horse at each rotation.

The transept is the best place to see the impressive scissor arches with their great curves which transfer weight from the west, where the foundations sank under the tower's weight, to the east where they remained firm. This dramatic solution of a structural problem in 1338 remains effective to this day. By contrast with the comparative plainness of the nave, the quire, where daily services are sung, presents a mass of colour. Here are embroidered stall-backs worked in 1937-1948 which attract needleworkers from far and near who come specially to examine them; embroidered cushions on the seats; medieval stalls with misericords underneath. High up in the east wall is the glorious east window of 1339, known as the Golden Window, with four windows, of five years later, flanking it.

Beyond the quire are the lady chapel, with its lovely but fragmented glass, and other chapels, used in turn for the daily eucharist throughout the week. Intriguing vaults are everywhere, including three ribs too many with a stone lion to bite them off.

From the north quire aisle lead the remarkable and much photographed steps up to the Chapter House and beyond. The Chapter House, a gem of the decorated style reduced to its simplest terms, is the official meeting place of the Canons. Beyond it the stairs lead on to the Chain Gate of 1459-1460.

The east walk of the Cloisters supports the Library of 1425. It is 168 feet long and possibly the largest medieval library building in England. Its contents suffered severely in the 16th and 17th centuries but the building was restored and refurnished in 1686. It contains a number of chained books as well as archives and documents from the 10th century onwards. An exhibition room is open to the public at a small charge on four days a week from Easter to the end of September.

In earlier days, the west Cloister supported the choir school, audit rooms and the grammar school. Young voices may yet be heard there because the Choristers' practice room is still above the west Cloister; but the Choir School and the Grammar School are now united in the Cathedral School of 700 pupils, occupying many buildings to the north of the Cathedral.

The 14th century Vicars' Close, where the Vicars Choral still live, is joined to the cathedral by the Chain Gate, mentioned above.

The Cathedral is open every day of the year and admission is free; but because it has few endowments and no state aid it is heavily dependent upon voluntary gifts. Visitors are invited to make a donation towards the maintenance of this great building and its day to day work. Cathedral guides are available by prior arrangement and there are regular guided tours from Easter to the end of October. The cathedral has a well stocked shop in which you can buy goods ranging from records of the Cathedral choir and organists to Caithness glass, Wedgwood pottery, pewter jewellery and small pieces of silver, as well as guide books, post cards and Christian literature of all kinds.

Beyond the cathedral shop is THE CLOISTER RESTAURANT in the West Cloister and whether you have spent time in these beautiful surroundings or come directly to the cathedral having explored Wells, there is one place you should make for and the Cloister Restaurant is that place. Opened in 1984 it was an immediate success and offers a first class menu supported by excellent service. Profits from the restaurant go exclusively to the upkeep of the Cathedral.

The moated palace and it associated buldings of this gem of a cathedral are what gives Wells a very special place in the hearts of all who come here. The fortified palace with its great ruined hall, its chapel and its early Gothic main living block show how feudal it all used to be. No less famous than the Palace are the swans who glide along the moat in their stately way, stopping only to raise their beaks to sound the gateway's bell when they are hungry; a trick they have learned from their ancestors. Some old glass from Nailsea Court suggests that the birds perfected this art almost five hundred years ago. The lawns are wonderfully manicured, the old walls mellow with age. The Palace is still the home of the Bishop of Bath and Wells and its garden contains the wells from which the city gets its name.

Stroll past the Georgianised medieval house in Vicar's Close and you will revel in the sheer quality and atmosphere in this housing area for minor clerics. It is blissfully quiet, totally car free and the gardens are beautiful.

It is not only the Cathedral and the Palace and its environs which are superb in Wells. There are many old houses, picturesquely medieval and tudor, some with Georgian fronts that stand close to the Cathedral quarter and close to the Liberties north of it.

You are spoilt for choice in Wells when it comes to places in which to stay, drink and eat. I have many favourites here and am never sure which one I like the best - usually the ones I am visiting. The Continental style CHAPELS CAFE BAR in Union Street is charmingly informal and some might think modern and trendy for Wells, but it fits in beautifully and offers something for people of all ages.

THE GOOD EARTH in Priory Road is a fascinating restaurant that once was a hotel, a past that has allowed its owner, Christopher Edwards, to use four informal inside rooms as eating areas and in addition he has created another charming spot in the sheltered paved courtyard. The charm of The Good Earth undoubtedly lies in the informality of the eating surroundings. The food is deliciously different and it is adjacent to a wholefood store specialising in dried fruits, nuts, cereals, pulses, 50 different varieties of tea plus many more specialised food items.

Situated on the junction of the B3139 to Bath and A371 to Shepton Mallet, just 50 yards from the Cathedral is THE FOUNTAIN INN built during the 16th century to house builders working on the Cathedral. The bar is panelled and full of atmosphere and above it is BOXERS RESTAURANT, renowned for its food and wine. If you love cheese you will be in your element; they have an award for their selection of West Country cheeses.

THE KINGS HEAD in the High Street is a wonderful inn, built in 1320 at the same time as the magnificent Cathedral. Its purpose was to be a refectory for the monks and so it was until it became an inn at the beginning of the 16th century. It is stone built with the 13th century gallery still encompassing the whole area of the pub at 1st floor level. People come here just for the sheer pleasure of its historical interest.

On the corner of Tucker Street and just five minutes walk from the Cathedral is THE MERMAID HOTEL, a solidly built 15th century hostery where genuine, traditional home cooking is the order of the day.

The elegant WHITE HART HOTEL was first described as an inn in 1497 and is thought to have been the Bishop's guest house. There are 13 en-suite rooms and a delightful dining room full of old world charm with a beamed ceiling which is the oldest of its kind left in this beautiful city.

Last on my list but by no means least, is the historic CROWN AT WELLS in the Market Place. Every room, every bar, is full of character. If you stay here you will find four-poster beds and a sense of history that enters your soul the moment you walk through the door.

Despite its wealth of history, Wells is also very much up to date in terms of its facilities, which includes a modern leisure centre and swimming pool, a cinema and an amateur theatre. Regular markets are held in the picturesque Market Square on Wednesdays and Saturdays.

Panborough is a pleasant place on the B3139 about five miles from Wells. It is truly rural within sight of Glastonbury Tor and in its midst is the village pub, THE PANBOROUGH INN. This peaceful pub is ideal for anyone who wants a respite from the absorbing beauty of Wells. It is very easy sometimes to have too much over powering beauty and it is good to return to the simple green countryside. Such a drive out to this pub for a drink or lunch will refresh you and enable you to return to exploring Wells and to appreciate it more.

Another gorgeous spot just 3 miles outside Wells is THE EASTON INN at **Easton** at the foot of the Mendip hills, overlooking the Somerset Levels and Moors. The food is particularly good and interesting. You will find all sorts of exciting dishes as well as the more traditional English fare. I will remember the Shrimp Creole for many a moon.

At WOOKEY HOLE, the Caves, one of Britain's oldest tourist attractions with recorded visits back to 189AD, are the main feature here. Vistors are taken on a half mile tour through the chambers, accompanied by a knowledgeable guide who can point out the amazing stalactites and stalagmites, including the famous Witch of Wookey. The new lighting uses state-of-the-art techniques to add dramatic interest to the caves and the *guides use remote controlled lighting to highlight geological features and illustrate the history and myths associated with the caves. It is almost incomprehensible to think that Roman coins carrying Christ's monogram from as far back as 341 AD were found in the caves. The caves have attracted famous visitors including Daniel Defoe, Alexander Pope and Oliver Goldsmith.*

Traditional Paper Making at Wookey Hole

The caves are not the only attraction at Wookey Hole Caves. Traditional papermaking is demonstrated showing the craft of paper making by hand in the Victorian Mill. Visitors can purchase a range of paper products from the Paper Shop adjoining the demonstration area. Also in the mill is Fairground Memories, a collection of late 19th century fairground rides together with a gigantic organ complete with original music. Then there is the Magical Mirror Maze. This is an enclosed passage of multiple image mirrors creating an illusion of endless reflections to enthral both adults and children. A visit to the Old Penny Arcade completes the mill tour. There is plenty of parking on site, a restaurant, GIFT SHOP selling all kinds of goods to please young and old alike and attractive picnic areas.

*The village of **Cheddar** is one of Somerset's many pretty villages, the original home of Cheddar Cheese and the awesome 40ft deep cleft in the rocks which covers two miles and is CHEDDAR GORGE. There are over 400 caverns and potholes in the area, some lit up and open to the* *public to see the stalactites and stalagmites. The largest cave is Gough's Cave which stretches for a quarter of a mile and contains wonderful stalagmites and pillared chambers. A 10,000 year old skeleton, the Cheddar Man was found in this cave and is now in the adjoining museum. At the head of the Gorge is the Black Rock nature reserve, 183 acres of land embracing grasslands, ash woods and coniferous forest. It is a fasinating are full of wild life.*

Close to the Gorge is a good pub which is a fitting finale to a visit to this designated area of natural beauty. THE GARDENERS ARMS is set in a quiet elevated street about five minutes walk away from the bottom of the Gorge. It is believed to be the oldest drinking house in Cheddar. Vine clad, it is definitely a local pub but it is also very popular with visitors who welcome the good, wholesome, reasonably priced food at lunchtime and the slightly more sophisticated meals at night.

I have had a wonderful time visiting the Mendip towns and the villages, revelling in the beauty of the countryside, the glory of Wells Cathedral, the sense of permanence in the five towns and the friendliness of the people.

THE BLUE BALL HOTEL

Hotel & Inn

2 Coombe Street,
Bruton, Somerset

Tel: (0749) 812315

Odd word association intrigues many people. Who would believe that this quiet, beautiful old Saxon town of Bruton would have a famous school called Sexeys in a suburb named Lusty? It is true; the school was founded by a local stable lad who made his name and fortune and returned to Bruton to found this fine school.There are many more tales about Bruton that you are quite likely to hear if you frequent The Blue Ball Hotel, a 17th-century coaching inn. It stands on the site of an earlier hostelry which was destroyed by fire in the mid 18th century which devastated the whole town. In the Forge Bar the fireplace is dated 1677 showing that it came from the earlier pub. It was in this hospitable bar that John Steinbeck reputedly wrote 'The Grapes of Wrath'. There are several golf courses nearby plus good walking including the Pilgrims and Leland Trails and coarse fishing - a wonderful centre for all outdoor pursuits.

Brian and Jane Hopkins, the landlords carry on this tradition of hospitality and many walkers who frequent the Blue Ball have found the drying room a boon. It is available for anyone staying and for those who come in at lunchtime out of the rain. In addition to walkers many other tourists come to Bruton to marvel at the town, its pretty and very ancient bridge and the houses which seem to cling to the hillside. For those wanting to stay a night or two the Hopkins make guests more than welcome in the five bedrooms. For those wanting a glass of Real Ale, they have come to the right place and Jane Hopkins cooks some excellent pub fare which is reasonably priced and generous in portion.

USEFUL INFORMATION

OPEN: Mon-Sat: 11-2.30pm & 6.30-11pm
   Sun: 12-3pm & 7-10.30pm
CHILDREN: Welcome, dogs also
CREDIT CARDS: Visa/Euro/Master
LICENSED: Full On
ACCOMMODATION: 1 twn, 1 fmly,
   1 sgl, 1 dbl en-suite

RESTAURANT: Good, wholesome fare room available for business/seminars & parties up to 35 covers
BAR FOOD: Good selection available
VEGETARIAN: Always 2 dishes
DISABLED ACCESS: Level entrance at rear
GARDEN: No

CLAIRE DE LUNE

2-4 High Street,
Bruton, Somerset.

Tel: (0749) 813395

Brasserie Restaurant & Accommodation

Bruton is the epitome of all that is small and beautiful and is a town of which Somerset is justifiably proud. It has one of the first fulling mills in England built around 1290 and it was here that Hugh Sexey was born; a man who started life as a stable boy, made good and invested his wealth in founding the famous Sexey's school in 1519. The town attracts thousands of visitors, many of whom will have discovered the pleasure of eating in the Claire de Lune restaurant in the High Street.

Run by Thomas and Kate Stewart, it is also somewhere one can stay. Since they opened this charming establishment in 1988, the Stewarts have been listed in The Good Food Guide, Michelin and Acherman. They are innovative, producing beautiful and delicious modern English food every day in the Restaurant and simpler but equally good, food in the Bistro/Bar. It is their Special Evenings which they have twice a month that makes them so popular locally. Sometimes Italian, Spanish or Oriental it can equally well be Lobster Gourmet, Roux Brother, Classic Cuisine or even a Casino evening. Visitors to Bruton should make sure they find out if one of the dates falls during the time of their stay, because the evenings are not to be missed. Naturally good wines are part of the occasion.

The two en-suite double rooms with colour TV, showers and tea/coffee making facilities are to be recommended. The whole operation is professional with an endearing intimacy.

USEFUL INFORMATION

OPEN: Tue-Sat: 7-10pm
    Sunday Lunch: 12-2pm
CHILDREN: Permitted. Limited highchairs
CREDIT CARDS: Visa/Access/Amex
LICENSED: Full On
ACCOMMODATION: 2 dbls. En-suite

RESTAURANT: Modern English, delicious
BAR FOOD: Simple food, no minimum spend
VEGETARIAN: Ample choice
DISABLED ACCESS: 2 steps
GARDEN: Sun Patio. BBQ

THE GARDENERS ARMS
Public House

Silver Street,
Cheddar, Somerset.

Tel: (0934) 742235

The vine clad Gardeners Arms is a local pub situated in the village of Cheddar, close to the famous Cheddar Gorge, a designated area of outstanding natural beauty. You will find it in a quiet, elevated street about five minutes walk away from the bottom of the Gorge.

The pub, believed to be the oldest drinking house in Cheddar, began life as a row of farm-workers cottages in the 16th century and later became a cider house. In 1899 the then Marquis of Bath, Frederick Thynne, ancestor of the present Marquis who is the owner of Longleat and the famous Cheddar Caves, sold the premises to a Shepton Mallet Brewery for £630. A copy of these deeds hang in the bar.

At lunchtime a popular selection of hot and cold snacks for all appetites is served at an average price of £2.50. In the evenings the extensive menu includes excellent local steaks, garlic chicken, a selection of fish dishes, giant Yorkshire puddings filled with home-made steak and kidney in ale and much more.

Customers are welcome to leave their cars in the car park whilst they walk and enjoy the beautiful countryside or visit the tourist attractions of Cheddar.

USEFUL INFORMATION

OPEN: Old fashioned pub hours
CHILDREN: Family room, suitable food
CREDIT CARDS: None taken
LICENSED: Full Licence
ACCOMMODATION: Not applicable

RESTAURANT: Not applicable
BAR FOOD: Wide range, sensible prices
VEGETARIAN: 6 dishes
DISABLED ACCESS: Yes, with help
GARDEN: Large beer garden. Wonderful views

THE BULL TERRIER

Village Inn

Croscombe,
Wells, Somerset.

Tel: (0749) 343658

Even if Croscombe were not the beautiful village that it is, standing in a valley with the pastures of the Mendips rising on either side, it would still be worth making the journey here to enjoy The Bull Terrier which was built in 1475-1500, and first licensed in 1612 when it was known as The Rose and Crown.

The Bull Terrier was originally a Priory belonging to Glastonbury Abbey. When you walk in you can not fail to feel the sense of history, the original beams are still in the bar and the flagstone floors are uneven and glistening with the patina of age. It is totally unspoiled and needs none of the sophistication of a restaurant to make it a good place to eat albeit informally in the bar. It is the sort of pub that is becoming harder and harder to find. You will find no games or vending machines at the Bull Terrier. It is a place to enjoy conversation with those who have also discovered the delights of the pub, and the conversation of the friendly owners, Stan and Pam Lea who have been here ten contented years.

Stay a night or two in one of the three rooms available, two of which are en-suite and you will have time to explore that place of timeless beauty, Wells Cathedral and its Bishop's Palace, Wookey Hole Caves, Cheddar Gorge and its caves and the legendary Glastonbury Abbey only eight miles distant. At the Bath and West showground at Shepton Mallett, apart from the annual Royal Bath and West Show in late May and June, there are events most weekends. The beer, the food and the company are super.

USEFUL INFORMATION

OPEN: 12-2.30pm & 7-11pm
   Closed Mondays October - March
CHILDREN: Not residential, but to eat
CREDIT CARDS: Access/Visa/Master
LICENSED: Full On and Off Licence
ACCOMMODATION: 3 rooms,
   2 en-suite

RESTAURANT: Not applicable
BAR FOOD: Cooked to order with care
VEGETARIAN: Always 6 dishes
DISABLED ACCESS: Yes. Not
   residential
GARDEN: Walled, splendid views,
   eating, drinking

THE EASTON INN
Public House & Restaurant

Easton (A371),
Wells, Somerset.

Tel: (0749) 870220

Easton, just three miles outside Wells is known not only for its beauty and its situation at the foot of the Mendip Hills, overlooking the Somerset Levels and Moors, but also for the Easton Inn. This charming hostelry delights all who visit it and is a triumph for its dedicated owners, John and Margaret Davidson, who have made the pub synonymous with the high quality of their English and International Cuisine, served in the comfortable restaurant.

You are invited to select from the exciting menu which includes such exotic favourites as Mexican enchilada filled with spicy beef and red beans, Chinese prawn and bamboo stir fry, Italian tortellini alla creme and shrimp creole. If your taste is for more traditional fare try The Easton's English steak and kidney pie, Lancashire hot pot or home-baked ham. There is also an interesting selection of vegetarian dishes with a variety of tempting salads and ploughman's snacks.

The Easton Inn is only a few minutes from Wells with its superb Cathedral and Bishop's Palace. The Somerset heritage towns of Frome, Glastonbury, Street, and Shepton Mallet are no distance and if you enjoy the coast, the seaside towns of Weston Super Mare and Burnham on Sea are only a short drive away. What better way to round off a trip to Cheddar Gorge and caves or Wookey Hole Caves than with a gorgeous meal at The Easton Inn!

USEFUL INFORMATION

OPEN: 11-2.30pm & 6-11pm. Normal Sunday hours
CHILDREN: Very welcome
CREDIT CARDS: Access/Visa/Master
LICENSED: Full Licence
ACCOMMODATION: Not applicable

RESTAURANT: Exciting English & international
BAR FOOD: Good, home-cooked daily specials
VEGETARIAN: Always available
DISABLED ACCESS: Level access
GARDEN: At rear, patio, play area

THE ANGEL INN

Public House & Restaurant

King Street,
Frome, Somerset.

Tel: (0373) 462469

This ancient pub is still obliged to take horses from all travellers by a law that has been on the statute books since the 17th century. It seems quite right and proper to have this fine hostelry which has been a public house since the 13th century, in the centre of a conservation area, with medieval streets which still have water running down the middle. The Angel stands at the head of King Street facing into the Market Square.

Hospitality would have been of paramount importance in those far off days when travelling was both dangerous and difficult. We have the means to get about more easily but we still need to feel welcome when we visit an inn. Sandra and James Heard, the landlords at The Angel have the right personalities to make you feel at home and their amiable staff follow suit.

The Angel Inn comes complete with the ghost of a serving wench, whose intimate relationship with the then landlord, produced an unwanted baby, which was buried in the wall of the restaurant. The tale goes that the mother, trying to expiate her guilt, walks around searching for her baby.

Sandra cooks all the traditional English fare herself and most of the menu has a Newcastle theme. Geordie Pie for instance and Black Pudding. At one time Sandra and James lived in America and so sometimes, an American recipe creeps in, but the beer is strictly British, James prides himself on the quality of his Real Ales.

USEFUL INFORMATION

OPEN: 10-11pm. Normal Sun hours
CHILDREN: Welcome
CREDIT CARDS: None taken
LICENSED: Normal pub & Off sales
ACCOMMODATION: Not applicable

RESTAURANT: Traditional English Fayre
BAR FOOD: Extensive range. Sensibly priced
VEGETARIAN: on request
DISABLED ACCESS: Level access
GARDEN: Beer Garden

LA BISALTA

Restaurant / Bistro

6 Vicarage Street,
Frome, Somerset.

Tel: (0373) 464238

Just out of the centre of the market town of Frome is La Bisalta, Italian restaurant. The building dates back to around 1750, and was originally a private house then a vegetable shop before becoming this charming little restaurant. La Bisalta is named after the mountain in the home town of Luigi Violino, your host, which is Boves in North West Italy.

During the summer months the well cared for romantic terrace is very popular with customers, to sit, eat and enjoy the sun. Luigi runs the restaurant with the help of his wife Susan and their chef; very much a family affair.

The food is delicious and excellently presented. Start with Cozze Arrosto - baked green-lip mussels with butter, parsley and garlic or Gamberoni in Tegame - Giant prawns in chilli and garlic finished with grappa. Then choose from the extensive main courses. Fish, including monkfish Provencal, a firm white fish diced and cooked in a tomato and pepper sauce, or a meat dish, Scaloppine al Marsala - veal escalopes pan fried in butter finished with marsala wine, or for the pasta lovers, one of their mouth watering dishes. Vegetables and salads are extras but well worth while. To follow, there is a generous cheese board and a choice of desserts from the trolley.

A good lunch should encourage you to explore the many places to visit around Frome. Longleat is not far, the east Somerset railway is nearby and Mells, an Elizabethan manor house is 2 miles to the west, and, not forgetting the mansion, Stourhead and its beautiful gardens only a few miles away.

USEFUL INFORMATION

OPEN: 12-2pm & 7- late
CHILDREN: Welcome
CREDIT CARDS: Master/Access/Visa/
Euro
LICENSED: Full Restaurant Licence
ACCOMMODATION: Not applicable

RESTAURANT: Specials available
Pasta, meat, fish
BAR FOOD: Light lunches,
Table d'Hote
VEGETARIAN: Always available
DISABLED ACCESS: Level access
GARDEN: Lovely terrace

CROFTS

21 Fromefield,
Frome, Somerset.

Restaurant

Tel: (0373) 472149

Crofts is on the main Bath-Frome road and is a restaurant not to be missed. It is situated in an attractive building that dates back to 1690 and is one of the many Listed buildings in this fine, medieval, market town.

Two small and very individual rooms make up the dining area. Each has a welcoming fireplace, which in winter throws out a wall of warmth. The small bar is designed to allow customers to enjoy pre-dinner drinks and an opportunity to relax whilst they study the interesting menu. Everything about Crofts gives you a sense of well-being from the decor, which is in keeping with the feel of the building, to the meticulous attention to detail that has brought it deserved renown very quickly. While you are taking a look at the fixed price menu and sipping your aperitif, you will be offered tiny little nibbles, a mouthful of crumbly pastry flavoured with anchovy or cheese; just enough to alert the tastebuds to what is to come. Everything is home-made including the bread, ice-creams, sorbets and sweetmeats. The emphasis is on English dishes with the occasional and always interesting Continental influence. For example you may be offered Monkfish with Leeks, Saffron and Coriander or Crudities with Tapenade.

Margaret Graham is the chef-proprietor and this is a lady with a wealth of experience which she delights in sharing with her customers. Wisely she has made her two dining rooms strictly non-smoking. Well worth seeking out, this delightful, intimate restaurant is open from Tuesday to Saturday in the evenings only.

USEFUL INFORMATION

OPEN: Tues-Sat: 7pm - last orders 9.45
CHILDREN: Allowed
CREDIT CARDS: Visa/Access/Master
/Euro
LICENSED: Restaurant
ACCOMMODATION: Not applicable

RESTAURANT: Everything home-made
BAR FOOD: Not applicable
VEGETARIAN: 2 changed weekly
DISABLED ACCESS: No special access
GARDEN: No

MARKET HOUSE INN

Public House & Hotel

Magdalene Street,
Glastonbury, Somerset.

Tel: (0458) 832220

This Victorian Market Inn situated directly opposite the ancient ruins of Glastonbury Abbey and with clear views of the Tor, remains a landmark in the town of Glastonbury. This is where a cross section of customers meet for fine restaurant meals, traditional ales, good company and entertainment. The warm and friendly staff and management maintain high standards of quality and service and with 7 single, double and family rooms will accommodate and entertain guests until the early hours.

Established sports touring sides are welcomed throughout the year. Golf, fishing, shooting and some hunting trips are arranged among many other activities, such as in-house skittles - in the longest alley in the district, visits to the local Cider Farm, picnics to the Tor, for example.

The garden boasts a 130 year old wysteria which is being trained to shade some of the beautiful suntrap of a garden where barbecues, parties and entertainments are staged from time to time. An unique inn, although architecturally typically Victorian, this inn oozes atmosphere and lightheartedness and is complemented by many a selective friendly local who, combined with the standard of service, will make anyone's stay whether for a drink or a week, a memorable one.

The usual facilities of private car park, satellite TV, telephone, full English breakfast, morning coffee and afternoon tea, take-aways and a laundry service to mention but a few are provided in this house and with such competitive pricing and room rates provides extremely good value.

USEFUL INFORMATION

OPEN: Mon-Sat: 11-11pm. Sun: 12-2.30 & 7-10.30pm
CHILDREN: Well behaved welcome
CREDIT CARDS: None
LICENSED: Full On
ACCOMMODATION: 7 rooms

RESTAURANT: A la carte & traditional Devon, Cornwall & Somerset dishes
BAR FOOD: O'Hagans specialist sausages, traditional baskets & platters
VEGETARIAN: 3-4 dishes
DISABLED ACCESS: No, unfortunately
GARDEN: Large with BBQ area

THE MITRE INN

Inn

27 Benedict Street,
Glastonbury, Somerset.

Tel: (0458) 831203

Glastonbury has a wealth of interesting places to visit including the Abbey ruins - reputedly the burial ground of King Arthur and his Queen Guinevere, beside the 11th century St Benedicts church. In a quiet side street just off the Market Cross is the Mitre Inn. Although not obvious from the front, this old pub has a beautiful walled garden, very tranquil and bathed in sun when the weather behaves.

Originally a coaching house, this 300 year old building is said to have the ghost of a highwayman, but Anne Chichowicz, your host, has never seen it. A medium, however, visiting the pub said she could feel its presence and some days later phoned to say other mediums, while holding a meeting had indeed seen the highwayman 'hanging around'.

Whilst you enjoy a good meal and one of their Real Ales, you sit at very unusual tables - the bases are antique sewing machines, Singer & Jones, treddle stands, in full working order.

The Mitre Inn has a good menu with a daily Specials board. Vegetarians and vegans have their own special board, and everything is home-cooked using fresh locally produced ingredients. To end a delicious meal, it is impossible to refuse one of their home-made sweets. For vegans there is a special ice-cream which has to be tried.

USEFUL INFORMATION

OPEN: 11.30-2.30pm & 5.30-11pm
Sun: 12-3pm & 7-10.30pm
CHILDREN: Welcome
CREDIT CARDS: None taken
LICENSED: Full Licence
ACCOMMODATION: Not applicable

RESTAURANT: Not applicable
BAR FOOD: Also served on Sunday evenings. Daily specials, good home cooked dishes
VEGETARIAN: Always 6 dishes
DISABLED ACCESS: No
GARDEN: Yes

PANBOROUGH INN

Public House & Restaurant

Panborough,
Wells, Somerst

Tel: (0934) 712554

Panborough is truly rural with Glastonbury Tor visible and just 5 miles from the great cathedral of Wells, 7 miles from Cheddar Gorge and 5 miles from Wookey Hole. At Wedmore, three miles away the remains of a Saxon village have recently been discovered. In the midst of Panborough is the 17th-century Panborough Inn, a charming, atmospheric hostelry in which you will always find a mixture of interesting people who have found their way there from quite a distance usually, although there are the faithful regulars who live in this lovely part of Somerset. The peaceful pub is just the place for refreshment after exploring the magnificence and awe inspiring beauty of Wells Cathedral.

The family partnership of John and Carol Halliwell and Kenneth and Catherine Hargreaves, have spent the last ten years constantly improving this well loved pub. They have made it into a very happy place; something one notices immediately on entering its old doors.

Real Ales, Ruddles Best Bitter, the local Butcombe Bitter and sometimes other Guest bitters attract the aficionados and for wine lovers, the wine list is extensive. The menu offers good, wholesome, home prepared dishes as well as simple snacks. Every day there are House Specials which are tempting and inexpensive. On Sunday the traditional lunch is a popular institution. In the summer the Beer Terrace is ideal for a quiet drink.

USEFUL INFORMATION

OPEN: 11.30-2.30pm & 6.30-11pm
CHILDREN: Welcome
CREDIT CARDS: Visa/Access
LICENSED: Full On licence
ACCOMMODATION: Not applicable

RESTAURANT: Full a la Carte. Home-cooked
BAR FOOD: Snacks, Specials, full menu
VEGETARIAN: Always 5 dishes
DISABLED ACCESS: Yes
GARDEN: Beer Terrace with tables

THE CAMELOT INN

Polsham (Main A39),
Wells, Somerset.

Public House & Restaurant

Tel: (0749) 673783

The very word Camelot conjures up the romanticism of the Arthurian legend. It was the seat of King Arthur's Court but where exactly was it? Over the centuries historians and experts have sited it in different parts of England and even Wales. But since 1967, when three years of excavation began which revealed some amazing discoveries, Cadbury Castle at South Cadbury, near Glastonbury, has emerged the clear favourite. This is reason enough for The Camelot Inn at Polsham, on the A39 midway between Wells and Glastonbury, to be called by this evocative name.

Although the area may be steeped in mystery, there is no mystery about what is on offer at The Camelot Inn. Good food, friendly service and excellent ales are the order of the day and the Inn has become a favourite eating and drinking place. It is popular with regulars, with people enjoying the occasional night out and is, of course, an ideally placed stop-over for tourists.

In February 1987 John and Margaret Davidson, also the owners of the Easton Inn, brought the Camelot and the result is that the Inn has something to offer everyone from tots to grandparents. The Camelot has an atmosphere which the whole family can enjoy. With Glastonbury and Wells both high on the list of foreign visitor's 'sights to see', The Camelot at times resembles a mini United Nations! To sum it all up, The Camelot bases its success on the importance of 'Food and Families' - a recipe for satisfaction.

USEFUL INFORMATION

OPEN: 11-3pm & 6-11pm
CHILDREN: Very welcome
CREDIT CARDS: Access/Barclaycard /Diners
LICENSED: Full licence
ACCOMMODATION: 3 rooms, not en-suite

RESTAURANT: Wide ranging, home-cooked
BAR FOOD: Excellent value, Daily specials
VEGETARIAN: Always available
DISABLED ACCESS: Yes
GARDEN: Very large, play area, Aviary

CANNARDS WELL INN

Inn

Cannards Grave,
Shepton Mallet, Somerset.

Tel: (0749) 346247

Just over a year ago Clive and Sharon King took over the 16th-century Cannard's Well Inn which stands on the junction of the A37 and A361 in the Mendips, just outside the market town of Shepton Mallett. It is an inn steeped in local history, at one end of the bar is a toft well, which is said to be of Roman origin. Certainly a Roman fortress was found about 500 yards from the pub. At the other end of the bar is the grave of Tom Giles, the last person in Shepton to be hung for sheep stealing. He has been seen walking the corridors and bedrooms of the pub ever since!

In the last twelve months the Cannard's Well has become steadily more and more popular. It is not just the excellence of the food, it is the happy, friendly atmosphere that prevails. Clive has a fund of good stories and his laughter once heard will never be forgotten. Sharon helps their excellent chef, Ivor Cross, in the kitchen; her speciality is curry. Ivor is well known for his presentation of good home-cooked food. In addition to the food and drink, there are 15 pleasant rooms for bed and breakfast - the latter is cooked by Clive and is an English breakfast of gargantuan proportion. Diners can eat in the Cottage Restaurant or in the bar. The bar menu, full of home-cooked dishes, is changed regularly and blackboard specials are changed daily. A separate a la carte menu operates in the Cottage Restaurant offering succulent and interesting dishes. On Sundays, Ivor's roast lunch served from noon is so popular that it is essential to book early.

USEFUL INFORMATION

OPEN: Mon-Sat: 11-2.30pm & 6-11pm
Sun: 12-3pm & 7-10.30pm
CHILDREN: Under strict control of
parents
CREDIT CARDS: Visa/Access/
Mastercard/Eurocard
LICENSED: Full Licence
ACCOMMODATION: 15 rooms

RESTAURANT: Good home-cooked
food, full a la carte menu
BAR FOOD: Comprehensive bar menu
Daily chef's specials
VEGETARIAN: 4 dishes
DISABLED ACCESS: Level entrance
& toilets
GARDEN: Patio

THE THATCHED COTTAGE INN

Inn

63-67 Charlton Road,
Shepton Mallet, Somerset.

Tel: (0749) 342058
Fax: (0749) 343265

This comparatively modern inn has enormous charm. From the day the first brick was laid it was almost a foregone conclusion that it would not be long before it was one of the most popular venues in the Shepton Mallett area. A great deal of thought went into the design of the spacious airy rooms and into the intimate atmosphere of the attractive restaurant. Its thatched roof gives it great character added to by the fascinating structure of the porch that leads inside from the garden. Covered by thatch it is supported by a structure of entwined tree limbs which have been varnished.

There are eight beautifully furnished and decorated bedrooms with enormous bathrooms. Each room is not numbered but called after a bird, somehow just right for an inn in this rural area. Dining in the intimate, panelled restaurant with its pretty drapes and table cloths is an experience not to be missed. The full menu has a particularly good fish section but there is also a three course set price menu which is excellent value for money. In the Main Bar area one can drink and sample the vast number of dishes available including some very tasty Daily Specials. Everything is well presented, the service is efficient and courteous and at the same time reassuringly friendly. The children have fun in the play area in the garden where tables and chairs are set out for their elders to have a drink in the sun. The Thatched Cottage lives up to its well deserved reputation.

USEFUL INFORMATION

OPEN: Mon-Sat: 11-11pm,
   Sun: 12-2.30pm & 7-10.30pm
CHILDREN: Welcome in Middle Room
CREDIT CARDS: Access/Visa
LICENSED: Full On
ACCOMMODATION: 8 en-suite

RESTAURANT: Intimate. Full menu.
   Speciality fish
BAR FOOD: Extensive menu & daily
   specials
VEGETARIAN: Several choices daily
DISABLED ACCESS: Not to
   accommodation
GARDEN: Large with play area

CHAPELS CAFE BAR

Cafe Bar

Unit 2, Union Street,
Wells, Somerset.

Tel: (0749) 675044

Chapels Cafe Bar is one of the few places in Wells that is licensed all day. It has many other benefits, not the least of which is its proximity to a car park. In the centre of Wells, you will find Chapels signposted from the High Street; you simply walk through a large alley to the cafe bar and the car park.

It is a Continental style Cafe Bar with a charmingly informal atmosphere. Sometimes, if one describes a place as modern and trendy, it is off putting for several reasons. The older generation might think it is not for them, parents with young children will view it with apprehension but whereas this might be true of some such establishments, it is definitely not so at Chapels Cafe Bar. Certainly it is refreshingly modern without being garish, but it is a place for all ages at any time of the year.

The small but selective menu is inexpensive and yet provides dishes with a difference. There is a children's menu. Most of the food is home-made. At night Chapels changes and becomes more of a Wine Bar drawing its customers from the younger generation. Its appeal to visitors must be its friendliness and the willingness to cater for everyone at sensible prices and at the same time offering generous portions. Ideal in fact if you have spent the day exploring Wells and its superb Cathedral. You can quite easily walk from Chapels to wherever you want to visit, returning later for a welcome break knowing that whether it is a glass of wine, a meal or just a coffee and croissant, it is going to be enjoyable and not hurt the pocket.

USEFUL INFORMATION

OPEN: Mon-Sat: 10am-11pm.
   Sun: 12-3pm & 7-10.30pm. Food until
   9pm Sun-Thurs, 6pm Fri-Sat
CHILDREN: Welcome until 7pm
CREDIT CARDS: Visa/Master/Euro
LICENSED: Full On & Off
ACCOMMODATION: Not applicable

RESTAURANT: Not applicable
BAR FOOD: Good interesting,
   inexpensive
VEGETARIAN: Always several dishes
DISABLED ACCESS: Level entrance
GARDEN: Small outside eating area

THE CLOISTER RESTAURANT

West Cloister,
Wells Cathedral, Wells.

Restaurant

Tel: (0749) 676543

The Restaurant is set in the cloisters of Wells Cathedral, an architectural gem in its own right with a beautiful vaulted roof and fascinating historic memorials. Wells Cathedral, one of the finest Cathedrals in England, or indeed in Europe, is somewhere that no one should miss. The Cathedral contains many unusual and attractive architectural features, such as the Chapter House - the only one in an English Cathedral which is 'upstairs'. The west front of the Cathedral, containing nearly 300 carved stone figures is world famous and much of the stone carving inside is equally fine as are the embroidered panels in the quire.

Whether you have spent time in these beautiful surroundings or whether you come directly to the Cathedral having explored Wells, there is one place you should make for and that is The Cloister Restaurant. Jenny Barnes has been the Manager here since the restaurant opened in 1984 and with her supportive and enthusiastic team, many of whom have connections with the Cathedral, she provides a first class menu and service.

There is something for everyone amongst the many attractive dishes. Hot dishes of the day might well be Somerset chicken casserole or a spinach and cottage cheese lasagne. There are home-made quiches, freshly prepared salads, cooked meats and ploughman's etc as well as some good desserts. Cakes and freshly baked scones, cream teas are available all day. Profits from the restaurant go exclusively to the upkeep of the Cathedral. The Restaurant closes for 2 weeks each year over Christmas and the New Year

USEFUL INFORMATION

OPEN: Mon-Sat: 10-5pm (4.30 Nov-Feb) Sun: 2-5pm. Closed Good Friday + 2 weeks at Christmas

CHILDREN: High chairs, Mother & Baby room nearby. Small portions

CREDIT CARDS: None taken

LICENSED: Wine & Cider with meals

ACCOMMODATION: Not applicable

RESTAURANT: Excellent home-made fare

BAR FOOD: Not applicable

VEGETARIAN: A choice of dishes

DISABLED ACCESS: Ramp, disabled toilet close by

GARDEN: Not applicable

THE CROWN AT WELLS

Hotel & Public House

The Market Place,
Wells, Somerset.

Tel: (0749) 673457

Wells without doubt is one of England's treasures. No one comes here without experiencing the thrill of being among so much history and beauty. The Crown at Wells in the medieval market place, which is adjacent to the Cathedral and the Bishop's Palace, is a delightful inn dating back to 1450 approximately and was then a medieval coaching inn. You can feel the sense of history the moment you enter its doors.

Many famous people have been here over the centuries and William Penn, the founder of Pennsylvania, once preached to a crowded market place from one of the hotel bedrooms. Every room, every bar is full of character. If you choose to stay here you will find that four of the fifteen en-suite bedrooms, have four-posters; naturally they have every modern facility but it is all in keeping with the age of the building. This is a family run business which at the moment is undergoing considerable refurbishment but none of it is being allowed to detract one iota from the charm of its old world appearance.

There is a private residents and diners bar. The Penn Bar and Eating House is open from ten in the morning until ten at night and serves light meals, morning coffee and afternoon teas. For residents there is an attractive lounge and in the summer the patio area is very popular for those who want to sit and enjoy the surroundings, have a drink or a meal. The hotel is able to offer excellent facilities for Conferences and is a favourite venue for wedding receptions.

USEFUL INFORMATION

OPEN: All year. Food: 10am-10pm
   Drink: 10am-11pm
CHILDREN: Welcome
CREDIT CARDS: Access/Visa/Amex
LICENSED: Full On
ACCOMMODATION: 15 rooms, 4 with
   four-posters

RESTAURANT: Bistro style menu
BAR FOOD: Interesting light meals
   served in Penn Eating House & Terrace
VEGETARIAN: 3-4 dishes
DISABLED ACCESS: Yes
GARDEN: Patio/Terrace for eating
   & drinking

FOUNTAIN INN & BOXERS RESTAURANT

1 St Thomas Street,
Wells, Somerset.

Public House & Restaurant

Tel: (0749) 672317

Adrian and Sarah Lawrence have been the proprietors of this very nice establishment for 12 years, and have built up an enviable reputation for food and wine using only the very best of local produce. If you happen to love cheese you will be in your element; they have an award for their selection of West Country cheese. To accompany your cheese, what better than a fine bottle of wine, from their great wine selection, of which they have received recognition winning the Mercier award.

The Fountain is situated on the junction of the B3139 to Bath and A371 to Shepton Mallet, just 50 yards from Wells Cathedral, surrounded by many beautiful buildings. After lunch what better pursuit than to wander around the moat to the Bishop's Palace.

The Inn was built during the 16th century to house builders working on the Cathedral. Above the bar is Boxers Restaurant, furnished attractively, with pine tables and Laura Ashley decor. The pub also has a function room which seats up to 30 people.

An extensive menu is available in both the bar and restaurant. There is a huge selection of delicious home-cooked food. There are vegetarian dishes and a childrens menu, also vegan dishes on request. In addition to the regular menu, the chef's blackboard specials include tempting dishes. Magret Duckling, venison steak in Cumberland sauce, Mussels or a whole sea bass are to name but a few. Sauces accompanying many of the dishes are very interesting and subtle, a little out of the ordinary and look superb.

USEFUL INFORMATION

OPEN: Weekdays:10.30-2.30pm & 6-11pm
    Sun: 12-3pm & 7-10.30pm
CHILDREN: Welcome. Own menu
CREDIT CARDS: Visa/Access/Amex
LICENSED: Full Licence
ACCOMMODATION: Not applicable

RESTAURANT: Anglo-French using
    local produce
BAR FOOD: Wide range as restaurant
VEGETARIAN: Approx 7 dishes daily
DISABLED ACCESS: Yes - toilets on
    first floor
GARDEN: No

THE GOOD EARTH
Restaurant

4 Priory Road,
Wells, Somerset.

Tel: (0749) 678600

Wells, known as the smallest city, has a wealth of beautiful buildings amongst which is the listed, red bricked Georgian building, in Priory Road, which houses The Good Earth. This fascinating restaurant was once a hotel, a past that has allowed its present owner, Christopher Edwards, to use four informal inside rooms as eating areas. In addition he has created another charming spot in the sheltered paved courtyard in which barelled tables and chairs are provided so that in good weather, people may enjoy the sunshine as well as the delicious food.

The charm of the Good Earth undoubtedly lies in the informality of the eating surroundings - wooden floors and oak tables allied to the home-made Vegetarian meals, all of which is adjacent to a wholefood store specialising in dried fruits, nuts, cereals, pulses, 50 different varieties of tea plus many more specialised food items. The restaurant has acquired a reputation for its food and has not gone unnoticed by Egon Ronay's 'Just a Bite', Family Choice and 'A Taste of Somerset'. It maintains a consistently high standard and is welcoming to people of all ages. There are high chairs for small children, a baby changing facility and a wheelchair access to all the inside eating areas. The constantly changing menu is all home-made and 100% Vegetarian although it does cater in a limited way for Vegans. Interestingly enough, you will find many non-Vegetarians eating here because the food is so good.

USEFUL INFORMATION

OPEN: Rest & Shop: Mon-Sat: 9.30-5.30
Closed Sundays & Bank Holidays
CHILDREN: Most welcome
CREDIT CARDS: Visa/Access/Master
LICENSED: Rest: Wine & Beer,
Shop: Off Licence
ACCOMMODATION: Not applicable

RESTAURANT: Home-made, 100%
vegetarian. Vegan menu
BAR FOOD: Not applicable
VEGETARIAN: Totally
DISABLED ACCESS: Yes
GARDEN: Paved courtyard seats 20

THE KINGS HEAD

Inn

36 High Street,
Wells, Somerset.

Tel: (0749) 672141

This wonderful inn was built in 1320 at the same time as the magnificent Cathedral. Its purpose was to be a refectory for the monks and so it was until it became an inn at the beginning of the 16th century. It is stone built with the 13th century gallery still encompassing the whole area of the pub at 1st floor level. No words can truly describe the magic of Wells and its wonderful buildings; they have to be seen and felt.

Today The Kings Head stands amidst the bustling activity of the High Street, but its beauty is unaffected. Of course it has been restored and altered over the centuries, the front room for example was built in the 1530's but still has the beautiful original 13th century beams and frequently brings people here just for the historical interest rather than to enjoy the hostelry - something they always stay to do after soaking in the atmosphere, vibrant with age. The hatch in the front bar used to be the original front door of the inn, and the stables have become a delightful courtyard garden. In the intimate, beamed restaurant, the soft drapes and pretty table covers add to the feeling of well-being.

The full menu offers an array of delicious dishes which come to the table beautifully presented and accompanied by wines, well chosen and at realistic prices. In the bar, food is served daily and provides a good choice of traditional fare with the addition of daily blackboard Specials. Children are welcome for meals and there are several choices of vegetarian dishes every day.

USEFUL INFORMATION

OPEN: Summer: 11-11pm,
    Winter: 11-2.30pm & 6-110m.
    Sun: 12-3pm & 7-10.30pm
CHILDREN: Welcome for meals
CREDIT CARDS: Access/Visa
LICENSED: Full On Licence
ACCOMMODATION: Not applicable

RESTAURANT: Intimate, full menu
BAR FOOD: Wide range, daily specials
VEGETARIAN: Several dishes daily
DISABLED ACCESS: No special
    facilities
GARDEN: Rear courtyard

THE MERMAID HOTEL

Public House with Accommodation

1 Tucker Street,
Wells, Somerset.

Tel: (0749) 672343

Solidly built, The Mermaid Hotel, has been a hostelry since the 15th century. Today not much is left of the past except the welcoming atmosphere and lurking in the Beer Garden, the old stocks, which no longer used for punishment, find themselves in great demand on Fun Days! The pub stands on the corner of Tucker Street and is just a five minute walk to Wells Cathedral and the Bishops Palace. Equally convenient for the good shopping centre in which it is a pleasure to browse. You will find Tucker Street just off the High Street in Old Wells.

Thomas and Irene Murray came from Edinburgh to become landlords of this attractive establishment. He was once a miner and knows a thing or two about good ale. You will find every pint of Founders and Ushers Best Bitter Real Ale, is well kept here. Irene is in charge of the catering which is genuinely home-cooked, unpretentious and excellent value. People who have stayed here in the letting bedrooms, which all have TV, satellite, and tea and coffee making facilities, will tell you that the breakfast she puts on the table is one of the best you will get anywhere. Children are welcome and families will find the separate sitting room very useful. No pets are allowed. Apart from the many visitors who have discovered The Mermaid, the pub has its regular locals who enjoy the fun of the pub. There is a skittle alley to amuse them. Local people also use the function room for parties and meetings.

USEFUL INFORMATION

OPEN: 11am-11pm
CHILDREN: Play area, pets corner.
    Children's room planned for 1994
CREDIT CARDS: None taken
LICENSED: Full On
ACCOMMODATION: 2 fmly, 1 dbl,
    1 sgl

RESTAURANT: Not applicable
BAR FOOD: Good home cooking
VEGETARIAN: On request
DISABLED ACCESS: Yes
GARDEN: Large Beer Garden

THE WHITE HART HOTEL

Sadler Street,
Wells, Somerset.

Hotel

Tel: (0749) 672056
Fax: (0749) 672056

The charming cathedral city of Wells is home to the elegant White Hart Hotel in Sadlers Street, with views of the cathedral green. The Hotel, was originally known as 'Harts Head' and was first described as an inn in 1497. It is thought to have been the Bishop's guest house.

The present owner, Peter Ayton is currently refurbishing the hotel and has discovered many interesting features which have been sympathetically restored. There are 13 en-suite rooms, with tea and coffee making facilities, colour TV and Satellite channels. There is a function suite overlooking the gothic spires, which holds up to 60 people. It has every facility needed for business meetings and conferences. An ideal base for anyone touring Somerset with Wookey Hole and Caves, the Gothic Cathedral city of Wells, Bath and Longleat, near by.

The Dining Room has an old world charm with its beamed ceilings and is the oldest original example of its kind left in this beautiful city. The menus are prepared by the Head Chef from local produce and are unusual but frequently traditional including dishes using wild boar, game casserole, quail and venison. The a la carte menu is noted for its fish dishes and delightful deserts, all at very reasonable prices. The bars are cosy and intimate although less formal. The open log fires and exposed beams make you feel very welcome and you can enjoy traditional bar food in these charming surroundings.

USEFUL INFORMATION

OPEN: 7.30-11.30pm. Lunch 12-2pm
Dinner 6-10pm
CHILDREN: Welcome
CREDIT CARDS: Visa/Access/Amex
Switch
LICENSED: Full On
ACCOMMODATION: 13 en-suite with
TV, satellite, trouser presses &
hairdryers

RESTAURANT: 25 covers . No
smoking only. Sunday Lunch
BAR FOOD: A la carte & table d'hote
VEGETARIAN: 4-5 available
DISABLED ACCESS: Ramp at
entrance. No special WC facilities
GARDEN: Not at present

The Famous Christmas Steps, Bristol

BRISTOL CITY

INCLUDES

"The Lord be praised
if my belly's raised
an inch above the table.
But I'll be damned,
if I'm not crammed
as full as I am able."

Anonymous

BRISTOL CITY

Let us imagine you are newly arrived in **Bristol**, *you have just enjoyed a light and refreshing meal at THE OLD CASTLE GREEN Public house, and having ordered your post prandial coffee you cross the old polished timber floor and take up your seat by the window. There is no cacophony of juke box or modern day intrusion and you are free to recover from your journey which may have been a long and wearisome one, possibly from a foreign country. Outside there is the bustle and hum of a very modern city, but inside all is peaceful and I would ask that as you relax you allow me to transport you on another journey, back through time to the 18th century and beyond.*

More than 250,000 years ago primitive man settled in the valley of the Bristol Avon, one can see the attraction, rich alluvial soil ripe for cultivation good clean spring water and a wealth of vegetation. The original settlement was built by Brennus a British Prince, in 380 BC. It was first mentioned as a fortified city in 430 AD. Variously called Caer Oder and Caer Brito British City, by far the most delightful name was the Saxon, Brightstowe or pleasant place. The name Avon appears elsewhere in the country, sometimes with a different spelling, but the origin is the same, from the Celtic word for river. This Avon is born in the South Eastern Cotswolds, near **Malmesbury** *from here it describes a wide arc through Chippenham, Melksham, Bradford on Avon and Bath. Over the Millenia the river has carved a deep narrow channel through the lime-stone ridge, and it makes its stately progress through Bristol until it spills past Avonmouth and relinquishes its identity at the confluence with the vast expanse of the Severn.*

From these auspicious beginings the vibrant Port of Bristol developed and continued to grow for the next 800 years. We will begin our story at the very hub of commerce.

It is a working day at the Tolsey, the centre of trade for the town and the crush of merchants and dealers is oppressive, but thrilling. The business of the day is conducted with speed, bargaining and bartering, undertaken with cut throat precision. When a deal is struck the cash is "paid on the nail', and the merchants count their money on ancient tables forged from bronze. Outside this throng gentlemen meet in the popular coffee houses, here they can discuss the latest news, a pastime much enriched since William Bonny intoduced the Bristol Post Boy, the first newspaper to be published outside London. It is far more comfortable off the streets for the populace is so increased that it becomes quite hazardous negotiating the narrow alleys, a situation not helped by the habit of the small traders who resort to dragging their wares through the town on 'geehoes,' or sleds, wheeled vehicles are not allowed in the streets because of the comb of cellars beneath them.

These cellars and wharves are brimful, but almost daily more and more ships arrive to discharge their cargoes into this overflowing cornucopea, at certain times of year the incoming merchant seamen report seeing over a thousand ships tied up at Kingroad and Hungroad, their masts like a forest along the river. The storehouses groan with hogsheads of wine from Spain and France, bales of wool, fine silks, flanders linen and skeins of thread. The exotic fragrance of almonds, saffron and liquorice fill the air. While the more prosaic, pots, pans, oil and tar are discussed in the same breath as the miserable pathetic human cargo of slaves, arriving in their hundreds to swell the coffers of the already fabulously wealthy.

*Often the throng of humanity in the town becomes unbearable, there are now almost 50,000 inhabitants all living cheek by jowl, the ramshackle dwellings of the poor sometimes only a stones throw from the grandly ornate mansions of the town's commercial fathers. It is a relief to venture out into the rural areas away from the foetid air. Thankfully the Merchant Venturers have donated vast sums to the Church, could it be they are mindful of the 'eye of the needle,' or are they motivated by consciences which occasionally remind them of the degree of human suffering upon which their fortunes depend? Whichever, within the shadows of the fine new churches some delightful Inns and public houses have appeared. One of these THE DUNDRY INN at **Dundry** occupies a lovely position, high above the clamour of the town. The officers navigating their way into the confines of the channel, no mean feat under sail, will use the churchtower which looms behind the pub to fix a bearing, no doubt the seamen below decks will be anticipating the good ale!*

*Another hostelry which lies adjacent to a church is the BOWL INN at **Almondsbury**, a short carriage drive from the estuary.*

*To the North of the town is **Westbury on Trym**, a thriving village community whose inhabitants still talk of the days when Prince Rupert and his Royalist army of 20,000 men marched through their midst, it is difficlt to imagine that only a few short decades ago this area was under seige and ravaged by plaque, but one cannot underestimate the importance of*

Bristol in the overall jigsaw of history, it was rightly believed that whoever controlled Bristol, controlled the West. Much has altered since John Wycliff was prebend of the college of priests, but the fine 15th century gatehouse still stands and other buildings would have a fascinating tale to tell, if walls could talk. THE FORRESTERS and THE PRINCE OF WALES have served the passing trade well and the FLEUR DE LYS probably holds many secrets within its foundation stones.

It is time to return to the town, and recall how in medieval days Bristol was enclosed by walls, pierced at intervals by gates. Above these gates were built churches and of these St Johns still stands. The four main streets met at an intersection to which the townspeople would flock to listen to the bellman read proclamations, here too stood the High Cross and any event of social interest took place beneath it. Visiting Monarchs received with great ceremony or an unfortunate vagrant dealt a flogging attracted the crowds equally, although the latter no doubt produced a somewhat less respectful response. Overseeing these events stood three of England's oldest churches, All Saints, Christchurch and St Ewens. The effigy of Edmund Blanket in St Stephens Church offers a good example of the characteristic dress of the wealthy merchants of the 14th century. Over his tight sleeved tunic he wears a 'cote lardie' across his shoulders is a small falling cape fastened in front. Below the waist he sports a handsome jewelled belt, this denoted him as a man of importance and substantial wealth. Under the sumptuary laws of Edward III the wearing of such belts was forbidden to anyone below the rank of knight or possessed of less than £200. If you think these laws were a little severe, I can assure you they were considerably worse in the days of 844 BC when it was ordained that, no woman should walk in the street attended by more than one maid, unless she were drunk!

It must have come as quite a shock to the gentry of Bristol when Henry VII imposed fines for the excessive finery worn by the merchants wives. Until then they had delighted in their conspicuous riches, far from hiding their light under a bushel, they were quite inclined to flaunt it and the bushel, or woolsack or wine barrel, anything for that matter by which they had earned their money, frequently commemorating these items on shields and merchant marks.

Of all the churches in the area St Mary Redcliff is renowned for its beauty and reputed to be one of the largest in the land, its massive tower is richly embellished and crowned with a spectacular spire which soars 285 feet toward heaven. It was in the muniment room above the north porch that the precocious teenager Thomas Chatterton was inspired to write the verses that would lead to his downfall. Discovering some suitably distressed materials, Chatterton put quill to parchment and began to compose poetry in the style of one Thomas Rowley, monk. These 'newly discovered' masterpieces were received with great excitement by the literati of the time, sadly for the entrepreneurial youth. Rowley was proved to be a fiction and Chatterton having travelled to London to make his fortune was so disillusioned he commited suicide in a Holborn Garret. A moral there for those who wish to see it! The fame he sought in life has been afforded him posthunously and his birthplace at CHATTERTON PLACE is now a museum.

If Chatterton created a minor stir in the literary world it was undoubtedly John Wesley who made a major one in the religious. John, his brother Charles and George Whitefield were friends at Oxford. While there they had been part of a group known as 'Methodists.' John spent two years in America and on his return, fired with a great revivalist zeal, attracted a crowd of 3,000 to hear him preach. The eloquence and fervent commitment that emanated from him not surprisingly produced a hostile reaction from the established church. His presence was not accepted in the parish churches, possibly because of this his followers grew rapidly in number. It became imperative for Wesley to find his own premises and when he eventually bought land at HORSEFAIR the first Methodist church was built. He travelled far and wide spreading the word and his famous Journal records the often depressing forays he made into the dismal underworld at KNOWLE where French prisoners were held in appalling conditions. He did much to improve education in the county. Despite this contribution to society he constantly met with hatred and suspicion, and it was not until after his death that the congregations became permanently established. 36, HORSEFAIR, the sight of his 'New Room', now has two fine bronze statues to John and Charles.

Before I introduce you to the townsfolk of Bristol, you may appreciate a visit to MULLIGANS FISH RESTAURANT at 43 College Green. It is a wise precaution to take refreshment before we launch into the hurly burly of streetlife.

Welcome to the 18th century! Bristol society displays the dichotomy one would expect in a fuedal society turned capitalist, and the atmosphere has produced a fertile breeding ground for dissent among the poorer classes. In October 1831 the catalyst appeared when Sir Charles Wetherall, the Recorder, entered the City. By opposing the reform Bill he had alienated himself from the people. The ensuing riots were catastrophic, The Mansion House was fired and looted as was the Customs house and other buildings in Queens Square, even the Bishops Palace went up in flames. The troops were called in and the Riot Act read, but Colonel Brereton refused to fire on the mob, for this act of compassion he was later rewarded by a court marshall, the shame of which resulted in his suicide, a sad time. The mob which had indulged freely of the wine liberated from the Mansion House rampaged on to the prisons and many convicts were released. After three days of looting and destruction they were finally brought to order, over one hundred homes had been raised to the ground and 500 people lost their lives. So great was the fire in the city that it could be seen in Cardiff. Charles Kingsley who was a schoolboy in Bristol at the time described the scene as being like Dante's Inferno.

This has been a dark period for the City, but we shall rally as usual. The world is expanding at a breathtaking pace, and in every quarter the conversation turns to exploration and adventure. This expeditionary zeal is seemingly inherent in the hearts of Bristolians, how else could the Venetian John Cabot have arrived in the city and, as a newly adopted son of Bristol convinced the merchants of the 15th century to sponsor his expedition across the uncharted Atlantic. On 2nd May 1497 his little ship, the Matthew, set sail. He and his crew of eighteen had embarked on a perilous voyage into the unknown, and I expect their families secretely despaired of ever seeing them alive again. Imagine their excitement when after a terrible period of waiting the ship was first sighted returning to her home port, fear and trepidation would have turned to pride when reports of the voyage became known. John Cabot had sighted land after fifty two days at sea, and on going ashore had ordered his men to hoist the flags of England and St Mark thereby claiming the 'new found land', for the King. So grateful was the Monarch for this gift of North America that he bestowed upon Cabot a reward of 10 pounds and a pension of 20 pounds a year. Henry VII was nothing if not munificent! Fortunately his peers were more benevolent and the CABOT TOWER in BRANDON HILL is a fitting tribute. Three centuries later ships are still leaving port to explore new territories and stretching long arms across the seven seas to claim the treasures of foreign lands. Surprisingly, although horizons are constantly being expanded and breached there remains a deeply parochial quality among the townspeople. The majority of men and women still choose to live in close knit communities and through this cautious crowd swaggers the Jolly Jack Tar.

There can be little about his chosen career to earn the average merchant seamen the epithet 'Jolly.' It probably has more to do with his

214

essence of bravado and occasionally altered emotional state after a brief exposure to alcohol. He carries about him the air of a true man of the world' for he has seen jungles and white beaches, the raging oceans and the deep blue seas of the West Indies. He stands apart from other men, and has developed characteristics and a uniform peculiar to himself. The wide bottomed trousers are tarred against insinuating damp, he wears a heavy 'fearnought' jacket and a Monmouth cap. On his forearms he displays tatoos made by scratching a design on the tough skin and rubbing in pigments or gunpowder. It is his face which proclaims him a seafarer battered by the salt winds, and burnt the colour of ochre by the sun; he is indeed a marked man, an occupational hazard which often results in him waking up on slave ships embarked on yet another voyage courtesy of the press gangs who roam the alleys searching out unwilling recipients of the Kings shilling. There are almost 2,000 seamen living in the town and as night falls more will be wandering the dark lanes looking for cheap lodgings, hot food and perhaps a jug of ale or two! As they stagger along between the close thronged houses past the doors of the LLANDOGER TROW whose lively clients spill onto the street, through the passages and into CHRISTMAS STEPS their carousing echoes of the walls causing some upstairs windows to be flung open and the helpful occupants call out alternative routes! They might even test the patience of the hospitable gentlewoman who runs McCREADIES WHOLEFOOD RESTAURANT at number 3, but I doubt it!

Llandoger Trow

The essence of a good restaurant is continuity and one of the best examples in the city is the RESTAURANT DU GOURMET in Whiteladies

Road, very close to the BBC studios, whose chef has created their classic cuisine for 21 years.

Outside the town at **Redcliff**, *THE BELL public house will be full of merriment, this area is known locally as Cathay and is becoming famous for the Bristol Blue Glass which is so popular. The health giving properties of Bristols spring waters is renowned worldwide now and the demand for bottles has provided more employment, the workers swell the numbers calling for ale. As they innocently sup their chosen brew, far beneath their feet in the deep cellars all manner of nefarious goings-on may be afoot for this is the golden age of smuggling and not only brandy and wine are contraband. Indeed it has been suggested that in England and America there is not a man or woman who has not drunk smuggled tea, smoked smuggled tobacco, or ever owned a silk handkerchief which has not passed through customs.*

This trading by stealth, acknowledges no social or economic barriers, and as such is similar to another form of free enterprise, poaching, and across the way toward Avonmouth at **Portishead** *the public house known as THE POACHER is undoubtedly doing a brisk trade. a caveat here, the streets are a good hunting ground for pickpockets, so I would suggest we repair to the comfort of the THEATRE ROYAL for a little entertainment or maybe we should take a carriage out to* **Hotwells***. Since Catherine of Braganza first visited the springs which gush out of the cliff near the mouth of the Avon Gorge, Hotwells has become quite the most fashionable place to be seen. Many of our great literary names frequent the spa. While we are there we could call at the ROSE OF DENMARK.*

Gradually the architecture of Bristol is changing, as the merchants pour money into improvement schemes a form of official planning has developed and the random structure makes way for a more formal design of elegant squares, fortunately the ancient city is not being swept away and it is still possible to see the COLSTON and ST NICHOLAS ALMSHOUSES, built by Edward Colston considered to be Britains greatest merchant. THE CATHEDRAL of course is the focal point of the city and its presence is largely due to one Robert Fitzharding. A man of great importance, he held the office of Reeve at the time when Bristol was under the control of Robert, Earl of Gloucester. Although the castle he had inherited was large and strongly built he set about rebuilding it on a grand scale. By adding a stone keep and encircling the whole with massive walls and bastions, he created a royal stronghold which dominated the town. Within these secure walls he gave shelter to the

Empress Matilda and her son Henry. Robert of Gloucester was a powerful supporter of the Empress in her bid for the throne, as a result no sooner had the castle been completed than it came under seige. Robert Fitzharding was also a loyal friend to Matilda and placed his considerable wealth at her disposal. Fitzharding was to buy the manor of Billeswick which lay without the city walls and it was here he founded the abbey of Augustinian Canons, and their church, after the dissolution became the cathedral church of Bristol. Among the architectural treasures of the Cathedral are the Stellar tomb reccesses which are unique to Bristol.

Bristol Cathdral

Before we know it the 19th century is upon us, and you should hold onto your hats for a breathtaking ride of discovery and invention.

The invention of the railway has been greeted with mixed feelings. For one they are proving an unwelcome competition to the canal companies. The Thames and Severn company are even attempting to form their own railway to rival that of the Great Western. Despite drastically cutting their tolls they are losing business at an alarming rate and they have had to watch their revenue drop from £11,000 to £2,874 in fourteen short years and are in danger of bankruptcy. There is talk of the Great Western buying the canal. There are grave misgivings at the suggestion that railways might one day carry passengers. It is considered that the effects of such a mode of transport would be extremely injurious to health.

217

Such suspicions as the public have voiced are being swept aside in the general thrust to develop a network of lines radiating out from Bristol and Gloucester. Our very own Temple Mead has become the centre for three railway companies, and one has to admit that the whole exercise has proved far more pleasant than could have been envisaged. On arrival at Temple Mead one discovers a most orderly and controlled scene as reported in Morgan's guide. 'A porter is ready to conduct you to the booking office, where you pay your fare and receive your ticket, you then ascend a flight of stairs to the platform. Having taken your place, and made all ready, you are now at ease to observe what is going on ... several engines with red hot fires in their bodies and volumes of condensed steam issuing from them: one of them moves slowly towards you. The huge piece bellows at first like an elephant; deep slow and terrific are the hoarse heavings that it makes. It is then linked to the carriages ...a whistle is sounded as a signal for starting - and you are off.' Many are being called upon to invest in the new railway companies some forward thinking embrace the idea wholeheartedly, but others decline to become involved.

A certain Charles Owen Cambridge of Whitminster felt that at the age of 80, it would not become him to become involved in adventurous speculations! The companies have also encountered difficulties when attempting to sight the new lines. Land owners are objecting to the idea of having their estates sliced in two, but few are as unyielding as Robert Gordon, squire at Kemble, who effectivly held the company to ransom refusing to allow them on his land until he had received substantial compensation, even then he insisted that the rail would be routed beneath his property through a quite unnecessary tunnel.

The papers are reporting that work has just begun on an engineering project of such enormous bravura. I find it difficult to believe that it is not in fact a figment of someone's imagination. They are to construct a railway tunnel under the Severn! In the unlikely event of this story proving true the works will no doubt be flooded and the attempt fail!

A few years ago I would hardly have believed it possible, but the railways are spreading across the country with remarkable success. They have brought with them interesting changes, in some areas they have proved a boon. The dormitory towns near the stations have expanded and prospered, but other towns which lack a main line or relied on stage coaches for good trade have stagnated. A colleaque writes from Teweksbury,'Whatever may be the ultimate effect of rail-roads it is evident that their introduction has hitherto been one of almost unmixed evil to the inhabitants of Tewkesbury". If one can believe what he says poor Tewkesbury has become a ghost town!

*One of the main protagonists of the day is a man of great vision, the name Isambard Kingdom Brunel is on everyones lips, not only was he instrumental in creating the railway link between Bristol and London, but his design has been chosen for a great suspension bridge to span the Avon Gorge at **Clifton**. Unbelievably Thomas*

The Clifton Suspension Bridge

Telford initially rejected the design on the grounds that he considered the spans too great, but as he then submitted his own designs there may have been an element of creative jealousy. Conversation in the drawing rooms of the town is so exciting, rumour has it that Brunel has persuaded the Directors of the Great Western Railway Company to make Bristol a stage en route to America, and that when one of the Directors complained that the length of the railway line was already excessive the irrepressable Brunel suggested extending it further by way of a steamboat connection to New York. This idea has been taken up by a man called Richard Guppy and there is talk of a ship being built at WAPPING WHARF she will be a wooden paddle wheel vessel and the first steamship built as an Atlantic liner. Of course there are some people who ridicule the idea even suggesting that one may as well talk of making a voyage from New York to the moon, but as everyone knows that is simply absurd!

It is now 1838 and following the success of the Great Westerns maiden voyage, New York in fifteen days, plans are underway to build a second ship. This will surely test the ingenuity of our engineers for she will

*be the first vessel built of iron and powered by screw propulsion. At 322
feet long and weighing 1,936 tons she will far outweigh any ship previously
built, it is claimed that her engines will be capable of attaining over 1,000
b.h.p. There will be accommodation aboard for 360 fortunate passengers,
I have no doubt there are certain members of Bristol society who are
clamouring for reservations even before her plans are drawn up.*

S.S. Great Britain at the Great Western Dock

*What a tumultuous crowd gathered at the docks today to bid
farewell to the S.S. Great Britain, bands played and the people cheered
and waved until she had sailed out of sight. Many amongst the gathering
would have offered up a silent prayer for the safety of their loved ones.
Fifteeen days later the following report arreared in The New York Herald:
The monster of the deep, sort of Mastadon of this age, the Great Britain
arrived on Sunday afternoon the 10th August. She was telegraphed
precisely at noon; the announcement threw the city into great excitment
and thousands rushed to the battery, to the wharves on the East River, to
the Brooklyn heights and to the Atlantic steamship pier at the foot of
Clinton street to get a sight of her ... this magnificent steamer came up the
bay in beautiful style ... the great problem whether or not a steamer of the
magnitude and construction of theGreat Britain, and incorporating her
principle of propulsion, could make a successful trip across the ocean is
now satisfactorily and happily solved. The engines were never stopped
until Captain Hosken had occasion to sound on St Georges Bank ... The
great vessel which carried the pride of Bristol with her whenever she
sailed was to make many crossings until 1850 when changing fortunes
sent her running between Liverpool and Australia, during this period she*

would carry the forebears of probably a quarter of a million Australians. Enthusiasts of the time honoured sound of leather on willow will be interested to know that she carried the first ever English cricket team to Australia, a fact which would be appreciated by the revered cricketer Doctor W.G. Grace who once resided at the WAGGON AND HORSES at **Upper Easton***.*

Meanwhile Brunels' spectacular bridge programme has run into difficulties, the project has been abandoned through lack of funds. In desperation the engineers are even utilising second hand chains from the recently demolished Hungerford Bridge in Berkshire. Sadly it is believed by some people that Brunel will not live to see his wonderful design come into operation.

The business men of Bristol are starting to complain at the decline in trade. It was once believed that the improvements made to the harbour would be sufficient to ensure healthy commerce for many years. So much time, money and effort has been invested to counteract the chaos caused by those two natural and fundamental problems that have beset the port since time immemorial, namely mud and tides. At **Kingroad** *off Portishead the ships were able to weigh anchor and wait for the right combination of wind and tide to carry them into port. Three miles further on the vessels had to rest on the mud until the tide turned sufficiently to carry them up river. Often smaller tenders ferried between the ships and men and cargoes were discharged onto them from these effectively beached whales. There were also pilot vessels to guide the ships up river, but so concoluted was the course of the channel and extreme the rise and fall of the tides that ships of any notable size were precluded from passing beyond Hungroad. This problem remained for centuries as though all concerned had resigned themselves to the situation, regardless of the fact that heavily laden ships settling their bulks awkwardly into the mud ran a grave risk of breaking their backs. Eventually our Merchant venturers galvanised themselves and constructed a dock at* **Sea Mills***, the first mercantile dock ever to be built in England. Commendable, but largely ineffectual as the dock remained tidal and by that virtue troubled until 1803 and Mr Jessops FLOATING HARBOUR. Brilliant in concept, it required three miles of river to be formed into a dock immediately dispensing with the problem of tides which were diverted into a new channel cut to the south of the city. This channel also allowed smaller craft to enter the harbour at* **Totterdon***. As a direct result of this scheme 85 acres of dock space has been created and a vast expanse of potential industrial zones opened up. As with most brilliant, innovative, sweeping changes, it cost a packet! Somehow the funds had to be recouped, does this sound familiar? We, the disgruntled* *voice of Bristol commerce now find that not only are we competing with the other ports around the country, but thanks to the massive increase in rates imposed by the Bristol Dock Company it actually costs twice as much for a ship to dock here as it does at our closest rival, Liverpool.*

*The situation looks grim and is further compounded by the effect of the American War and the loss of our trade from the West Indies. I think I shall retire to the CAMBRIDGE ARMS at **Redland** and drown my sorrows!*

Things are looking up! We have recently managed to resolve a ridiculous situation whereby our two new docks at Portishead and Avonmouth were set in competition against one another, each being privately owned. Thankfully the Corporation has moved in and assumed control of the entire Port of Bristol, now perhaps we can see some sensible revenue returning to the city. Who knows we may even be looking towards a period of great expansion, with new industries, manufacturing, smelting plants. Possibly vast networks of rail and roads will fan out to the far corners of the country. Maybe I should consider taking a short holiday, this time travel can play havoc with ones imagination!

*That's better, a stroll along the Esplanade at **Clevedon**, lunch at MURRAYS, followed by a visit to the PIER and I am completely relaxed. The Victorians with their fondness for creating seaside resorts have been responsible for this lovely area and very grateful I am to them. The pretty Victorian villas look out over the channel to distant Newport. There is so much to enjoy, the CRAFT CENTRE for example has all manner of artifacts on display and it is open throughout the year from 11am to 5pm, with no charge for admission. I love to watch the parade of fashionable ladies as they wander along the promenade, with their funny little dogs and light hearted chatter about the latest society parties, their parasols protecting peach complexions against the sun and dresses which are a display of the exquisite workmanship of the local seamstresses they are as pretty as a picture. Some of the bicycles one sees nowadays defy description.*

*A little further South is the popular resort of **Weston-Super-Mare**. A perfect place this for families with young children, they can ride donkeys along the wide beach and watch artists creating huge models in the sand. Maybe they will watch a Punch and Judy show and then retire tired but happy to one of the many guest houses, all of which boast nothing less than the comforts of home are on offer. I could leave you here if you wish, to enjoy the sunshine, ozone and sparkling sea, or you* could accompany me to two more wonderful places of sheer mouth watering delight before we enter the twentieth century and things really start to hot up!

For me no holiday would be complete without a trip to the HIPPODROME and close by the stage door there is the scrumptious HARVEYS WINE MUSEUM, housed in the cellars beneath 12 Denmark street, these same cellars were once used as part of the Hospital of the Gaunts. It is open on weekdays 10am-1pm and 2-5pm. Weekends pm only, and here is the best news - admission for adults includes a free glass of Harveys sherry. They also have a fascinating display of wine related exhibits, including early glasses, corkscrews and silverware, a museum worthy of the company which first came into being in 1796.

The Bristol region has also been responsible for what can best be described as one of the worlds most influential commodities, it also happens to taste excellent! In 1729 Walter Churchman took out a patent for a recipe, he later sold this patent to Joseph Fry and confectionary history was made. Never mind Ambrosia, to my mind chocolate is the food of Gods! A combination of sugar refineries, first grade imported cocoa and some of the finest milk in the country resulted in chocolate production on a large and profitable scale. The area North of **Keynsham** is the sight of a fine factory which can provide for the sweetest tooth. I wonder if the TROUT TAVERN nearby has any chocolate puddings on the menu today?

Travelling about the county is much improved since the introduction of the turnpikes, a simple carriage ride could become a nightmare in the past. The historian Samuel Rudder recorded that the main road between Gloucester and Bristol, was so deep in mud on one occasion that a horse had nearly been smothered. Conditions were little better elsewhere. The local stone was too soft for the degree of traffic and the practice of excavating stone from the roadside converted them to causeways bordered by dangerous pits. Hardly surprising therefore that it can take a stage coach three days to travel from Bristol to London. The hauliers objected strongly to the turnpikes and tore down a number of toll houses, despite their violent opposition turnpikes have become common place, mercifully for the traveller and the post. More often than not the mail bags were entrusted to the hands of young, ill- mounted and dishonest boys. Bad enough that the mail run often took two days, but to allow these juveniles to ride with valuable mail, into the countryside was tantamount to criminal, and that was the inevitable outcome if they were apprehended by one of the local outlaw gangs.

The most extensive and notorious band of thieves, highway robbers and general ne'er-do-wells, that the county ever had the misfortune to spawn was the infamous Cock Road Gang of Bitton and Kingswood. They terrorised the annual Lansdown Fair and demanded protection money from the local farmers. Despite numerous hangings and transportations they flourished for more than 50 years, leading one exasperated circuit judge to remark darkly, 'I thought I had hanged the whole of that parish years ago'. Many an unfortunate mail boy fell foul of their evil. Finally, Palmer, the post office comptroller decided to revolutionise this parlous service by introducing the fast and efficient light mail coaches. Restricting the number of inside passengers to four and providing a guard armed with loaded blunderbus to deter raiders, the coaches now sped across the country unmolested. The driver would sound a horn to warn the toll keepers to open his gates. Palmer encountered much critiscism when he mooted his suggestions, but on the 3rd of August 1784 as the first mail coach hammered into London on schedule he was rightfully vindicated. The journey from Bristol had taken just 16 hours.

Further interesting plans were underway in an attempt to alleviate the transport problems and expedite the movement of goods and people around the city. An important step came toward the end of the century when the Government passed an act authorising the construction of tramways as a method of transport. At last the voice of the people had been heard, not only in Bristol, but throughout the country where large numbers were moving out to the suburbs. A reliable form of transport within the cities had become essential. August 1875 saw the first of Bristols tramways come into operation, initially these were horse trams, pity the poor horses, as most of the city consisted of hills it soon became apparent that a mechanical form of propulsion would prove more effective. Fortunately The Bristol Tramway Company had as its chief promoter, Mr George White, an inspired and inventive man. Under his control the tramway system was converted to electric traction and the electric trams became a feature of the city for many years.

To the trains and boats of the past we can now with the arrival of the twentieth century, add planes. Just as Bristol set the precedent with steamships and locomotives it has also been in the forefront of development in air transport: In 1908 Bleriot made his famous flight across the English Channel, a mere two years later Sir George White founded the Bristol Aeroplane Company and instigated the manufacture of aircraft. In

September of 1910 the British Army were proudly putting the Bristol Boxkite through its manoeuvres. This was the first heavier than air machine to be used in such exercises.

*World WAR I wrought many changes to the rural life around Bristol. The 1914-18 War memorials give testimony to the many men who prematurely lost their lives. The farming communities were sadly depleted and as a result many of the traditions disappeared with them. Some farmhouse cheeses and ciders were lost forever. RADFORD FARM and SHIRE HORSE STABLES at **Radford** nr Bath still has a fine team of working shire horses, a nostalgic reminder of the days when these noble beasts could be seen drawing their ploughs across the rolling green fields of the county. They are open every day between the 1st April until the end of October, tel (0761) 470106.*

The blitz of World War II, tore the heart out of Bristol and much that was lost proved to be irreplaceable. The destruction whether directly as a result of the bombing or in the clearing up process swept away over 90,000 homes, but with the indomitable spirit of the British a new city arose from the devestation. The advances made in aircraft design at Filton were crucial to the course of the war, and the 'Blenheims','Beaufighters' and 'Beauforts' all bore the name of Bristol. When the men on the production lines had a lull between working on aero engines they turned their hands to making the Bristol motor car, destined to become something of a collectors item. With the knowledge gained during the war years the designers at Filton began to prepare the way for a major expansion in the demand for commercial aviation. The Bristol Britannia appeared on the line and became one of the best known passenger aircraft. Not widely known is that during the fifties they were also working on the first titanium built Mach III plane, and had produced a twin rotor helicopter. This technology culminated on the 9th April 1969 with the inaugral flight of Concorde 002, the worlds only passenger airliner to break the sound barrier, another first for Bristol.

We have nearly come full circle, but there is one poignant note to record before we continue. We had left the S.S. Great Britain in 1850 running between England and Australia, for a short time after that she was converted to a sailing ship and then ignominiously passed her old age as a hulk off the Falkland Islands, where it was believed she would ultimately break up, she was not to give up without a fight. The grand old lady who had carried thousands out to the new lands to seek their fortunes, who had seen active service as a troopship during the Crimean War and the Indian Mutiny was to find salvation. The operation to bring her back to her home port touched the hearts of millions around the world, and on 19th July 1970 she rested once more in the dock from which she was first launched,127 years to the day, a fitting testimony to the skill of Bristol ship-builders throughout the centuries. The S.S. Great Britain has undergone extensive restoration and you may now visit her at the GREAT WESTERN DOCKS (0272 260680) Hours of opening daily 10am-6pm (summer) 10am-5pm(winter). By contacting The Purser it is possible to hire the exquisite dining saloon for the evening.

I will now interrupt your reverie. Our tour through the pages of history is complete and we can begin to explore the present and possibly glimpse the future.

One of the Chimpanzees of Clifton Zoo

*If the weather is kind, and doesn't the sun always shine on Bristol? You may like to visit the zoo. There are some who hold the belief that keeping animals in captivity is cruel and detrimental to their well being. I would urge them to visit CLIFTON ZOO before they generalise. Set among twelve acres of beautifully landscaped gardens and rare trees from around the world **Clifton** is more sanctuary than prison. We spoke earlier of the world expanding as travel opened up vast new colonies, now we all are made aware that the world has started to shrink, to close in upon its inhabitants at an alarming rate. Those that suffer first are the silent minority, the Sumatran Orang Utan lives mainly in rain forests, which are vanishing. The Iranian Leopard roams the mountains on the Iran\Afghanistan border, there are probably less than 250 left in the wild. The Cotton-Top Tamarin live in the forest areas of South America, there* *is barely any forest left. At Clifton these species are given a second chance, there is a worldwide breeding programme underway with co-operation from many other zoos. The enclosures are constantly monitored and updated to provide the most reassuring environment possible . Children will love the Zoo-Olympics and the hands-on activity centre where they will have the chance get really close to some of the animals, what child or adult for that matter could resist stroking Wendy the elephant. Finally there is no comedy programme on the television as entertaining as the antics of a colony of meerkats. Don't miss them.!*

If you still have the energy after your zoo visit CLIFTON is a lovely place to explore. It is full of contrast from the wide sweeping DOWNS which offer some 400 verdant acres of country to roam, to the gracious terraces and crescents of Regency houses. Royal York Crescent and Windsor Terrace are built dramatically on a cliff over the Gorge. Clifton still manages to retain a village like quality, yet is only a short drive from the city centre.

Theatre, music and the arts have a long pedigree in this area. The Bristol Old Vic has the longest history of any working theatre in Britain, quite an accolade. During its heyday it enjoyed a reputation for staging elaborate plays and musicals. If you will excuse the thespian overtones, whats in a name...? In the case of the Old Vic, survival virtually. The name still carries sufficient cachet to interest commercial investors and producers, and after the drought years of underfunding this is vital if the theatre is to remain viable. The range and breadth of productions is impressive. THE SIDDONS BAR is open for pre show meals and drinks. Call the Box Office (0272 250250)

In June of 1993 'CATS' came to Bristol. Not a feline invasion, but the breathtaking extravaganza of Sir Andrew Lloyd Webber's musical based on the old possums book of practical cats by T.S.Eliot. THE BRISTOL HIPPODROME at St Augustines Parade is the perfect venue for this wonderous show which has delighted audiences around the globe. To date it is the longest running musical in the history of the British Theatre. The CATS HOTLINE is open on (0272) 297799.

After this stunning and cosmopolitan show why not continue on to THE CHINA PALACE in Baldwin Street, its exotic interior will suitably compliment the performance.

Do you enjoy riddles? If so I will quote you this one from a brochure recently given to me. Question; Which Bristol building can boast a 400 year history during which it has been a home, a lecture theatre, a finishing school for young ladies, a mecca for scientists and the first girls reform school in the country - and perhaps the world? Which Bristol building can boast one of the finest rooms in the South West? Answer: The Red Lodge ... Such a remarkable and varied career would suggest a quite special piece of architecture and THE RED LODGE will not disapoint. The Lodge is one of Bristols few remaining 16th century buildings, once forming part of a great estate and the 'finest room', is an astonishing example of interior decoration. From the icing sugar plasterwork of the ceiling to the carved oak wall panels there is seemingly no end to the intricate embelishments. When you have become quite dizzy with the splendour it is well to remember the walled Tudor garden which has been lovingly created outside. In June and July the garden is open to visitors and where better to sit and unwind than among the wafting perfume of old roses and honeysuckle?

THE REDWOOD LODGE HOTEL AND COUNTRY CLUB is situated just three minutes from the Clifton Suspension Bridge, in woodland bordering on the Ashton Court Estate, the panelled room situated within the restaurant is used for private dining there is also a large conference centre and a 175 seat cinema . Major snooker tournaments attracting some of the best names in the sport are often held here.

It is always pleasant to sit near a river and often riverside Inns have fascinating histories. THE CHEQUERS INN at Hanham-on-the-River is no exception. It used to be the haunt of barge men, who quenched their thirst with rough ales and cider from pewter tankards . The Inn became involved in the Duke of Monmouths Protestant uprising against King James and Conan Doyles novel Mica Clark describes how the Dukes rebel army was drawn up alongside The Chequers while the Kings army was on the other side of the river. The atmosphere is certainly less tense these days!

A short walk along Park Row will take you from the Red Lodge to the BRISTOL CITY MUSEUM AND ART GALLERY where you will discover exhibits and collections representing the arts and natural sciences. These are excitingly diverse, from Chinese brocade-woven silk to metal sculpture from Zimbabwe, and if by now you are suffering a degree of cultural overload I can assure you they also mount exhibitions of a less esoteric nature. How does the Great Rubbish Show sound?. It was in fact aimed specifically at children and families and intended to give a new perspective on domestic rubbish! During my investigations of the City I have frequently discovered invitations to enjoy a cup of tea with the Bristol

Magpies, not I was relieved to discover, the thieving variety, but a conscientous band of folks who constitute one of the Museums vital support groups.

If your taste is for the avant garde a visit to THE WATERSHED MEDIA CENTRE should be high on your list of priorities. Looking at their current brochure I realise I have underestimated, a dozen visits could hardly do justice to this stimulating feast of art, music and film. Box Office (0272) 253845.

Bristol is blessed with dozens of important art galleries and the exhibitions range from Old Masters to contempory artists, ceramics, jewellery,sculpture, the list is infinite. So too is the variety of music which can be enjoyed throughout the City. Colston Hall offers performances which cannot fail to appeal to the most catholic of tastes. Where else could one expect to find The Bristol Bach Choir and Cambridge Baroque Camerata one week and Pat 'love letters in the sand,' Boone the next?

There comes a time when one needs to leave pavement pounding behind and the countryside around Bristol has been carefully preserved and nurtured, it is still possible to find places where wild flowers grow undisturbed and the best of these is the AVON GORGE NATURE RESERVE. This haven stretches along the West side of the Avon and it is one of the most important lowland limestone reserves in the country. The ancient broad leafed oak predominates, but you will also see Ash, Birch, small leaved lime and sycamore. In the North of the reserve Yew and Holly cleave together and if you are lucky or knowledgeable enough to seek them out the rare British Whitebeam grows here, the only place in the world where you will see them. If you visit during a misty autumn you will be rewarded with a fine show of funghi, beware! Dont touch for the highly poisonous fly agaric thrives here. Archeologists among you can see the Iron age hill fort of Stockleigh camp which lies within the boundary.

There are other attractions for nature lovers. It is possible to arrange a guided tour around the lovely long Ashton Cider orchards near Abbots Leigh and be reminded of the golden days apple orchards and farmhouse cider in stone jars. The English Nature Warden will accompany you on seasonal walks through Leigh Woods and you are reccommended to wear stout shoes and bring binoculars for an ornithological tour of Blaise.

All this wonderful fresh air will no doubt make you hungry for wholesome country style fare. In the triangle close by the University tower is the ROWAN TREE, on a sunny day you can sit in the garden and listen to the gentle play of a fountain. The organically grown vegetables, home made bread and free range eggs will ensure you leave replete with food and nostalgia! This is an excellent place to buy gifts or souveniers which will remind you of your visit to Bristol.

After lunch you are well positioned to visit the QUAKERS FRIAR which is part of the domestic buildings of the Dominican Friary founded in 1227. Part of the building houses the planning exhibition which also contains the Bristol Historic Tapestry which shows a pictorial description of the city's history.

If you have some serious shopping to do the BROADMEAD shopping centre is the place to visit. There was an element of resistence to this project initially. Many believed that some of the buildings planned for demolition should be spared, however there comes a time when new and innovative schemes have to be introduced to prevent a place stagnating. Broadmead is a success, it contains virtually every major department store and literally hundreds of smaller shops many of which are housed undercover in the GALLERIES. It is mainly pedestrianised which makes shopping so much safer and easier especially for families with young children and the less able-bodied.

The HOUSE OF FRASER store DINGLES is situated in the exclusive Queens road area of the city. It occupies an imposing site within view of the University and Cathedral. A temptingly lovely department store arranged on many floors with a restaurant and comfortable coffee shop, the food is of a consistently high standard and well presented. A good place to meet your friends for lunch. The fashion departments carry some of the best names in couture and there are wonderful gifts to be found in the well laid out china, glass and jewellery sections.

The frenetic times we inhabit of noise, fumes, schedules, financial crisis and seemingly perpetual motion, it can sometimes be quite difficult to find a quiet place to repair to and restore ones sanity. Often in an attempt to get away from it all, we find ourselves knee deep among others desperatly trying to do the same thing! At such times the only place to be is up, high up, drifting away from the turmoil in the basket of a hot air balloon, travelling gently with the air and of the air. Over the trees and chimneys and fields of grazing animals. Disturbing no-one and remaining undisturbed. Bristol Balloons offer champagne flights, weather permitting these flights leave from Ashton Court, a manificent park and mansion house. To win a friend for life why not give them a balloon ride as a unique birthday present? Contact (0272) 637858 for further details.

*Hotwells may no longer be the fashionable spa town to which the gentry flocked for revival, but it is certainly the perfect place if you want to visit the S.S. Great Britain and HOWARDS is just around the corner. An elegant Georgian building occupies a perfect waterside position and every window gives a view of the Clifton Suspension Bridge.Tel(0272 262921).There is another Howards at **Nailsea** which is only ten minutes drive from Bristol, this bistro is housed in a pretty white washed cottage and simply decorated to complement the exquisite French menu; goats cheese with basil and pine kernels is a favourite of mine.*

By night the streets of Bristol come alive there are cafes,bars and clubs catering for every taste. 'Happy hour,' seems to stretch from 5.30p.m onwards. The flavours are multi national, Mexican, Japanese, Thai, Chinese, Indian. The world comes to you. LOS IQUANAS advertises itself as the best Mexican restaurant, in Bristol, how many others are there I wonder? Why not try to find them all and enjoy make your own comparisons.

As you will have learnt it has taken many centuries to perfect the transport system which serves Bristol. Long gone are the days of horse and cart! It is now possible to travel here with ease from all parts of country, via the M5 which stretches from Devon to the North of Birmingham and becomes the M6 reaching to the Borders and beyond. The M4 which bisects the country from Wales to London. The Railway is fast, comfortable and still brings you to the heart of the City. To complete the picture Lulsgate Airfield is now Bristol International Airport ... Brunel would have been impressed!

We have come to the end of this potted history of one of England's richest and most diverse cities, but as with any good ending it also marks a new begining for you the visitor. I hope the story has inspired you to explore further, to make your own discoveries and in doing so carry on the tradition of adventure which is fundamental to the people of Bristol.

CHINA PALACE

Restaurant

18a Baldwin Street,
Bristol, Avon.

Tel: (0272) 262719
Fax: (0272) 256168

Open seven days a week, the China Palace has a superb range of 188 Chinese dishes, cooked to perfection by the Cantonese Chef; one of the top three in this country. It is right in the heart of the city just 100 yards from the centre. Close by is the 2,000 seat Bristol Hippodrome and the historic Theatre Royal, Britain's oldest theatre.

The restaurant is large and luxurious, yet intimate and relaxing with a spacious Mandarin Bar separated from it by a few stairs. Kam Wong, the owner, personally designed all the decor of the China Palace and, drawing on his previous experience as an aircraft engineer, he also designed the unique multi-burner 'Turbo Wok' which is the secret of how so many wonderful Chinese dishes can be cooked so expertly and quickly. The restaurant is air-conditioned, has facilities for dancing and is ideal for parties, receptions and banquets. It has won virtually every award for excellence and has a tradition of organising charity galas with cabaret, live bands and dancing.

Sea food and Chinese fondues are specialities. The most popular dishes of all are aromatic Crispy Peking Duck and sizzling Cantonese Fillet Steak. Dim Sum, the traditional Chinese delicacy is also available seven days a week, with a specially wide choice on Sundays. The wine list is comprehensive and the choice of de-luxe brandies finishes a meal superbly. Because The China Palace is open from 12 noon - 11.30pm every Sunday, lunch can be almost anytime.

USEFUL INFORMATION

OPEN: Mon-Sat: 12-2.30pm & 6-11.30pm
 Sun: 12-11.30pm
CHILDREN: Yes
CREDIT CARDS: Visa/Access/Amex
LICENSED: Spirits & wines & public
 entertainment
ACCOMMODATION: Not applicable

RESTAURANT: Gourmet Chinese
 traditional dishes
BAR FOOD: Not applicable
VEGETARIAN: Yes. About 8 dishes
DISABLED ACCESS: No but wide
 staircase
GARDEN: No. City centre location

RESTAURANT DU GOURMET

Restaurant

43 Whiteladies Road,
Bristol, Avon.

Tel: (0272) 736230
Fax: (0272) 237394

For twenty one years this attractive restaurant with an elegant frontage has been under the same professional and sympathetic management of Serge Francolini and his partner Lucien Parussina. In all these years they have had the talented and creative support of the same chef. This must be quite a record and no doubt accounts for the unchanging standards of The Restaurant du Gourmet which is not only renowned in Bristol but has a worldwide following. These two restaurateurs are accomplished chefs in their own right and trained in Switzerland. They are more than capable of taking over in the kitchen and frequently do, but what they enjoy most is being in the front of house, caring for their clientele and delighting in the pleasure the food brings to diners.

It is not only food that is good here; the wine list is extra special. There are some 120 wines on the list, each carefully selected. Frequently the restaurant hosts wine tastings. The menu is a pleasure to read and the choice of thirteen starters makes it difficult to decide. Each dish is tempting. An equal number of dishes for the main course makes the choice even more difficult. Perhaps one would start with a Salade de Concombre au fromage de Chevre, French style cucumber salad with goats cheese and walnuts and follow that with Filet Mignon de Porc Parisienne - slices of Pork tenderloin, white wine sauce, diced bacon, shallots, mushrooms. The delicious desserts are equally tempting. This is a memorable restaurant.

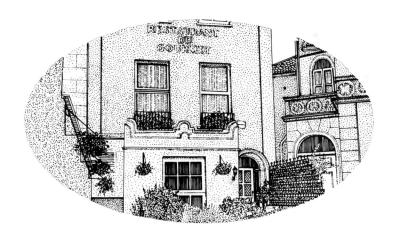

USEFUL INFORMATION

OPEN: Mon-Fri: 12-2pm & 7-11.30pm
    Sat: 7-12.30am
CHILDREN: Very welcome
CREDIT CARDS: All major cards
LICENSED: Restaurant
ACCOMMODATION: Not applicable

RESTAURANT: Wide choice, excellent,
    plus daily specials
BAR FOOD: Not applicable
VEGETARIAN: Always available
DISABLED ACCESS: Level & Toilets
GARDEN: No

THE ROWAN TREE

Cafe

The Triangle,
Bristol, Avon.

Tel: (0272) 277030

The Rowan Tree is a fascinating place. It houses a splendid shop which is not unlike an Aladdin's Cave, full of gifts that are both sensibly priced and attractive. The Rudolf Steiner Bookshop is also there with its wonderful selection of New Age and beautifully illustrated children's books. A recent addition is a selection of second hand books at reasonable prices. The Cafe is a meeting place for all manner of people who have learnt to enjoy the conversation, read the thoughtfully left newspapers and generally appreciate an unusual eaterie.

You will find The Rowan Tree on the tip of The Triangle at the top of Park Street, a hundred yards from the University Tower with the Victoria Rooms on one side and the West of England Academy on the other. Before the building was taken over in 1980 by Claude and Geraldine Hayn, the building had been derelict for ten years but patient and loving care has made it the most attractive of places with a garden terrace and a fountain which customers describe as an oasis of peace. It has an interesting history having once been a Nun's dining room and chapel, part of the Pro-Cathedral complex.

The food is organically grown. The vegetables and the bread are wonderful. Free range eggs are always used and you will find an interesting variety of salads, savouries, and cakes. There are speciality teas, coffees and herbal Teas. Vegetarian lunches are served every day.

USEFUL INFORMATION

OPEN: Mon-Sat: 9.30-5.30pm
CHILDREN: Welcome, High chairs
CREDIT CARDS: Access/Visa
LICENSED: Not licensed
ACCOMMODATION: Not applicable

RESTAURANT: Wholesome, delicious
BAR FOOD: Not applicable
VEGETARIAN: Entirely. Some Vegan
DISABLED ACCESS: Ramp
GARDEN: Sunny terrace with seating

McCREADIES WHOLEFOOD RESTAURANT

Restaurant

3 Christmas Steps,
Bristol, Avon.

Tel: (0272) 298387

It must be everyone's hearts desire to own a business in Christmas Steps, the oldest part of Bristol. The buildings here are all 14th century and the Fish Shop at the bottom of the steps is the oldest building in Bristol. Every building on the steps is different from the other and each has its own character. It is a wonderful place to be and at Number 3 is McCreadies Wholefood Restaurant, an experience in itself. Bearing in mind that Christmas Steps was the centre of the Bristol Slave Trade, it was not surprising that when Number 3 was gutted for refurbishment, they found slave hooks still in the basement which now seats 16 people. The counter here is the original from when it was a button shop. This Grade 2 Listed Building, which is as fascinating as any in the street, still has the well between floors from the time when flour was milled upstairs and lowered down on a hoist.

The food is Kosher vegetarian and vegan. It is a delicious experience for everyone, even the non-vegetarians whose jaded palates react with enthusiasm to the new and unexpected tastes and textures. You will find as many non-vegetarians here as anyone else. Something you will notice about this remarkable restaurant is that Julia, the owner is a warm friendly person herself and somehow she generates the same warmth in her customers who chat to each other quite happily even if this is the first time they have met. If you are a stranger to Bristol they will tell you all sorts of tit bits about its history. This genuinely nice woman and she and her restaurant are good to know.

USEFUL INFORMATION

OPEN: Tues & Wed: 8am-7pm,
 Thurs-Sat: 8am-10pm, Sun: 11-5pm
CHILDREN: Welcome
CREDIT CARDS: No
LICENSED: Restaurant
ACCOMMODATION: Not applicable

RESTAURANT: Kosher Vegetarian &
 Vegan. Super food
BAR FOOD: Not applicable
VEGETARIAN: Totally, plus vegan
DISABLED ACCESS: No
GARDEN: Small patio eating area

MULLIGAN'S FISH RESTAURANT

Restaurant

43 College Green,
Bristol, Avon.

Tel: (0272) 226460

Surrounded by restaurants and wine bars of all nationalities, Mulligan's Fish and Chip Restaurant, Oyster Bar & Charcoal Grill is definitely different. Your first introduction to it will be a vast pool in the window full of water plants. Inside it is a specious welcome bar where you can drink before going further into the restaurant. Whilst there is plenty of room Mulligans still remains an intimate place.

The specialities of the house are traditional English Fish and Chips, and speciality dishes such as Oysters, Lobsters and Crab. The menu, however, caters for all tastes and palates. Only the finest fish and seafood is used and if anything is not up to standard or unavailable in the market daily, it will not appear on the menu. You will notice that there is a blackboard which states what items are unavailable. It also tells you what daily specialities have been produced. The staff are all young and friendly and obviously enjoy the ambience of Mulligans.

For non-fish lovers, Mulligan's offers various dishes from their Charcoal Grill, for example Sirloin steaks either simply grilled or 'Marchand du Vin' (red wine and shallot sauce), spiced chicken, and the homely sausage and mash. The starters are tempting with a good selection of puddings and sweets, followed by a cheese board. Mulligans is fun, the food is excellent and the price is fair.

USEFUL INFORMATION

OPEN: Mon-Sun: 12-2.15pm (last orders)
Eve: 5.30-1.45pm, Sun: 5.30-10.30pm
CHILDREN: Welcome to eat
CREDIT CARDS: Visa/Access/Amex
LICENSED: Full Licence
ACCOMMODATION: Not applicable

RESTAURANT: Fish & seafood a
speciality
BAR FOOD: Yes, available
VEGETARIAN: Yes (not vegan)
DISABLED ACCESS: Level entrance
GARDEN: No

THE OLD CASTLE GREEN

Gloucester Lane,
Old Market, Bristol.

Public House

Tel: (0272) 550925

Situated in Old Market, which used to be a real street market in the last century, The Old Castle Green is a gem of an old traditional pub with wooden floors and its polished mahogany bar. These days, Old Market is a thriving business area just a stones throw from Broadmead, which is the main shopping area in Bristol. Park around here and avoid the hassle of central Bristol traffic.

The pub has no juke box, so avoiding that endless racket which spoils many pubs these days. At lunchtime, food service is very fast, straight off the hotplate, so that if your time is limited you can still get your lunch without that agonising wait! Real ales by Marstons are complemented by a full range of spirits and soft drinks, low alcohol drinks and an interesting selection of wines. Food is served all day from 12.15 until 10.30pm.

All the food is daily prepared at the pub from fresh ingredients. The hot dishes of the day, which always include at least two vegetarian dishes, are served with a choice of Basmati rice or Dauphinoise potatoes. Chillie con Carne, and Chicken Neapolitan in a creamy sauce made with wine, herbs and tomatoes, are regulars on the menu. Fresh Pasta, Onion Bhajias, Stuffed Naan and huge salad rolls are also available, together with Landlord, David Legg's famous real Indian curries.

USEFUL INFORMATION

OPEN: 11.30-11pm. Weekends: closed 3-7pm

CHILDREN: Allowed until 8pm

CREDIT CARDS: None taken

LICENSED: Marstons Real Ales, quality largers, wines, spirits

ACCOMMODATION: Not applicable

RESTAURANT: All one bar, same menu

BAR FOOD: All fresh & varied. Reasonably priced

VEGETARIAN: Yes, at least 2 plus snacks

DISABLED ACCESS: Level through garden

GARDEN: Yes, with swings

MURRAY'S
Restaurant

91 Hill Road,
Clevedon, Avon.

Tel: (0275) 874058

Hill Road is in the old part of Clevedon and is a secondary shopping area. It has an air of graciousness about it which is no doubt why Murray's was used in the television series 'The House of Eliott'. The restaurant has great charm and readily lent itself to the tea room scenes. The road has many individual shops and still retains much of its 18th century appeal. For over twenty years the name Murray's has been synonymous with good food; a fact of which the owners John and Gail Murray are understandably proud. Only the finest ingredients are used in their baking and they pride themselves in the knowledge that their food is wholesome, fresh and tasty. The variety of cakes and pies are baked here every morning and lunches, are made using locally grown vegetables, most of which are organic. Delicious and freshly cut sandwiches are served with a salad garnish, Pizzas are made on the premises and come with a wide range of toppings. You can choose from Eggs Florentine, Steak Medici, Cannelloni, Chicken Tagliatelle and many other tempting dishes.

The sunny restaurant undergoes a remarkable transformation from a lovely tea room in the daytime to an evening restaurant which is remarkable; it then becomes an intimate Bistro. It is the skill of the owners which makes it possible and at whichever time of day you go there you will find it pleasurable.

USEFUL INFORMATION

OPEN: Daytime: Mon-Sat: 10-5.30pm
    Eve: Tues-Sat: 7-10.30pm
CHILDREN: Welcome
CREDIT CARDS: None
LICENSED: Restaurant Licence
ACCOMMODATION: Not applicable

RESTAURANT: Tearooms during day,
    Bistro at night
BAR FOOD: Not applicable
VEGETARIAN: Always avaiable
DISABLED ACCESS: Limited
GARDEN: No

THE DUNDRY INN

Church Road, Dundry,
Bristol, Avon.

Public House

Tel: (0272) 641722

No one coming to Bristol should be allowed to leave without visiting Dundry, a well known beauty spot. It looks right out over Bristol and is dominated by the tower of the church which was built with money donated by the Merchant Venturers of Bristol and provided a Navigational point for ships in the Bristol Channel and those entering the safety of the City Docks. Legend has it that The Dundry Inn is as old as the tower which seems highly probable although there is no firm evidence to support this theory.

What is fact is that this pub is everything one dreams of. Its age gives it a wonderful feeling of stability, the walls seem to have soaked in the history of the centuries and the local people who use it are not so different from their ancestors - maybe in dress and hairstyles, but the conversation is still topical, fun to listen to and for the stranger, arriving, an instant welcome. Real Ale is of prime importance and beautifully kept as indeed is all the beer. The food is good, wholesome, pub fare with a range of dishes that allows for everyone's palate. Everyday in addition to the general menu there are several very tasty Daily Specials, cooked freshly and at sensible prices. Children are very welcome if they are accompanied by well behaved parents . There is a family room but in the summer months the large garden is particularly popular with parents and their children.

USEFUL INFORMATION

OPEN: 11-3pm & 6-11pm daily. Normal Sunday hours
CHILDREN: Welcome
CREDIT CARDS: All major cards
LICENSED: Full On Licence
ACCOMMODATION: Not applicable

RESTAURANT: Not applicable
BAR FOOD: Wide range of good wholesome food
VEGETARIAN: Always available
DISABLED ACCESS: Level access, no toilets
GARDEN: Large with seating

THE TROUT TAVERN

Public House

46 Temple Street,
Keynsham, Bristol, Avon.

Tel: (0272) 862754

Halfway between Bristol and Bath, Keynsham has long been a popular place in which to live. It has a great community spirit and the focal point is the local pub, The Trout Tavern just off the high street.

The present building has been offering a welcome and hospitality since the 1760's but prior to that it was also licensed premises used for what was known as 'The Carriage Trade'. That building was knocked down but it is of little importance because the present Trout Tavern carries on the tradition of good inn-keeping without any need of help from the past.

If you enjoy the old traditional pub games like dominoes and darts then this is the place for you. On Friday evenings there is live music and there are both Quiz nights and Karoke nights. It is always a lively place and no doubt the well kept Real Ales and traditional Ciders have a lot to do with keeping a happy clientele.

Food is available both in the lounge and the bar. There is nothing pretentious about the dishes on offer; it is good, traditional pub grub. In the summer the small garden with a patio area is quite regularly used for Barbecues.

USEFUL INFORMATION

OPEN: Mon-Fri: 10-11pm, Sat: 10-4pm
7-11pm. Sun: Normal hours
CHILDREN: Lounge only
CREDIT CARDS: None
LICENSED: Full On Licence
ACCOMMODATION: Not applicable

RESTAURANT: Not applicable
BAR FOOD: Traditional pub grub
VEGETARIAN: On request
DISABLED ACCESS: Step entrance
GARDEN: Small garden. Patio, BBQ

ROSE OF DENMARK

Public House

6 Dowry Place,
Hotwells, Bristol.

Tel: (0272) 290472

The Rose of Denmark is an elegant Georgian building named after an equally elegant lady, Princess Alexandra of Denmark who became the wife of Edward VII. She was reputedly a friend of Lord Dowry. You will find the pub close to the Brunel Lock on the Cumberland Basin and within walking distance of Clifton Suspension Bridge, built by that genius, Isambard Kingdom Brunel. The pub is also a ferry ride across the Floating Harbour to the City Centre, close to Ashton Court and Bristol Football Ground.

With such a convenient and enviable position The Rose of Denmark is the watering hole of many devoted regulars. However it is not just the position; it is the bonhomie, the atmosphere, the excellence of its Ales - including Burton, Smiles and Tetleys - and the sensibly priced, well cooked food which continues to bring people back.

In addition there are three letting rooms which people working in the area find ideal. The menu every day consists of many time honoured favourites including some very good home-made pies. Specials of the day are on offer for less than two pounds and a 16oz steak is amazingly cheap. On Sundays a two course lunch is served. For anyone staying you will find the full English breakfast will set you up for the day.

USEFUL INFORMATION

OPEN: Mon-Sat: 11-11pm, Sun: 12-3pm & 7-10.30pm
CHILDREN: Allowed for meals
CREDIT CARDS: None taken
LICENSED: Full On
ACCOMMODATION: 1 dbl, 1twin, 1 sgl

RESTAURANT: Not applicable
BAR FOOD: Wide range. Very reasonable
VEGETARIAN: Always three dishes
DISABLED ACCESS: Yes
GARDEN: No

THE BOWL INN

Inn & Restaurant

Church Road, Almondsbury,
Bristol, Avon.

Tel: (0454) 612757/613717
Fax: (0454) 619910

Almondsbury is a delightful place, as pretty as its name and deserves to have a good hostelry. The Bowl Inn answers this need admirably. Built by Monks centuries ago it has aged well and has both a great atmosphere and a warmth that has built up over the years.

The eight en-suite bedrooms are recommended by the English Tourist Board ; three crowns - commended. Comfortably furnished they provide an excellent place in which to stay either for business or pleasure. For most people though this is the place to eat and drink in attractive and historic surroundings. People of all age groups seem to make up the clientele. The inn is always busy with people in the bars enjoying the well kept Real Ales and in the Restaurant the wide ranging menu tempts even the most pernickety of diners.

Fourteen starters make the choice difficult but exciting. Stilton and garlic mushrooms - button mushrooms sauted in Stilton and garlic butter and succulent slices of smoked chicken breasts served with a quince and orange jelly, are two very popular choices. Fish, fresh from the market, prime Scotch beer, English lamb and veal, and a range of Bowl Specialities together with vegetarian main courses, make up the menu in the restaurant. An equally good selection of dishes is on offer in the bar. With the comprehensive and fine selection of wines, you will leave The Bowl totally contented.

USEFUL INFORMATION

OPEN: 11-3pm & 5-11pm,
  Saturday: 11-3pm & 6-11pm,
  Sundays: 12-3pm & 7-10.30pm
CHILDREN: Welcome
CREDIT CARDS: All major cards
LICENSED: Full On Licence
ACCOMMODATION: 6 twn, 2 dbl
  en-suite

RESTAURANT: A la carte. Home-
  cooked. International cuisine
BAR FOOD: Full Bar menu
VEGETARIAN: 7 dishes
DISABLED ACCESS: Level & loos
GARDEN: Patio. Barbecues

THE POACHER

106 High Street,
Portishead, Bristol, Avon.

Public House

Tel: (0275) 844002

Portishead has grown from a village into a town but still has just one main street, the High Street, with The Poacher in the centre. It is an attractive, grey stone building with a large car park and frontage, set in the midst of shops and offices.

The first licence was granted in 1683 when it was known as the Blew Anchor. During the 1720's, a widow lady, Mary Whitwood, ran the pub and had stocks and a whipping post outside with which to dispense justice! The pub has changed its name several times: in 1850 it became the Gordon Arms, to appease the local squire; a little later it was renamed The Anchor, and became The Poacher 14 years ago, some nine years before the present landlord, Mr Hazelton, and his wife took over.

The Hazeltons are a convivial couple whose aim has always been to make people welcome. They have achieved a wonderful atmosphere which not only attracts customers but their caring attitude has meant also, that the staff have stayed with them over the years.

The food is excellent. There are about 30 home-made dishes from which to choose, including many favourites such as: Somerset chicken in cider, braised steak and onions, beef stew and dumplings, pork hot pot and lamb stew. If you decide to stay a night or two in one of the three letting rooms you will be able to enjoy a great English breakfast and return at the end of the day to an equally good evening meal.

USEFUL INFORMATION

OPEN: 11-2.30pm & 6-11pm
CHILDREN: Not allowed
CREDIT CARDS: Cheques with Bank card
LICENSED: Full Licence
ACCOMMODATION: 2 twin, 1 sgl

RESTAURANT: Evening meals
BAR FOOD: 30+ home-made dishes
VEGETARIAN: Cold dishes only
DISABLED ACCESS: level entrance
GARDEN: None

THE BELL

Public House

7 Prewitt Street, Redcliff,
Bristol, Avon.

Tel: (0272) 291167

It was not until we discovered The Bell, right opposite The Bristol International Hilton, in the heart of Temple Mead that we found out this was an area, the real name of which is Cathay, because of the Bristol Blue Glass Glazing that has been carried out here for many years. The Bell has been a pub since 1729 at which time it had a huge courtyard. This has now been covered in and become an attractive part of the hostelry. Deep underground are the cellars which probably housed smuggled brandy and wines at one time; Bristol had a strong connection with those who wished to outwit the Excise Men! Those days are long gone but the pub does keep an excellent stock of wines and brandy as well as a range of Real Ales which will please even the most discerning of beer drinkers.

Christopher and Linda Walter are your hosts. A couple who thoroughly enjoy their business and their enthusiasm spills over to their staff. If you are looking for food you will find it good honest pub grub with generous portions and sensible prices. Here there are popular Daily Specials, a range of freshly made and well filled sandwiches, jacket potatoes with a variety of fillings and a substantial Ploughmans. This centrally situated pub is the haunt of many business people and is not the place for children. There is no garden but what it lacks in this is more than recompensed by the general warmth and happy atmosphere of the establishment.

USEFUL INFORMATION

OPEN: Mon-Sat: 11am-11pm. Normal Sunday hours
CHILDREN: No
CREDIT CARDS: Not applicable
LICENSED: Full On Licence
ACCOMMODATION: Not applicable

RESTAURANT: Not applicable
BAR FOOD: Traditional Pub fare
VEGETARIAN: On request
DISABLED ACCESS: Level Access, No toilets
GARDEN: No

THE CAMBRIDGE ARMS

Cold Harbour Road,
Redland, Bristol, Avon.

Public House

Tel: (0272) 735754

Just 200 yards from the famous Whiteladies Road and close to the hotels, shopping area and five minutes from the centre of Bristol, The Cambridge Arms is one of Bristol's most popular pubs. It is surrounded by famous listed buildings but has a unique quality of its own. The proprietor also owns the excellent hostelry, The Prince of Wales in Westbury-on-Trym in which he has a Royal theme, this ideal he has copied at The Cambridge with maps and memorabilia pertinent to the University. He has a knack of creating atmospheric and happy establishments and this is certainly true of The Cambridge which is run by Val and Rod Duckett. The sporting instinct is very apparent here with football, cricket and local charity events.

The pub attracts a wide range of people both for its ambience and for its excellent Real Ales and wines. On Monday nights there is always live music from local bands. Every day there is a good range of traditional pub fare with a touch of international cuisine added to it. The emphasis on home-cooking comes over every day, but is probably strongest on Sundays when it would be very hard to fault the traditional Sunday roast complete with Yorkshire Pudding, crisp roast potatoes and a choice of fresh vegetables.

Children will be happy here but in the garden only, where there are slides, a wendy house, climbing frame, a bouncy castle and an undercover Barbecue area.

USEFUL INFORMATION

OPEN: Mon-Sat: 11-11pm. Normal Sunday hours

CHILDREN: Garden only. Climbing frame, bouncy castle

CREDIT CARDS: None taken

LICENSED: Full On Licence

ACCOMMODATION: Not applicable

RESTAURANT: Traditional Pub fare

BAR FOOD: Home-cooked. Sunday Lunch

VEGETARIAN: Many choices

DISABLED ACCESS: Level entrance

GARDEN: Large and pretty. BBQ area

WAGGON AND HORSES

Public House

83 Stapleton Road,
Upper Easton, Bristol, Avon.

Tel: (0272) 553036

This lively and well loved pub has seen some famous people in its time. An episode of 'Only Fools and Horses' with David Jason was filmed here and the revered cricketer, Doctor W.G. Grace lived here.

The Waggon and Horses is one minute from the M32 which connects to the M4/M5 and is ten minutes from Broadmead Shopping Centre. It has a happy band of regulars, but is equally welcoming to those who enter its doors for the first time. There is always something happening with the occasional band practice taking part in the room which is also used for meetings. Bands play every Friday night and you will also find great fun with the comedians, singers and duos who take part. There is a skittle alley and a pool room.

The floodlit Beer Garden with a built in Barbecue is the venue for many a good evening during summer months. The Wadsworth 6X, Tetley Bitter and Burton is well kept for anyone who is hungry. The home-cooked, traditional pub grub is excellent value and the portions are more than generous. A very inexpensive Sunday lunch is available complete with all the trimmings. Bob and Sue Anderson are mine hosts and they make everyone, including children very welcome. Pets are only allowed in the bar.

USEFUL INFORMATION

OPEN: Mon-Thurs: 11-3pm & 6-11pm
   Fri-Sat: All day, Sun: Normal hours
CHILDREN: Welcome
CREDIT CARDS: None taken
LICENSED: Full On Licence
ACCOMMODATION: Not applicable

RESTAURANT: Not applicable
BAR FOOD: Home-cooked pub grub
VEGETARIAN: On request
DISABLED ACCESS: Level entrance
GARDEN: Floodlit. Barbecues

THE FLEUR DE LYS

238 Henleaze Road,
Westbury-on-Trym, Bristol, Avon.

Restaurant

Tel: (0272) 624458

It is only an experienced chef-proprietor, ably supported by a dedicated wife who could produce this homely, welcoming and prettily decorated restaurant, Fleur de Lys. Gilbert and Christine Schneider have been at the Fleur de Lys for over seven years now and their regular clientele have come to expect good food both at lunchtime and in the evenings served to them at the attractively laid tables. Gilbert had achieved considerable success in both the French and English restaurant trades, including some time at The Chester Grosvenor before he came to Westbury-on-Trym.

Considerable thought has gone into the planning of the menus which divide neatly into French dishes in the evenings and English at lunchtime. The dishes change constantly but one of the favourites is French duck breast with oyster mushrooms served in a cream sauce. Another is a succulent, slightly pink, fillet of lamb in puff pastry. Seafood platters are always available and so too are some delectable home-made desserts. There are few people who can resist Gilbert's Pavlova with a fresh blackcurrant sauce.

You will not find a vast wine list here but the chosen wines are a good cross section and acceptable to the palate and the pocket. The Fleur de Lys has a very happy atmosphere and is to be recommended.

USEFUL INFORMATION

OPEN: Lunch: Sat & Sun. Eve: Wed-Sat
CHILDREN: Welcome
CREDIT CARDS: Barclays/Access/Master
LICENSED: Restaurant Licence
ACCOMMODATION: Not applicable

RESTAURANT: French and English
BAR FOOD: Not applicable
VEGETARIAN: On request
DISABLED ACCESS: Limited. No WC
GARDEN: None

THE FORESTERS

Public House & Restaurant

77 Westbury Hill,
Westbury on Trym, Bristol Avon.

Tel: (0272) 622899

Westbury Hill is the main road through Westbury on Trym and in the days of the coach and horse it must have been a welcome relief for the driver, his horses and his passengers when they reached the doors of The Foresters. Sadly the old pub is no more and a new one arose in the 1940's but what it lost in antiquity has more than been accounted for by the tremendous atmosphere and welcome that is forthcoming from the present landlords, Adrian Beddows and Johnathon Anstee. These two men have created a super hostelry in which, whilst the Real Ales and Beers are kept excellently, the emphasis is on good, exciting food. With their keen appreciation of food they set about acquiring a first class chef who had much the same ideas as themselves. He reigns supreme and is justifying their faith in him when they see the contented faces of their clientele after they have eaten. At lunchtime the dishes on the menu are added to by a range of Specials, all prepared beautifully but with an awareness that many of the people lunching work and do not have too much time.

In the evenings everything changes. The choice of starters is never less than thirteen, the main courses, which include fish, poultry and excellent steaks as well as Vegetarian dishes, are nothing short of gourmet standard, and yet the prices are very fair. On Saturdays there is a special Gourmet Menu with three courses at a fixed price. The choice is varied and delicious. The days of the coaches have gone but those travellers would be envious of The Foresters today.

USEFUL INFORMATION

OPEN: 10.30-3pm & 5-11pm. Normal Sunday hours
CHILDREN: Well behaved
CREDIT CARDS: None taken
LICENSED: Full On Licence
ACCOMMODATION: Not applicable

RESTAURANT: Excellent menu. Gourmet meal every Saturday
BAR FOOD: Wide range, sensible prices
VEGETARIAN: Always available
DISABLED ACCESS: Limited
GARDEN: Courtyard with seating

PRINCE OF WALES
Public House

84 Stoke Lane,
Westbury-on-Trym, Bristol, Avon.

Tel: (0272) 623715

Whilst Westbury these days is very much a part of Bristol it has still managed to retain the feel of a village, and has a good hostelry, The Prince of Wales, in Stoke Lane. What makes this pub particularly attractive to its regular clientele is that is only ten minutes from the City Centre and five minutes from the M5. It is also blessed with good parking space.

In keeping with its name the pub has a Royal Theme. There is memorabilia everywhere of the present and past Princes of Wales. Richard Ellis, the landlord, has spent twelve years collecting all the interesting bits and pieces and obviously has a fondness for Edward VII when he was Prince of Wales. The pub is full of character and very welcoming. You are as likely to be greeted, robustly, by Ginny, the dog - short for Guinness, as you are by Richard and his staff. The Prince of Wales has a strong Rugby team following and is frequently lively and sometimes partisan! On Saturdays the television is turned on solely for sport. On sunny evenings, the clink of 'Boule' can be heard in the garden.

This is a Real Ale pub and also has a very extensive wine list. Hopefully a new addition to The Prince of Wales will be an upstairs wine bar and a supper room which seats 30. This is also available as a meeting room, complete with fax machine, coffee, etc.

A fair description of the food available would be traditional pub grub with an international flavour. Whatever one calls it, it is good, home-made and imaginative.

USEFUL INFORMATION

OPEN: Mon-Fri: 11-3pm & 5.30-11pm
Sat: 11-11pm
CHILDREN: Welcome. Lots of games
CREDIT CARDS: Not at present
LICENSED: Full On Licence
ACCOMMODATION: Not applicable

RESTAURANT: Traditional Pub Grub
with an international flavour
BAR FOOD: Yes. Not in the evening
VEGETARIAN: Lots of choices
DISABLED ACCESS: Level entrance
GARDEN: Large. BBQ, games, boule
court, bouncy castle, slide,

The Roman Baths and Abbey in Bath

BATH AND AVON

INCLUDES

"Never eat anything at one sitting that you can't lift.
Always use one of the new - and far more reliable -
elastic measuring tapes to check on your waistline."

Miss Piggy

BATH AND AVON

The chapter heading puts Bath first followed by Avon, and excludes Bristol, but I am perverse and intend to keep Bath, this jewel in the crown of Britain, until last. It is one of the loveliest places in the world, inspite of the planning monstrosities that occurred after World War II. Avon has struggled for years to acquire its own identity but what has always been there, whatever the name of the county, are some charming small towns and villages. This journey of mine will take me from the north of the county where it adjoins Gloucestershire and then south and west until we reach the coast at Weston-super-Mare.

__Thornbury__ to the immediate north of Bristol is one such town. Whenever I see it signposted as I drive down the M5 I always think I have reached Bristol, but near as it is, Thornbury has not been encroached by its ever lengthening tentacles.

Thornbury is a thriving country town and yet has managed to achieve a certain isolation. Yes, it does have traffic problems, but they are home grown ones. The A38 passes to the east of the town, and long before its existence, the old turnpike road avoided it as far back as 1769. It has become a splendid backwater, keeping its old streets and buildings. The main street layout, which forms the letter Y, by the junction of Castle Street, High Street and the Plane, has not changed since medieval times. In the High Street you will see two fine 18th-century inns, THE SWAN and THE WHITE LION, both excellent places to visit, and at number 24, THE COFFEE LOUNGE AT HERITAGE SHOPS, a place that is regarded by the local civic society as being of special architectural interest. The shop, selling fine china, crystal and gifts has retained and incorporated the original black oak beams and low ceilings into its fittings. Built partly from local stone, as an extension to the rear some 15 years ago, the coffee lounge allows superb views from two wide sets of sliding doors of the garden and beyond across the valley to the river and to Wales. There is a well-preserved old Market House and a small Greek Temple built in 1839 which was the old Registry Office.

In 1511 Edward Stafford, 3rd Duke of Buckingham, started to build his castle at Thornbury. Ten years later he was beheaded for treason and the castle appropriated by Henry VIII, who stayed here in 1535 with Anne Boleyn. Mary Tudor lived here for some years and when she became Queen she returned the castle to the descendants of the late Duke. Today, with its own vineyard and the oldest Tudor garden in England, THORNBURY CASTLE is the only Tudor Castle to be run as an hotel. As you would suspect it is superb, and it is rated as one of the best 300 hotels in the world. Quite a reputation to uphold. The resident proprietor, the Baron of Portlethen has a fine appreciation of old buildings and cultural heritage. Since he bought it in 1986 it has thrived and been lovingly cared for. You will still find reminders of Buckingham everywhere. A stone carved doorway bears his emblem in relief, the Brecknock Mantle, the Stafford Knot, among other devices. The Knot even appears on the mounting block in the courtyard. Fireplaces too, display the emblems. A wonderful place to stay and it would be insulting to suppose that the food, the wines and the service would be anything other than superb. It is unashamedly expensive and deserves to be.

Thornbury High Street

*We cannot all afford such an expensive hotel but lunch perhaps might be an option after which it would be an ideal opportunity to set forth and take a look at Aust and Elberton. From Roman times **Aust** was the main ferry route to Chepstow and so to Wales. For the geologist the cliffs, with their various coloured strata and examples of faulting, are wonderful hunting grounds, particularly the Rhaetic bone bed, famous for fossils of prehistoric reptiles. I read somewhere that 'Aust' was no more than a hamlet with a scenic motorway service centre on the north side of the M4". Not quite fair but I have to admit it does not have much to offer other than its historical interest. Unless, of course, you are enthusiastic about collecting fossils.*

Elberton *is just east of Aust, with a church dedicated to St John. Much restoration took place in 1858 and again in 1900 but nothing can mar the beauty of the 14th-century tower. I like the Jacobean manorial box pew, with carved panelling and four holes for inserting holly at Christmas time. The manor is right next door, in fact a door from the churchyard leads into the garden of the manor. It is a graceful house built in the 16th-17th century, with three storeys and a cupola on the roof, probably erected to be used for keeping a watchful eye on the labourers working in the fields, for this manor was once a farmhouse.*

Both **Littleton upon Severn** *and* **Oldbury upon Severn** *are a mile or so from the river. In the past they would have been named more accurately for they were villages of the marshland subject to severe flooding.*

It is very flat around Oldbury but every now and again there are knolls and it is on such knolls that the churches were built to protect them from flooding. This is true of Oldbury church. It is worth a climb up to see it rather more for the view than the church. You will see the Severn Bridge downstream and the great concrete towers of Oldbury Nuclear Power Station in the opposite direction. More to my liking is the view of Chepstow, the Forest of Dean and the foothills of the Welsh Mountains. The church was destroyed by fire in 1897 and rebuilt, but a legend lingers about the first church built there. It was the intention to build it in the village but every night it was destroyed. The villagers consulted an aged hermit, who told them to yoke together two maiden heifers and to build the church where they stopped. The heifers obviously preferred the grazing on the knoll so they stopped there! It is a pretty village with old world cottages and flowering gardens clustering around THE SHIP and THE ANCHOR, two fine hostelries named for their connection with the Severn.

Littleton has a little church with a saddleback roof, dedicated to St Mary de Malmesbury. It was virtually demolished in the 19th century because of its state of repair, but several items from the old church remain including the fine Norman font with its chevron design and the two piscinas inserted in the wall by the altar table. Around the foot of the font are tiles from Thornbury Castle.

It is not far down the A38 from Thornbury to **Tockington***, a charming village where, surrounding the green, are old houses and the 300 year old pub, THE SWAN, whose beer is kept cool by a natural spring in the cellar. Another excellent establishment here is THE KITCHEN*

GARDEN, a restaurant with a gift shop and a farm shop, all housed in the converted stables and coach house of Old Down House. The restaurant gets its name from the large walled garden just outside where the fruit and vegetables are grown. It is quite impressive and very reasonable.

The motorways are a blessing in many ways for they allow you to travel more easily from one place to another and do not prevent you from slipping off at various junctions to explore. **Winterbourne** *is one such place, although it has really become part of Bristol today. Its oldest part has managed to stay untouched. In the quiet area around the church are a few cottages. and the adjoining Winterbourne Court Farm. I like to think of Winterbourne when hat-making was a cottage industry and between 1770 and 1870 the whole place flourished with the trade brought to them because fashion dictated the wearing of beaver hats. The church too has a romantic story surrounding a knight whose effigy lies by the north wall. The knight is thought to be Hugo de Sturden who eloped with a fair lady but was a bit of a rogue. He made a pact with the devil in return for certain favours. He agreed that when he died he would not be carried into the church,, or buried in the churchyard, feet or head forward. He managed to cheat even on that and gave instructions for his coffin to be carried in sideways and be buried in the wall. On one wall is a brass which I found fascinating. It is about 1370 and one of the Bradestone ladies whose family were lords of the manor. Her dress has pocket holes which show part of the girdle beneath. It is thought to be the oldest brass in the county. I popped into a nice pub, THE WHEATSHEAF while I was here. Good food and well kept ale make it a good watering hole.*

Three miles from Yate, there is an extraordinary business, at **Rangeworthy** *- RANGEWORTHY NURSERIES AND BIG BEN RESTAURANT & MOTEL. Nothing particularly strange on the face of it but it has a story to tell. Here you have not only the restaurant and motel, both of them good, and Rangeworthy Nursery which is first class at its job, you also have an animal park and children's playground, the proceeds from which all go to THE ELEANOR CHILDREN'S CHARITABLE TRUST founded by Mrs Eleanor Bartlett, mother of the Ben Bartlett, whose business it is. This is a remarkable lady, who with the help of friends and anyone else she can press-gang in to help, raises money for the children of Romania. She works tirelessly and many a Romanian child has food and clothing, medicine and that other missing ingredient, somebody who cares, as a result of this brave lady's work. Entrance fee for adults is £1 and for children 75p plus whatever clothing, goods, offers of help and prayers you care to donate. It is a wonderful cause and worthy of your support.*

*On the fringe of the Cotswolds there are a number of delightful places such as Marshfield, Dyrham and Tormarton all built of Cotswold stone with its lovely mellowness. Each has its charm and I particularly like **Tormarton** with its long main street and nice pub, THE PORTCULLIS. There is little development round here because all three villages are within a conservation area. From any one of them you can set forth to explore places as DODINGTON PARK which is a children's paradise - and not bad for their elders either. There is a wonderful adventure playground, a carriage museum and many exhibitions which are either held in the grounds or in Dodington House with its great porticoed front.*

DYRHAM PARK belongs to the National Trust. The west front has glorious views over the countryside towards Bristol. It is a delightful building crowned with a balustrade and has a courtyard terrace flanked by one-storey wings, one of which leads to the medieval church. You will find the interior much influenced by the Dutch fashions. It is lovely and I do not know which is more beautiful, the magnificent 18th-century park with groves and clumps of beeches, chestnuts and cedars, or the house. The little village clusters round the church and the walled grounds of the manor house.

*The quiet village of **Hinton** is close to Dyrham and it is somewhere of which I have fond memories. I stayed here some four years ago at THE HINTON GRANGE HOTEL in a degree of comfort and well-being that is difficult to emulate. This immaculate hotel was once a stone farmhouse built somewhere about 1416 with additions made to it in the 18th century. My arrival almost coincided with the opening of the hotel after its stunning conversion by the owners, John and May Lindsay-Walker. They opted for an exquisite Victorian decor - even extending this theme to the bathrooms. Mullioned windows, four-posters, roaring fires and wonderful views across the Cotswolds aligned with memorable food, wines and service, is it any wonder that I have never forgotten the experience?*

One can wine and dine in the wooden beamed CROFTERS bar which dates back to the 15th century. May is an International chef and totally unafraid to display her culinary brilliance with dishes from all over the world. Possibly more intimately, the Old Inglenook restaurant may be your preference. For fun you can take off in a small boat and dine al fresco on One Tree Island. If this is insufficient choice then the Tropical Conservatory enables you to dine poolside with a choice from the menu or a 'Do it Yourself' barbecue.

Incorporated in the 'things to do' whilst staying here is an opportunity to try out the fully equipped gym, play tennis, croquet, golf on the nine hole course, fish or go ballooning. The latter is one of the most astonishing experiences I have ever had. Seeing Somerset and Avon from above in total peace is unforgettable and so too is staying at Hinton Grange.

Doddington Park, Close to Chipping Sodbury

One of the great equestrian occasions of the year is the horse trials at **Badminton**. People come from all round the world to spectate and to take part. It is also one of the rare times in the year when the great house is open to the public and the opportunity to see it should not be missed. It has always been a jealously guarded house by the Dukes of Beaufort and is hardly visible from the village.

Thomas Somerset, Viscount Somerset of Cashel, bought the house in 1608 and through his daughter it passed to Henry Somerset, Lord Herbert. In consideration of his noble descent from Edward III through John de Beaufort, eldest son of John of Gaunt and Catherine Swynford, Henry was created Duke of Beaufort. The family has sometimes been in Royal favour and at others distinctly unpopular. For example Henry the 5th Earl, supported the Crown in the Civil War, gallantly defended Raglan Castle, and was created Marquess of Worcester. His son Edward was sentenced to death by the House of Commons for his royalism, but was later imprisoned in the Tower and pensioned by Cromwell who held some of his confiscated estates. Charles I once wrote to the Duke of Ormonde that Edward's honesty or affection to Royal service would not deceive him,

257

but that he would not answer for Edward's judgement. As if to prove the point Edward once produced forged papers creating him Duke of Somerset and Beaufort.

The oldest part of BADMINTON HOUSE is the work of the 1st Duke of Beaufort and his father. It began with the central block and was enlarged somewhere in the mid 17th century by William Kent who also designed Worcester Lodge, a gateway on the northern boundary of the park. It is here that the Beaufort Hunt meet on Boxing Day morning. A sight worth seeing, you will always find a large number of people there to enjoy the spectacle and watch the riders and hounds depart. Capability Brown had a hand in alterations to the Lodge and inside the big house there is work by Grinling Gibbons and Wyatville.

The church of St Michael is attached to the house and came into being in 1785 in a simple rectangular with a tower, replacing the earlier medieval church. As one might expect the church is dominated by Beaufort memorials. I found the estate village delightful with its houses either side of a wide street. It includes a pedimented terrace dating from 1714 for retired servants, interesting houses of the late 18th and 19th century and small cottages whose diamond paned windows twinkle away in the sunshine.

The horse trials are always held in April and frequently attended by members of the Royal Family. Indeed the Princess Royal was a winner here one year.

Chipping Sodbury *was a 12th century property speculation! It lies at the edge of Old Sodbury parish and was primarily a market centre. The property developers laid out the plots in a regular pattern on each side of the road and so it has remained. It has some wonderful street names - Hatters Lane, Horse Street, Rouncival Street, Hounds Lane and Shoutinge Lane. It really is an attractive place in which to wander and while the population has grown, little has been built to its detriment.*

The M4 with its unceasing traffic crosses the county a little to the south of Chipping Sodbury and just below that is Marshfield, surrounded by cornfields and at one time a place that supplied malt to Bristol and Bath. Those days have long gone but not so the attractive malthouses. The town thrived on the wool trade and many of the fine 17th and 18th century houses reflect the wealth of the citizens in that era.

Its ancient traditions are carried on by the Marshfield Mummers, whose play is performed on Boxing Day each year. The play never varies in its presentation of the traditional conflict between Good and Evil.

*Only six miles from Bath but set amidst lawns and gardens with uninterrupted views through the Cam Valley, is THE OLD MALT HOUSE at **Radford**, Timsbury. The hamlet is quite beautiful and this delightful, family run hotel will give even the fussiest visitor nothing but pleasure. Nearby is RADFORD FARM, run by the Horlers who own the hotel. Here you can see older breeds of pigs, sheep, goats, poultry and, of course, the famous Radford shire horses. I always think there is something very permanent and reassuring about these gentle giants.*

***Radstock** to the south east of Radford will not please everybody but it is of great interest to the industrial archaeologist and to railway historians. Both of these industries were for many years the main providers of work and money in the town. The last coal mine closed in 1973 but well before that great thought had been given to grassing and planting the batches - spoil tips for those who have not heard this word used in this context before - I always associate it with cooking and baking! You will want a comfortable place in which to eat and drink when you have taken a look around Radstock and I can cheerfully recommend THE FIRTREE in Frome Road.*

THE RADSTOCK, MIDSOMER NORTON & DISTRICT MUSEUM at Barton Meade House, Haydon, Radstock is an 18th century converted barn and outbuildings standing in beautiful countryside in the former North Somerset Coalfield. You can see how a Victorian miner lived and worked with a re-constructed coalface and cottage. You can see where the colliery children went to school and where the family shopped at the co-op. There are displays covering 200 years of farming and railways, complete with a model layout. Everywhere there are reminders of the past including an early Methodist meeting room, blacksmith shop, and Saxon artefacts. Temporary exhibitions relating to local themes are held throughout the year. The tea room produces an excellent cup of tea but on a fine day you may prefer the picnic area. There is a souvenir shop and free car parking.

*It is only open at the weekends on Saturdays from 10-4pm and Sundays and Bank Holidays from 2-5pm. It is possible to book appointments for Groups by ringing (0761) 437722. It is quite easy to get here from Radstock. Just take the Kilmersdon Road and it is a mere mile away. There is an admission charge. Not far from Radstock at **Wellow** you will find WELLOW TREKKING CENTRE who invite you to come trekking with them to explore the countryside surrounding the ancient city of Bath on horseback. Wellow is pretty enough in its own right but they are quite right in saying that the bridle ways lead you high up on the hills giving you breath-taking views of the unspoilt landscape.*

There are horses to suit all the family, from beginners to experienced riders. A large selection of rides allow you to ride deep in the heart of the countryside. They are friendly people with a great deal of experience and you may well find yourself taken to a good country pub for lunch or even a barbecue somewhere. At the centre there is a children's play area and somewhere for you to have a picnic. For further details and bookings ring (0225) 834376.

*Going westwards you come close to the CHEW VALLEY LAKE, a place of infinite beauty. It is a great place for anglers and for those who just want to stroll along its banks. Chew Valley has two villages worthy of note, **Chew Magna** and **Chew Stoke**. At Chew Magna you enter it by traversing one medieval bridge and leave it by another.*

*Back on the main A368 you will come to **Blagdon** which also has a beautiful lake attracting tourists from afar for its trout fishing. It is also lucky enough to have a cosy and typically English village inn, THE SEYMOUR ARMS. Because of its situation in such close proximity to Bath and Weston-Super-Mare a goodly number of people have found it a good place to stay and use as a base while they go exploring. There are five letting rooms, three of which are en-suite.*

*You will either love **Weston-Super-Mare** or hate it; there seem to be very few people who feel indifferently about it. There is no doubt that it has much to offer the visitor in every conceivable way. The question is where to start.*

My researchers stayed at TIMBERTOP HOTEL & APARTMENTS at 8, Victoria Park, where for a reasonable price they were more than well cared for. It is quite small but the service was excellent and the food good. It enabled them to get to all their ports of call very easily and so the same would apply for visitors.

DAUNCEY'S HOTEL in Claremont Crescent is highly rated by some friends of mine who would not dream of staying anywhere else when they come to Weston. Its position is marvellous overlooking Weston Bay. Privately owned it offers extremely comfortable accommodation. I sat in their attractive lounge eating a delicious cream tea and with such a magnificent view to complement it, I certainly felt that all was well with my world. There were several people in the room and they all looked happy and contented.

Situated right on the sea front with easy access to all the many amenities and attractions that Weston has to offer is SMITHS HOTEL. Open to non-residents, it is a good family hotel, caring for its guests and laying on good food, drink and nightly live entertainment.

One lively hostelry is THE CAPTAIN'S CABIN in Birnbeck Road. This Freehouse is appreciated by all Real Ale enthusiasts and by those who enjoy good seafood. In the summer the large terrace can seat 100 people comfortably at tables overlooking the sea.

Naturally Weston has a multitude of hotels, guest houses, restaurants and pubs which are all centred close to the beach and the shops. You will be spoilt for choice.

I read one of the promotional brochures put out by the local Tourist Board and it describes the town as 'Miles of Smiles'. It is true that as a good family resort it has something to put a smile on every face whether young or not so young, with its attractive setting and choice of things to do and places to visit. The two miles of clean golden sandy beach and the Grand Pier, with its large amusement centre and Blizzard white knuckle ride certainly delight people.

Windsurfing at Weston-Super-Mare

For those who enjoy leisure complexes you will not find a better one than the TROPICANA PLEASURE BEACH with its heated swimming pool, wave machine, water chutes and children's adventure equipment, based on a tropical fruit theme.

The Marine Lake should not be forgotten, here there is always shallow water for children to bathe and splash around in complete safety. I was delighted to discover that Knightstone landing has once again captured the oldest and most famous paddle steamer, S.S. Waverley. This summer it is calling in here and providing full day trips along the Bristol

Channel coast and shorter sails around the bay and across to South Wales. It is a wonderful boat and I have enjoyed sailing on her many times but always before from Ilfracombe and Minehead.

When you are sailing along aboard the Waverley look out for Flat Holm and Steep Holm, not far from the shore. As a child I used to think they were partly submerged whales. It was a bitter disappointment to me when I found out they were just two rather curious shaped small islands sticking out of the sea. In those days I did not appreciate that Steep Holm is the home to rare plants, sea birds and other wildlife. It also has some historic and military remains. The Victorian barracks has been converted into a visitor centre with comfortable seating, snack bar and souvenir counter. Sailings to the island are arranged most Saturdays, Bank Holidays and some Wednesdays between April and October. The schedule is available from the secretary of the Kenneth Allsop Trust who can be contacted on Weston-Super-Mare 632307.

I am not sure whether the Weston Council is responsible for the flower displays in the town or whether, like many other places today, they put it out to contractors but whoever deals with it does the town proud. The spacious beach lawns add a touch of charm to the seafront and the attractive parks and gardens around the resort have superb colourful displays. Just sitting looking at them is joyous and therapeutic.

WOODSPRING MUSEUM should not be missed. Right in the town centre it is a re-creation of everyday life at the turn of the century. Having recently been to the dentist and suffered hardly at all, thank heavens, for I am a miserable coward, I was more than appreciative of the techniques today when I saw a replica of an Edwardian dentist's surgery complete with the most horrendous implements. There is an old fashioned chemist's shop, a farm dairy and a cider-making room. If you ever wondered what our Victorian ancestors did when they went to the seaside you can soon find out by examining one area of the museum which is devoted to this very subject. One display features Mendip mining and another the Worlebury Iron Age Hill Fort as it would have been two thousand years ago. As well as various collections of antiquities there is also an indoor nature trail complete with a running stream and two ponds, one freshwater and the other salt. The Museum is open all the year round.

CLARA'S COTTAGE is another museum in its own way. This time it is a restored Weston seaside landlady's lodging of the 1890's which also includes the Peggy Nesbet doll collection. It is open daily except Sundays from 10am-5pm and admission is free.

You can ride in style along the Marine Parade daily during the season in a horse drawn Landau. It makes you feel very important and is quite delightful. If you have small children with you it will take them some time to be lured away from the land train which services the whole length of the promenade every day from April to September, weather permitting. It costs something like 50p single and 70p return - a worthwhile investment. For those who want to walk with a purpose I would suggest collecting a series of leaflets published by the Civic Society which will help you to follow trails around the town at your own pace and allow you to appreciate the various aspects of the resort's history and architecture. You will find them on sale at both the Tourist Information Centre and the Heritage Centre.

THE INTERNATIONAL HELICOPTER MUSEUM at Weston Airport holds the world's largest collection of helicopters and autogyros, unique to Great Britain. There are indoor and outdoor displays, you can see restoration work in progress and nobody seems to mind your asking questions in this friendly place. It is open from March to October daily from 10am-6pm and from November to March 10am-4pm. It is closed on Christmas Day, Boxing Day and New Years Day.

*Before I left Weston, I was invited to dinner with some friends who lived in **Congresbury**, a few miles outside the town on the A370 going towards Bristol. They suggested we met at their favourite pub in the village, THE BELL. Recently refurbished, the very attractive restaurant which seated about 50 people was ideal for a meal. The food seemed to cover a wide range from the well presented home-cooked traditional dishes to the more exotic. I thoroughly enjoyed my evening and I hope the new owners do well. They deserve to.*

*And so to **Bath**. A frisson of excitement courses through me whenever I think about this wonderful city. I treat it like an old friend but always with a decorum and an awareness that Beau Nash together with the Master of Ceremonies at the assembly and pump room insisted on the highest degree of civility and manners. It is always with a certain amount of impatience and eager anticipation that I seek out this incomparable city. I prefer to behave in the manner of an ostrich and bury my head in the sand when it comes to the outskirts or the 'new' Bath which arose because of indifferent planning. Thankfully, Georgian Bath still remains. It is not the individual buildings that make this city so wonderful but the whole architectural assembly. Take a walk down through Laura Place looking at the houses in which society used to dwell in its heyday when Bath was a fashionable watering hole, cross Argyle Street and so to Pulteney Bridge which spans the Avon. You could be forgiven for thinking you were in Florence as you cross this enchanting bridge which has small* *shops on either side of it not unlike the Ponte Vecchio. The Abbey must come on your list of places to see. It is probably the most beautiful place in the city. There is more glass than stone in the walls which fill it with light. It is sometimes called the Lantern of the West.*

Bath's Pultney Bridge

It is the West front that is its greatest glory. It looks down on the square where all the visitors gather outside the Roman Baths. The West door itself is heavily carved with heraldic shields set in a triple arch, and on each side are wonderful stone canopies covering ancient figures of St Peter and St Paul. The Abbey will give hours of pleasure to the visitor and especially if you seek out the hidden treasures. I have been visiting there for years and see something new to me every time.

Bath owes its abbey to the energy of Oliver King, Bishop of Bath and Wells, who had a dream in which angels climbed up and down ladders to heaven and a voice exhorted a 'king to restore the church' which he did between 1495 and 1503. His dream is carved in stone in the abbey. There is so much to see and do that it is probably easier if I make a sort of shopping list. The list is in no order of priority - it is all wonderful!

In Broad Street there is THE BATH POSTAL MUSEUM. The first known posting of a Penny Black, the world's first stamp took place from this historic building on the 2nd May 1840. The ground floor displays introduce the story of letter writing and the carriage of mail throughout the ages. There are working machines and a life-size Victorian post office as well as a children's activities room. A film room, tea room and further exhibition areas can be found on the first floor. The Museum opens every day from 11-5pm throughout the year and on Sundays from April to October from 2-5pm.

THE VICTORIA ART GALLERY in Bridge Street is a major venue for touring exhibitions of national importance which are shown in the recently opened temporary exhibition gallery. A smaller gallery shows displays of works by local or contemporary artists. A fine permanent collection of European Masters, 18th-20th century British paintings and drawings together with decorative art, is also on display. Highlights include the famous topographical views of Thomas Malton, Thomas Rowlandson's 'Comforts of Bath', and work by Walter Sickert, Matthew Smith and Rex Whistler. Lectures are a regular feature here.

THE BATH BOATING STATION in Forester Road, is a unique surviving Victorian boating station with tea gardens and licensed restaurant, a living museum with traditional wooden skiffs, punts and canoes for hire by hour or by day. A pleasant way for the family to spend a summer day on the river Avon. Abundant wildlife, kingfishers, heron, wild geese, moorhens, cormorants etc. Punting is a speciality and you need have no fear if this demanding science is foreign to you; there is tuition! You can find bed and breakfast here and somewhere to park your car - no easy matter in Bath.

Take a Birds-Eye View in a Hot Air Balloon

I talked of Ballooning when I wrote about Hinton Grange. Here in the heart of Bath at Kingston House, Pierrepoint Street you can arrange with *HERITAGE BALLOONS to take a magical flight yourself. The magic is inescapable and I promise that a trip in a hot-air balloon offers the adventure of a lifetime. From the air, the city of Bath and the surrounding countryside,take on an entirely new dimension. Only from the air can you truly appreciate the beauty of the designs of John Wood, the architect and his son, whose vision came to life in the shape of the Royal Crescent and The Circus. Flights take place early in the morning and early evening and the whole excursion lasts about three hours. In the oldest tradition of ballooning, each flight is celebrated with a glass or two of chilled champagne. The take off site is Victoria Park and to book your flight which must be between March and October please ring (0225) 318747.*

THE ROMAN BATHS MUSEUM is in the Pump Room, Abbey Churchyard. The Roman bathing establishment with its magnificent Great Bath flourished in Aquae Sulis between the first and fifth centuries AD. It was built around the natural hot spring which rises at 46.5 C. The remains are remarkably complete and among the finest in Europe. Sculpture, coins, jewellery and the gilt bronze head of the goddess Sulis Minerva can be seen. The waters can be tasted in the 18th century pump room above the museum. Opening Hours, March-October 9am-6pm. August 9am-6pm and 8pm-10pm. November-February 9am-5pm - 10am on Sundays.

BECKFORD'S TOWER AND MUSEUM stands on the summit of Lansdown, with extensive views from its Belvedere, reached by 156 easy steps. The Tower was built in 1825-7 by the architect H.E. Goodridge for William Beckford, to house part of his magnificent collection of works of art. Today, after recent restoration, it contains two museum rooms which illustrate in fascinating detail - with pictures, prints and models - Beckford's life at Fonthill and Bath. It is open from April until the end of October, Saturday, Sunday and Bank Holiday Monday from 2-5pm.

No one should come to Bath without experiencing SALLY LUNN'S REFRESHMENT HOUSE AND MUSEUM. It is the oldest house in Bath. Excavations in the Cellar Museum show remains of Roman, Saxon and Medieval buildings, together with the ancient kitchen. In 1680 Sally Lunn worked in this charming building, creating the legendary bun, that carries her name. Today, the licensed refreshment rooms serve an intriguing menu, based on the famous Sally Lunn during the day and are open for dinner during the evenings. It is open every day except Christmas Day from 10am and in the evenings from Tuesday-Sunday the restaurant opens from 6pm. You will find it close to the Abbey in a narrow passageway between Abbey Green and North Parade.

Abbey Green, Bath

THE MUSEUM OF COSTUME AND ASSEMBLY ROOMS *in Bennett Street tells the story of fashion over the last 400 years and is brought alive with one of the finest collections of its kind in the world. The displays include 200 dressed figures and up to a thousand other items of costume, accessories and jewellery to illustrate the changing styles in fashionable men's, women's and children's clothes from the late 16th century to the present day.*

The museum is open from March-October from 9.30am-6pm and between November and February from 10am-5pm. On Sunday mornings throughout the year it opens one hour later.

NO 1 ROYAL CRESCENT *provides one with the opportunity to see how a house in this wonderful crescent might have appeared when it was first built. First of all one needs to know something about the Royal Crescent which is popularly regarded as the climax of the Palladian achievement in this most classical of English cities. It is the culmination of a grand plan which takes you from John Wood the Elder's Queen Square built in the 1730's, up Gay Street to The Circus and then along Brock Street to the Royal Crescent itself. It was John Wood the younger who completed The Circus after the death of his father and then went on to design the Royal Crescent. When he first envisaged this majestic sweep it was to look out over unspoilt countryside and not as it was later*

267

developed as part of the expanding 19th century city. The Crescent comprises 30 houses of three or four bays each of which are divided by a giant ionic half column. Wood decreed that no one should be allowed to vary the external treatment of the Royal Crescent but he could not stop it occurring inside which has meant that there is an enormous variety in the internal arrangement and decoration of the individual houses.

The Royal Crescent, Bath

The Bath Preservation Trust has scrupulously restored No.1. and so we are able to see how it would have been. A flight of steps leads you over a bridge, which crosses the basement area and on into the house through the main door. It took considerable skill and a great deal of money to ensure that we can see rooms on the ground floor and the first floor decorated and furnished as accurately as possible in the manner of the late 18th century Bath Town House.

The dining room on the left as you enter has a mid-Georgian table beautifully laid for dessert and the walls are covered with an interesting selection of 18th century portraits. In the study on the right of the hall, a port decanter is laid out ready for the master of the house to repair to after dinner, possibly with his friends. There are playing cards on the table, a clay pipe and a twist of tobacco. The drawing room upstairs is the most elaborately decorated and furnished and has a fine view of the Crescent. Milady's bedroom is a picture of femininity and in total contrast to the very masculine study downstairs. The kitchen brings home how hard staff must have worked in those days and not lived too comfortably either below stairs. This is a fascinating museum and even in a city so full of things to see, it should not be missed.

No.1. Royal Crescent is open from the beginning of March until the end of October from Tuesday to Sunday from 10.30am-5pm and from November 1st until mid-December, Tuesday to Sunday from 10.30am-4pm.

The building of BATH MUSEUM in the Countess of Huntingdon Chapel, The Vineyards, The Paragon is somewhere in which you will discover how one of the architectural masterpieces of Europe was created and how each house was put together from the laying of the foundation stone to the last coat of paint. Exhibits include full scale mock-ups and a series of spectacular models, including that of the entire city with push button illumination. No trip to Bath is complete without a visit. A must for the visitor whatever your interests. You will find it open every day except Monday from 11.30am-5pm. It is also open on Bank Holidays but not between December 16th-28th.

At the same address is THE MUSEUM OF ENGLISH NAIVE ART (1750-1900). This is the first museum of English folk painting, by travelling artists of the 18th and 19th century. The paintings depict ordinary people, pursuits and incidents with a direct simplicity which is both revealing and entertaining; they illustrate a preoccupation with livestock, county furniture and pottery. This is a friendly, unintimidating collection, to be enjoyed by all the family. The opening hours are 10.30am-5pm daily and 2pm-5pm on Sundays from Easter to Christmas but is closed on Sundays in November and December. There is an entrance charge and also a good shop which sells prints, postcards and hand-made crafts.

THE AMERICAN MUSEUM at Claverton has 18 period furnished rooms from the 17th-19th centuries. There are galleries of silver, pewter, glass, textiles, folk art and maps. Sections devoted to the American Indians, Shakers and Pennsylvania Germans. Seasonal exhibitions in the New Gallery. The gardens are beautiful with an American arboretum. You can also spoil yourself with tea and American cookies. The opening hours are from the end of March until the beginning of November from 2-5pm every day except Monday. The gardens open 1-6pm every day except Mondays and are also open on Sunday and Monday Bank Holidays Weekends from 11am-5pm.

Without doubt one of the best ways of seeing Bath is on the splendid KENNET AND AVON CANAL. Run by the Bath and Dundas Canal Company you can join a boat at Brass Knocker Bottom, opposite the Viaduct Inn in Warminster Road, Monkton Combe. From this historic base near the famous Dundas Aqueduct in the beautiful Limpley Stoke Valley, 5 miles from Bath, attractive self-drive electric boats are available for the hour, day or evening hire. Picnicking becomes a delight or you can visit the canalside pubs and tea gardens along the delightful stretch between Bath and Bradford-on-Avon. You will find a number of these pubs also have bed and breakfast accommodation. The normal availability is from Easter until the end of September from 9am-5.30pm. Advance booking is advisable.

At Sydney Wharf, Bathwick Hill, you can join the JOHN RENNIE, named after the architect and engineer who designed the 87 mile long canal which joins the River Avon at Bath with the River Thames at Reading. This really is a magical cruise with the opportunity of dining on board. The John Rennie is available not only for luxurious candlelit dinner cruises but also for charter bookings, business entertaining, wedding receptions, meetings and in fact celebrations of any kind. As you begin your journey and pass through Bathwick Hill road bridge look to your left at Sydney Wharf which was one of the most important unloading areas for the stone used in building many of Bath's imposing houses and coal used to heat these elegant houses.

The car park at the rear of Sydney Wharf was excavated some years ago and found to have been a Roman soldier's burial ground. After this you will pass the wider pond or "winding hole" used originally and to this day to turn boats. Those facing the River Severn for instance turning to face the Thames and vice-versa. Immediately after this you come to Sydney Gardens. This lovely secluded area brings you to Sydney Road Bridge on top of which can be seen Cleveland House, built by the Duke of Cleveland and was the original canal company's headquarters. You then come to the tunnel where you are encouraged to hunt the missing stone to the left of the arch. This forms a shaft up into the heart of the building. Letters or packages could be dropped down this shaft to the barges below for onward carriage to their final destinations. Owing to the peculiar acoustic properties, messages could also be called down to the barge from any floor of the building upwards from the barge.

Continuing through the tunnel you will see strange markings on many of the stone blocks. These are the masons marks, each man, after cutting a stone by hand to a particular shape would make his own mark upon that stone. Between this and the second tunnel are two cast iron foot bridges erected about 1800. By now you are in one of the most fashionable areas of Bath - also a very awkward spot for large boats to navigate, I am told so you must excuse any slight bumps!

The second stone tunnel carries the modern Warminster Road, and you will see part way through on the right hand side an iron ring set into the wall. It was known as "The Sunday Ring" because during the times of strong religious revivals, the Great Western Railway tried to stop night and day working seven days a week and installed these rings so that on Sunday they could hang a heavy chain across the canal to prevent anyone working.

Emerging from this bridge you will see on the port side, what was known as a "lengthmans" cottage. These lengthmen each had charge of approximately 2 miles of canal and reported any leakages or damage to the canl company for repair. What is now the modern extension to the house was once the stable block where barge horses were housed.

Some say that Little Solsbury Hill ahead and to the left, which is actually an Iron Age Fort, was the site of one of King Arthur's battles. Who knows?

If you become addicted to travelling on the canal as many do you will see that there are stretches where it is obvious that work still needs to be done and more time and money spent, especially on the width and dredging, but in the 1950s and 60s parts of the "cut" were merely wet ditches and but for the totally voluntary work of the Kennet and Avon Canal Trust, would still remain un-navigable.

These days the canals are in the hands of the British Waterways Board, a government body who do much hard work but, who, of course, are badly underfunded and still need the assistance of such stalwarts as the Kennet and Avon Trust. A wooden footbridge will come to your attention next. This is a recent replacement for one of John Rennie's original swing bridges. We take ball bearings for granted but these swing bridges were one of the first commercial uses for this invention. Misuse of a swing bridge was a criminal offence and the fine was heavy - 40 shillings. Two pounds in our money today but worth considerably more then when a man's wages would only have been a few shillings.

The beauty of the wildlife on the canal thrills everyone and there is an abundance of swans, mallards and kingfishers. At one spot in particular, at the site of the old Harbutts Plasticine factory, some of the modern day residents of the new houses feed the ducks and swans all the year round which has encouraged a colony of mallards to make it their home.

On every bend there is something to see, a row of cottages next to the GEORGE INN was probably built in the 14th century and originally a hostelry for the monks of the priory of Hampton - now known as Bathampton.

The Canal is wonderful and I cannot urge you enough to make sure you do not miss this rare treat.

Also near Bradford-on-Avon is IFORD MANOR GARDENS. The Tudor Manor House with an 18th century facade, stands beside a medieval bridge over the River Frome. Once a busy centre of the woollen trade, it is now surrounded by a peaceful terraced garden of unique character. Designed in the Italian style, it was the home of Harold Peto, the Edwardian landscape architect. There are pools, statues, a colonnade, antique carvings, cloisters and many plants of botanical interest. Don't rely on getting any form of refreshment here except on Sundays. Opening hours from May-September are from 2-5pm daily except Monday and Friday. In April and October it is only open on Sundays and Bank Holidays. There is free parking.

A visit to the THEATRE ROYAL is one of the delights of Bath. It is one of Britain's oldest and most beautiful theatres, situated in the heart of the city with numerous interesting and attractive shops on the doorstep and immediately adjacent to the delightful new Seven Dials Centre. Whatever your tastes, theatrically might be, you will find the wide ranging programme has something for everyone from opera to ballet, Sunday night concerts and frequently pre West End productions. There is something very special about an evening spent here and it is no bad thing to combine it with a meal in the Theatre Vaults Restaurant - now with tables outside on the Piazza, where you can enjoy a coffee or a snack during the day, or a drink in the historic GARRICK'S HEAD pub.

Here is a pub set in a house that was the first to be built outside the City Walls. The pub was built especially for Beau Nash who made Bath so popular and famous. It shares a ghost, the Grey Lady, with the Theatre Royal and Ghost Walks commence from the pub every weekday night during the summer and on Fridays during the winter. It is a splendid place to visit just for the sheer pleasure of enjoying its ambience let alone its superb food and drink. It is the haunt of both business people and those from the theatre. During the summer months there are tables and chairs outside giving the whole area a Continental air.

In the Bath Industrial Heritage Centre you will find MR BOWLER'S BUSINESS. It is the fascinating story of a family firm which was involved in many aspects of Bath life for nearly 100 years, during which time virtually nothing was thrown away! Walk through a re-creation of Mr Bowler's workshops and aerated water manufactory. Partake of drinks such as Cherry Ciderette and Lemon Juice Soda from Mr Bowler's soda fountain. Other displays of working Bath include the story of Bath Stone and cabinet making. Opening hours from Easter until October 31st are 10am-5pm seven days a week. From November 1st until Easter it is only open from 10am-5pm on Saturdays and Sundays.

My last suggestion is a visit to the HOLBURNE MUSEUM & CRAFTS STUDY CENTRE where, in a lovely garden setting this historic 18th century building uniquely displays superb collections of English and Continental silver, porcelain, Italian Majolica, bronzes, miniatures, glass, furniture and fine old master paintings, including Gainsborough, together with wide ranging work by 20th century British artist-craftsmen. The Crafts Study Centre shows Bernard Leach pottery, woven and printed textiles, furniture and calligraphy. Lively events and temporary exhibitions on varied themes are held throughout the year. There is an educational programme for schools.

Opening hours are Monday to Saturday from 11am-5pm including Bank Holidays and Sundays from 2.30pm-6pm. Closed mid-December until the end of February and on Mondays from November to Easter. The Museum has a charming teahouse and garden. I am being selfish enough to include only my most favourite places to stay, eat and drink. There are many more naturally but I behave a bit like a homing pigeon and return to well tried and tested venues.

Since the advent of the delightful QUEENSBERRY HOTEL in Russel Street, I have stayed there on occasions. It is so luxurious. You sleep in a vast, beautifully furnished room, full of antiques, overlooking a quiet street. The size of the draped bed matches the room. Breakfast appears in your room, and you are ready to sally forth on a day full of expectation and knowing you will not be disappointed. Stephen and Penny Ross have created this award winning hotel which must be considered upmarket although it is not in the least pompous. Cleverly they have married together three fine period houses with 18th-century stucco ceilings and cornices, and an attractive drawing room.

Another hotel of distinction is the small NEWBRIDGE HOUSE in Kelston Road, Newbridge, Bath. Here the brothers Day, Colin and Nigel have achieved a hotel and restaurant from the former residence of Lord and Lady Kirkwood. It is a house noted for its true Georgian Architecture and is a Georgian 1770 Graded Listed Building. The location is one of peace and everything about the running of this establishment is restful. The Restaurant is open to non-residents and a meal there overlooking the gardens is a joy. Fresh flowers are everywhere and to their scent is added the gentle fragrance of big bowls of pot-pourri. Someone said to me that the hotel has a touch of the old Colonial Singapore. I think they had "Raffles" in mind and, yes, I agree.

THE REDCAR HOTEL in Henrietta Street is another excellent establishment and it is here I come when I want to be spoiled in BENTLEYS RESTAURANT. When you make your choice from the menu you may rest assured that the ingredients are fresh whenever possible and carefully prepared by their master chef. The venue is charming and the food lives up to one's expectations.

The history of the buildings in which the Redcar and Bentleys are housed is interesting. The hotel was once three houses, numbers 27, 28 and 29 Henrietta Street. Henrietta Street is situated at the end of Laura Place, a row of houses beloved by the society ladies who came to Bath to take the waters and to be seen in the fashionable Assembly and Pump Rooms. The two streets have more in common than one might think. Henrietta Street was designed between 1788 and 1792 by Sir William

Pulteney, designer of Great Pulteney Street, who was also involved in the design of Laura Place, built between 1788-1789. Both Henrietta Street and Laura Place were named after Sir William's daughter, Henrietta Laura Pulteney.

The occupants of the three houses in 1892 were Mrs Henry Williams a dressmaker, at Number 27, Number 28 housed Mrs Edward Forshall, a teacher and in Number 29 Miss Harriet Thewrnti pursued her trade as a seamstress. In 1902 the occupancy of Number 27 changed and a London artist, Mr C. Hodges took up residence until 1912. Number 28 became vacant in 1904 and remained so until 1907 when it was taken over by another well known artist of the time, Alfred Jones, who remained there until his death in 1912. In 1912 both 27 and 28 became vacant until 1915 when it became the home of the Girls Friendly Society and they remained there until World War II when the houses were used as safe houses for refugees, who shared the houses with the residents. Finally the Redcar Hotel was opened and has flourished ever since.

Everyone who vists DUKES' HOTEL in Great Pulteney Street leaves it enriched. It is elegant, luxurious, comfortable and hospitable. The resident owners, Tim and Rosalind Forester have zealously preserved its 18th century beauty and at the same time have managed to incorporate the modern facilities that we demand. It is a hotel that has won acclaim throughout the world and it is not unusual to find celebrities staying here. Who could possibly find anything but pleasure in an hotel situated in Great Pulteney Street, Europe's most elegant and grandest Georgian thoroughfare - just a few minutes level stroll from the city centre. The ingenious way that Sainsbury's managed to convert the old LMS Railway Station into a restaurant has always intrigued me.

GREEN PARK BRASSERIE is both pleasing from a food point of view and to the eye as well. It answers the needs of many people every day and from Wednesday to Saturday it opens in the evenings as well with live music to add to the atmosphere on Friday and Saturday evenings. An added bonus is the use, for those eating in the Brasserie to be able to park their cars in Sainsbury's car park - remember to get the ticket stamped before you leave the restaurant.

One hundred yards from the Theatre Royal is THE WALRUS AND THE CARPENTER, one of Bath's most popular restaurants.It was built *in 1740 and gives the impression of a typical French Bistro. When you walk in there is a wonderfully warm and friendly atmosphere. The food is excellent and the price is right.*

In Cleveland Place West, THE CURFEW has a devoted band of followers who use the pub almost on a daily basis because of its friendly hospitality, the well kept ales and the enjoyable food, which is readily available and at a price that does not hurt the pocket.

CLARETS at 7a Kingsmead Square is a delicious place, a stylish restaurant and wine bar dedicated to the delights of drinking and dining - what could be better! The restaurant and bar occupy four vaults in this lovely Georgian terrace in Kingsmead Square. It is the perfect place to meet friends, enjoy a leisurely bottle of wine and be offered free canapes presented to you by the courtesy of the chef.

THE WIFE OF BATH is a Bistro at the garden level of a property in Pierrepont street, It was converted from three cellars over the last twenty years and it is a very special place with lots of individual eating areas, each with its own personality. It is said that Acker Bilk made his debut in one of the eating rooms just off the bar.

I have now reached a moment I hate - the time to leave Bath, but God willing it will not be too long before I return.

THE REDCAR HOTEL & BENTLEY'S RESTAURANT

Hotel & Restaurant

27-29 Henrietta Street,
Bath, Avon.

Tel: (0225) 469151
Fax: (0225 461424

Apart from the undoubted comfort and service of staying in a hotel of this calibre, there is the added pleasure in learning about its history. Its architect and designer, the redoubtable Sir William Pultney, who also designed Great Pultney Street, would no doubt be very surprised that the three houses numbers 27-29 had changed from individual buildings into this elegant establishment which gives pleasure to visitors from all over the world, all the year round.

Centrally situated at the end of Laura Place, a street beloved by Regency society, The Redcar is versatile. It has 31 bedrooms each furnished beautifully and with every modern facility. It is an ideal venue for small conferences, where meetings can be held in quiet surroundings. It accommodates 70 people theatre style and 50 boardroom. The rooms are also excellent for a dinner dance or a wedding reception.

Bentley's Restaurant is somewhere that is popular with residents of Bath. They know it is tranquil, delightfully appointed and it is somewhere that they can be sure of the freshest of ingredients in all the interesting dishes that are produced by the Head Chef and his Brigade. Every dish on the a la carte menu is a masterpiece and an excellent table d'hote menu is also available. The Bar is a meeting place for friends who want to enjoy comfort, a drink and probably indulge in one of the tasty lunchtime specials.

USEFUL INFORMATION

OPEN: All day
CHILDREN: Welcome
CREDIT CARDS: All Major Cards
LICENSED: Full On Licence
ACCOMMODATION: 31 rooms,
    22 en-suite

RESTAURANT: A la Carte &
    Table d'Hote
BAR FOOD: Lunchtime Specials
VEGETARIAN: Always available
DISABLED ACCESS: No
GARDEN: Henrietta Park next door

CLARETS

Restaurant & Wine Bar

7a Kingsmead Square,
Bath, Avon.

Tel: (0225) 466688

Clarets is a stylish restaurant and wine bar dedicated to the delights of drinking and dining. It is situated beneath the lovely Georgian terrace in Kingsmead Square. The restaurant and bar occupy four attractive vaults (one a strictly no-smoking area). The wine bar is the perfect place to meet friends and enjoy a leisurely bottle of excellent wine from the well chosen list. In warm weather tables and chairs are placed in the square for Clarets customers to enjoy alfresco drinking and dining.

The imaginative and delicious modern English food is attractively presented and excellent value providing a wide choice including fresh fish and vegetarian dishes. The chef's creative chicken, fillet mignon and salmon dishes are firm favourites amongst both regulars and visitors as are the delectable traditional bread and butter pudding and the brilliant baked cheesecakes.

In addition to the a la carte menu, changing daily specials and excellent value fixed price lunch, Clarets also offers fondues. You can freak out on a full fondue feast for four (comprising cheese, chicken, steak and chocolate for only £15.95 per head or enjoy a marvellous melting cheese fondue for only £8.95. Clarets is very near the Theatre Royal and Bath's three cinemas. The restaurant and bar are open lunchtimes and evenings from 5.30pm for drinks, full meals and snacks. Clarets Curtain Call Club for concert, theatre and cinema goers is one of Bath's great institutions.

USEFUL INFORMATION

OPEN: Lunch 12-2pm.
Dinner 5.30-10.30/11pm
CHILDREN: Allowed in restaurant
CREDIT CARDS: Mastercard and Visa
LICENSED: Full On Licence
ACCOMMODATION: Not applicable

RESTAURANT: Imaginative, modern English
BAR FOOD: Delicious snacks
VEGETARIAN: Choice of ten
DISABLED ACCESS: No
GARDEN: Alfresco drinking and dining in Square

THE CURFEW

Public House

11 Cleveland Place,
Bath, Avon.

Tel: (0225) 424210

Another unusual name for a pub, The Curfew, which stands on the main London Road just before the Cleveland Bridge, acquired its name from the Second World War. If you happened to be in the pub when the curfew or the air raid alarm sounded you were allowed to stay in the building, no matter what time of the night it was. Hence the name of the hostelry. There were many good parties held in this pub. 'H' & Sue Collins are the landlords who moved here quite recently. They have spent time and loving care on refurbishing the interior which has a great olde worlde atmosphere. Old beams and roaring, open fires help to add to the charm of the pub.

Whilst 'H' cares for the Real Ales and the Guest Beers, Sue does all the cooking; a task she relishes. She brought with her an old, cast iron skillet in which she cooks and serves from as well. The result is delicious - It could be anything from Saute of Bacon and Mushrooms to Chicken Avocado or a Vegetarian pasta with oriental vegetables stir fried in a creamy white sauce and wine. There are simple Oven Baked Potatoes with a variety of fillings and a splendid hot Chilli Beef. It is not a vast menu but every dish is beautifully cooked and the price is incredibly reasonable. So centrally placed, The Curfew is ideal for people exploring Bath.

USEFUL INFORMATION

OPEN: 11-3pm & 6-11pm.
CHILDREN: Upstairs in daytime & early evening
CREDIT CARDS: None taken
LICENSED: Full On Licence
ACCOMMODATION: Not applicable

RESTAURANT: Not applicable
BAR FOOD: Unusual, delicious & inexpensive
VEGETARIAN: Always available
DISABLED ACCESS: No
GARDEN: Beer garden

DUKES' HOTEL

Hotel

Great Pulteney Street,
Bath, Avon.

Tel: (0225) 463512
Fax: (0225) 483733

There is nowhere in Bath that exemplifies its architecture more than Great Pulteney Street, a classical Georgian parade without a single building dating from later than the 18th century. It is here that you will find Dukes' Hotel. Until you experience it for yourself you will find it difficult to envisage how zealously it has been preserved inside and out. It is truly beautiful in every way. You can enter through an elegant doorway with an impressive staircase almost immediately ahead of you. The bar is warm and friendly, the drawing room impressive but restful. It is a hotel that has won acclaim throughout the world and it is not unusual to find celebrities staying here.

It is never easy to adapt old buildings to cope with the demands of modern day life. Somehow Tim and Rosalind Forester, the resident proprietors, have managed to incorporate private bathrooms and showers, central heating and superb modern kitchens without in anyway detracting from the beauty of the house.

You will dine here on beautifully presented food, sleep peacefully in comfortable beds and awake in the morning looking forward to a day in this lovely Georgian city, after breakfasting exceedingly well. As part of their tariff, Duke's offers 'Daysaway' breaks, which include accommodation, breakfast and dinner for two nights at generous rates; an offer that is well worth taking. There is no doubt that you will be well cared for here.

USEFUL INFORMATION

OPEN: All year
CHILDREN: Welcome
CREDIT CARDS: All major cards
LICENSED: Full On Licence
ACCOMMODATION: 22 en-suite
   3 star rating

RESTAURANT: Fixed Price, delicious
BAR FOOD: Not applicable
VEGETARIAN: Always available
DISABLED ACCESS: No
GARDEN: Two parks very close

THE GARRICKS HEAD

Public House

6 St Johns Place,
Saw Close, Bath, Avon.

Tel: (0225) 448819

This wonderful pub, right next to the new Theatre Royal and just five minutes from the main shopping centre, was built for Beau Nash in the 18th century. It was he who made this Spa town so fashionable and had London Society flocking to the city. The Garricks Head is essentially a city centre pub but when it was built it was on the boundary of the old city limits.

With its proximity to the theatre, the interior designed by Carl Toms, the international theatre set designer, seems a fit setting in the evenings, when frequently it takes on a 'theatrical' air with the visiting company and actors using the Pub as the 'Green Room bar - which perversely is decorated red - there are many photographs of some very famous actors and actresses. Five years ago the pub was totally refurbished and re-opened by Charlton Heston.

During the summer there are tables and chairs outside and the area takes on a Continental atmosphere. Good wholesome, traditional pub food with generous portions and excellent value is available between 12-2pm Monday to Saturday and although children are unable to go into the bars they are welcome outside.

USEFUL INFORMATION

OPEN: Mon-Sat: 11-11pm,
Sun: 12-3pm & 7-10.30pm
CHILDREN: Outside only
CREDIT CARDS: None taken
LICENSED: Full On Licence
ACCOMMODATION: Not applicable

RESTAURANT: Not applicable
BAR FOOD: Wholesome, traditional
good sized portions, excellent value
VEGETARIAN: Eight dishes
DISABLED ACCESS: Unfortunately,
no - 3 steps at entrance
GARDEN: 'Patio' outside during
summer

GREEN PARK BRASSERIE

*Restaurant, Wine Bar,
Coffee House*

Old Green Park Station,
Green Park, Bath, Avon.

Tel: (0225) 338565

The Green Park Brasserie is open from 10am-3.30pm Sunday to Tuesday and from 10am-10.30pm Wednesday to Saturday. This gives you ample time to discover the pleasure of eating in an unlikely venue if one remembers that the building was the old L.M.S. Somerset and Dorset Railway Station until the Beeching cuts of 1966. It was then purchased and restored by Sainsburys, who permit customers of the Brasserie to use their car park - remember to have your ticket stamped behind the bar when you leave. It has been a restaurant since 1985 and has established itself firmly in Bath as one of the best places to eat.

The menu is not vast but it does have a well selected choice of dishes at very reasonable prices. There are eight starters, four of which are suitable for vegetarians and the list also includes Pasta of the Day which is also available as the main course. Three exciting salads are served daily. The main course is served with pommes frites, or potato of the day. You may choose fish of the day, prime Aberdeen Angus fillet 'au poivre' or perhaps breast of duck, coated in sea salt, honey and cracked black pepper with a caramelised Madeira sauce. Those are just three from a choice of 11 dishes. The Brasserie has the benefit of an entertainments licence and a supper hours certificate and on Friday and Saturday evenings there is always live background music.

USEFUL INFORMATION

OPEN: Sun-Tues: 10am-3.30pm
   Wed-Sat: 10am-10.30pm
   Open for Sunday lunch
CHILDREN: Welcome
CREDIT CARDS: All but Diners
LICENSED: Restaurant Licence
ACCOMMODATION: Not applicable

RESTAURANT: Well chosen, selective
   menu
BAR FOOD: As above
VEGETARIAN: Always available
DISABLED ACCESS: Level & toilets
GARDEN: Seating at front & rear

Sydney Wharf, Bathwick Hill,
Bath, Avon.

Tel: (0225) 447276

THE JOHN RENNIE CANAL CRUISES

Canal Cruises

If you fancy a relaxing day enjoying the beauties of the countryside where you can watch swans, mallards and kingfishers, without having to lift a finger yourself, then a cruise along the Kennet and Avon Canal has to be the perfect answer.

John Rennie, named after the man who designed the Canal, offers a day of luxury on the water. Your journey starts at Sydney Wharf and from there, the Broad Beam boat meanders quietly along, under bridges and through tunnels passing some amazing scenery. It is hard to believe that the men who worked these canals, often laboured from three or four in the morning until nine or ten o'clock at night, and children as young as three or four years were expected to work even if it was just to walk behind the horse.

Maureen and Peter Tattersall run the John Rennie and they are Past Masters at providing comfort. There is plenty of room for 60 people and an open deck at the bow allows passengers to enjoy the views and the sunshine. The boat is an ideal setting for a special occasion, a private party, a wedding reception, school groups and corporate functions. The cruise lasts up to four and a half hours and the catering on board is a special experience; everything from sandwiches, home-made scones, to a delicious buffet or a five course dinner. The bar is fully stocked with Wadworths beers, wines, spirits and soft drinks. For whatever reason you take this cruise, it will be memorable.

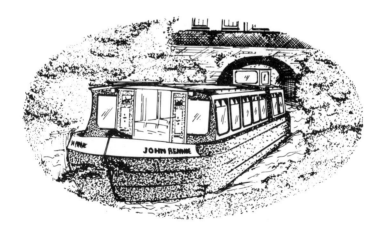

USEFUL INFORMATION

OPEN: All year
    Takes 60 people
CHILDREN: Welcome
CREDIT CARDS: Not applicable
LICENSED: Yes
ACCOMMODATION: Not applicable

RESTAURANT: From sandwiches to
    five course dinner
BAR FOOD: Not applicable
VEGETARIAN: On request
DISABLED ACCESS: Yes. Welcome
GARDEN: Not applicable

THE NEWBRIDGE HOUSE HOTEL

Hotel & Restaurant

35 Kelston Road,
Newbridge, Bath, Avon.

Tel: (0225) 446676
Fax: (0225) 447541

Newbridge House was one the home of Lord and Lady Kirkwood and is noted within the City for its true Georgian Architecture. It is a period Georgian 1770 Graded Listed Building, set in a peaceful location and those who stay within its hallowed portals feel privileged. Of course, much of the pleasure is in staying in such an elegant building but that pleasure would be severely diminished if one did not have all the other ingredients that brothers, Colin and Nigel Day have brought to the hotel.

Some people describe the hotel as a reminder of old Colonial Singapore - Raffles perhaps. In the Reception room is a splendid grand piano, vast and very comfortable settees invite people to sit down and everywhere there are fresh flowers, and added to their scent is the gentle fragrance from bowls of pot-pourri. There are eleven en-suite bedrooms, some with open fires and four-poster beds. The charming restaurant, which is open to non-residents, overlooks the gardens and the breakfast room opens out onto a terrace where pergolas, water fountains, Chinese Buddhas and figurines bedeck the lawns. The beef trolley on Sunday is something that the people of Bath will tell you is not to be missed.

This truly beautiful hotel has three rooms available for small meetings and conferences. There are two formal dining rooms with open fires and one of these has a full length balcony commanding stunning views of the countryside.

USEFUL INFORMATION

OPEN: All year
CHILDREN: Any age welcome
CREDIT CARDS: All major cards
LICENSED: Full On Licence
ACCOMMODATION: 11 en-suite rooms

RESTAURANT: Superb cuisine
BAR FOOD: Not applicable
VEGETARIAN: On request
DISABLED ACCESS: 2 ground floor rooms
GARDEN: Beautiful garden & terrace. No playing!

QUEENSBERRY HOTEL

Hotel & Restaurant

Russel Street,
Bath, Avon.

Tel: (0225) 447928
Fax: (0225) 446065

The very name of Bath conjures up a vision of elegance both materially and architecturally. The Queensberry Hotel is the epitome of this style and charm. Your bedroom will be huge, beautifully furnished with a vast draped bed and well appointed bathroom. The whole house is quietly luxurious.

The house was built in 1722 for the Marquis of Queensberry who employed the renowned architect, John Wood to create a unique town house. Little did the Marquess know that he would be giving so much pleasure to so many people in this era; people who come to stay find themselves supremely cared for in a quiet, un-pompous but efficient manner. The position is marvellous too for you are just a few minutes walk from the Royal Crescent, Circus, and the Assembly Rooms, yet it is sublimely quiet.

In 1992 the hotel won the 'Best Newcomer Award for the South West. Sitting in the courtyard garden on a warm summer evening, you may forget that you are in the middle of Bath. You may not know that the Queensberry is rather less traditional than its surroundings; whether it is first class bathrooms, laundry and room service or up-to-date office support for executives, the hotel-keeping is certainly contemporary. The Olive Tree is what Stephen and Penny Ross, the owners, conceive as a contemporary restaurant - informal, modestly priced with English cooking that combines their own excellent produce with the robustness of the Mediterranean.

USEFUL INFORMATION

OPEN: All Year
CHILDREN: All ages welcome
CREDIT CARDS: All major cards except Diners
LICENSED: Full on Licence
ACCOMMODATION: 22 en-suite rooms

RESTAURANT: Contemporary - informal
BAR FOOD: Not applicable
VEGETARIAN: Always available
DISABLED ACCESS: Limited
GARDEN: Yes with seating. Not playing

THE WALRUS AND THE CARPENTER

Restaurant & Bistro

28 Barton Street,
Bath, Avon.

Tel: (0225) 314864

This is one of Bath's oldest and most popular restaurants. Built in 1740 it stands just 100 yards from the Theatre Royal. What strikes you most when you walk through the door is the impression of a typical French Bistro sitting happily in a building of very English, Georgian grandeur. It is the most warm and friendly place and it is no wonder that it has so many regular and devoted customers. The welcome is just as great if you have never set foot in The Walrus and The Carpenter before. In my experience this sort of genuine, welcoming atmosphere always stems from the top and in this case it is the proprietor, Andrew Robinson, whose enthusiasm and love of his business which he treats in a professional but informal manner, spreads to his staff who make you feel equally wanted.

The menu is wide ranging but everything is home-made. What ever you decide upon will be of the best quality and cooked to perfection. The Walrus is famed too for its traditional and luscious puddings. There is an extensive range for Vegetarians and Vegan meals are available, all home-made on the premises.

It is here also that you realise the art of cocktail mixing and shaking is still alive and kicking! You will be hard put to think up one that the bartender has not heard of and you will also be introduced to some you did not know existed. I use the word 'kicking' advisedly - each and every one of them is potent - beware!

USEFUL INFORMATION

OPEN: Lunch: Mon-Sat:12-2.30pm &
 Dinner: Every evening 6-11pm
CHILDREN: Welcome
CREDIT CARDS: Visa/Access/Amex
LICENSED: Restaurant Licence
ACCOMMODATION: Not applicable

RESTAURANT: Super, home-made
 Superb puddings
BAR FOOD: Not applicable
VEGETARIAN: Extensive range &
 vegan
DISABLED ACCESS: Yes but restricted,
 no special WC's
GARDEN: No

THE WIFE OF BATH

Bistro

12 Pierrepont Street,
Bath, Avon.

Tel: (0225) 461745

Chaucer's Canterbury Tales told of 'The Wife of Bath', a most hospitable lady, and what better name could there be for this attractive, welcoming establishment, owned and run by Richard and Ainslie Ensom, whose inborn enjoyment of people makes them ideal hosts. The Bistro, which is in the centre of Bath, very close to the Abbey, the railway and bus station, was built by John Wood on the site of the orchard of Bath Abbey and is an elegant, Georgian terrace house. It always has been an attractive house and has lost none of its charm and character.

The Bistro is at the garden level of the property and was converted from three cellars and over the last twenty years the Ensom's have made it a very special place. There are lots of individual eating areas, each with its own personality. It is said that Acker Bilk made his debut in one of the eating rooms just off the bar.

The staff at The Wife of Bath have been with the Ensoms for years, a factor that adds to the contented and happy atmosphere. It is only a lover of wine who could produce such an excellent selection. From Spain there is a good Rioja, from Australia a Koonunga Hill Shiraz Cabernet 1991. France, New Zealand and the U.S.A. provide many bottles at varying prices but never indifferent and never unaffordable. The menu has something for everyone with fresh fish a speciality. A delightful place to be among friends or even on your own you will not feel alone for long.

USEFUL INFORMATION

OPEN: 12-2.30 Mon-Sat & 5.30-11pm daily 10.30 Sundays
CHILDREN: Very welcome. Small portions
CREDIT CARDS: Barclay/Access/Visa/ Amex
LICENSED: Restaurant Licence
ACCOMMODATION: Not applicable

RESTAURANT: Wide range, fresh fish a speciality
BAR FOOD: Daily specials
VEGETARIAN: Always available
DISABLED ACCESS: No
GARDEN: Patio area, dining only

THE SEYMOUR ARMS
Inn

Bath Road,
Blagdon, Avon.

Tel: (0761) 462279

This is a friendly, cosy and typical English village inn and situated in the small village of Blagdon. It is a place that attracts visitors from far and wide because of its sparkling lake which has an abundance of trout.

The Seymour Arms was built around 1900 and has been cleverly designed to allow a large proportion of table seating which gives it the look of a restaurant without destroying the pub image. For anyone who is a collector of antique plates, the collection on the walls is fascinating. For parents with children a step up area which is semi sectioned off by a stone wall is a godsend. The children are happy and their elders do not feel cut off.

Sue and Dave Moir run The Seymour and make every one welcome in the bar, they also cater for people coming to stay. They have five rooms, three of which are en-suite and all of them have TV and coffee making facilities.

This is a very food orientated pub with the emphasis on home-cooking and reasonable prices. Senior citizens are provided with lunchtime Specials, children have their own menu and on Sunday lunchtime the traditional roast is extremely popular. Food is available seven days a week at lunchtime and in the evenings.

USEFUL INFORMATION

OPEN: Mon-Sat: 11-2.30pm & 6-11pm
  Sun: 12-3pm & 7-10.30pm
CHILDREN: Welcome. Family area
CREDIT CARDS: Not at the moment
LICENSED: Full On Licence
ACCOMMODATION: 5 room,
  3 en-suite

RESTAURANT: Generous portions,
  Sunday roast
BAR FOOD: Home-cooked. Reasonably
  priced
VEGETARIAN: Good selection
DISABLED ACCESS: Level entrance
GARDEN: No

THE BELL INN

Inn & Restaurant

Kent Road,
Congresbury, Avon.

Tel: (0934) 833110

The Bell Inn is set in the small, picturesque country village of Congresbury, yet within 15 minutes drive you can find yourself in the heart of bustling Bristol. The inn has the Mendips in the background and open farmland to the front. It certainly is a place that tempts one to call in for a drink or a meal.

The main part of the Bell Inn was built in the early 1800's but with the advent of the A370 in the early 1950's, the rear of the Inn was completely rebuilt to become a front! It is quite fascinating inside with an extensive collection of Bells of all kinds from Warships to Fire Engines, together with a number of artefacts collected over a number of years.

Quite recently a new restaurant has been opened. This attractive venue seats 50 people comfortably and it is here the skill of the talented chef makes every meal a pleasure. Everything is home-cooked and ranges from simple bar snacks to extravagant 6 course banquets, all prepared and cooked on the premises. The large Beer Garden and Children's Activity Centre, Pets Corner and aviary ensures that the youngsters can have as much fun as their parents. Steven Peters is the justly proud and welcoming, mine host in this very agreeable hostelry.

USEFUL INFORMATION

OPEN: Mon-Sat: 11-11pm
    Sun: 12-3pm & 7-10.30pm
CHILDREN: Allowed. Activity centre
CREDIT CARDS: Access/Visa/Switch
LICENSED: Full on Licence
ACCOMMODATION: Not applicable

RESTAURANT: Superb range, all
    home-cooked from fresh ingredients
BAR FOOD: Well priced & unusual,
    home-cooked
VEGETARIAN: Always available
DISABLED ACCESS: Level,
    all facilities
GARDEN: Large. Aviary, pets corner,
    BBQ on Sundays in summer

OLD MALT HOUSE HOTEL
Hotel & Restaurant

Radford, Timsbury,
Bath, Avon.

Tel: (0761) 470106
Fax: (0761) 472616

The Horler family who own and run this delightful hotel in the hamlet of Radford on the fringe of the Mendip Hills, combine management of the hotel with running the successful Radford Farm where you can see older breeds of pigs, sheep, goats, poultry and, of course, the famous Radford Shire Horses. It is the winning rosettes and certificates for these splendid beasts that one can see proudly attached to the beams in the bar of the Old Malt House. It would take you hours to study them but it produces many comments and starts people talking in this friendly establishment.

The hotel has 10 en-suite rooms complete with all the comforts you could possibly want including the very welcome tea and coffee making facility. Daughter Julie is the Chef and she has a love of creative cooking which gives her customers great pleasure. In addition to the main meals of the day, Julie conjures up some very tasty Specials every day for those who want a Bar Meal. Both the Bar and the Restaurant are open to non-residents.

Throughout the Hotel the emphasis is on comfort and a relaxing atmosphere, resulting in a 'home from home' feeling. It is beautifully warm in winter and the lawns and gardens with uninterrupted views through the Cam Valley make it a wonderful place to be in summer. There is ample car parking within the hotel's grounds. Apart from the beautiful walks one can take, a visit to Radford Farm is a must.

USEFUL INFORMATION

OPEN: All year, all day
CHILDREN: Welcome
CREDIT CARDS: All major cards
LICENSED: Full On Licence
ACCOMMODATION: 10 en-suite

RESTAURANT: High standard of
  English Cuisine
BAR FOOD: Tasty Daily Specials
VEGETARIAN: Always available
DISABLED ACCESS: Yes.
  Not bedrooms
GARDEN: Yes & Terrace. Seating

THE FIRTREE

Frome Road,
Writhlington, Radstock.

Pub with Accommodation

Tel: (0761) 433139

There is a romantic atmosphere about The Firtree, a little pub built from local stone which during the summer months boasts beautiful hanging baskets and colourful window boxes in the beer garden and the veranda. Situated on the main road between Midsomer Norton and Frome, the pub is at the cross roads of Writhlington and enclosed on two sides by fields.

Approximately 180 years old this purpose built inn originally had stables attached to the premises. These out-buildings have had many uses over the years, once upon a time providing sleeping areas for ostlers and stable boys. The ghost of a horseman murdered in one of the stables, which are now garages, is a regular visitor!

The Inn has three family letting rooms, tastefully decorated and cosy, all of which have tea and coffee making facilities and are close to the bathroom. There is a well kept bar with pool, darts and live entertainment every Saturday night. Breakfast is served in the comfortable lounge come dining area. A large function room and skittle alley is available for parties.

All the wholesome, traditional food is home-cooked. Dishes like Boozy Beef - steak marinated in Guinness with onion and mushroom is a firm favourite on the menu. Try to leave room for the traditional puddings - a rare treat.

USEFUL INFORMATION

OPEN: All day
CHILDREN: Yes + accommodation
CREDIT CARDS: None taken
LICENSED: Full On
ACCOMMODATION: 3 family rooms

RESTAURANT: Traditional home-cooked fare, generous portions
BAR FOOD: All home-cooked
VEGETARIAN: Half dozen, home-made
DISABLED ACCESS: Yes
GARDEN: Attractive beer garden. BBQ's

RANGEWORTHY NURSERIES & BIG BEN RESTAURANT & MOTEL

Pool Farm, Wotton Road,
Rangeworthy, Bristol

Restaurant & Motel & Nurseries

Tel: (0454) 228209
Fax: (0454) 228938

This is a fascinating place, a mixture of sophistication, nature and Christian Charity. Owned by the Bartlett family, Rangeworthy Nurseries is only ten miles from Bristol, three miles from Yate and four miles from the M4/M5. Here you can stay in one of the excellently appointed Motel rooms, all en-suite naturally. There is a delightful Bridal Suite complete with a Four-poster. In fact, The Big Ben Restaurant specialises in wedding receptions, as well as offering coffee, tea, cakes and snacks. One of the rooms has disabled facilities. Pets are allowed .

Here you have not only the Restaurant and Motel, but one of the best Nurseries in this part of the county, offering a wonderful range of bedding plants, Fuschias, Geraniums, hanging baskets, trees, shrubs, Herbaceous and rockery plants. This is not all. The children's playground is well equipped and there is an enchanting animal park with many small animals including Vietnamese Pot-Bellied Pigs and Angora goats, Shetland ponies, Ducks, Rabbits and Chipmunks. What is unique is that all the proceeds from the Animal Park and the Children's Playground go to the Eleanor Children's Charitable Trust founded by Mrs Eleanor Bartlett in support of suffering Romanian children. Entrance for adults is £1 and for children 75p plus whatever clothing, goods, offers of help and prayers you care to donate. It is a wonderful effort by dedicated and caring people. Go and see for yourselves.

USEFUL INFORMATION

OPEN: Every day 10-5.30pm except Mon
CHILDREN: Welcome. Special playground
CREDIT CARDS: None taken
LICENSED: Residential Licence
ACCOMMODATION: 7 en-suite rooms
  Bridal Suite

RESTAURANT: Specialising in Wedding
  receptions. Coffee Shop
BAR FOOD: Snacks and light bites
VEGETARIAN: On request
DISABLED ACCESS: Yes. Level.
  Loos etc
GARDEN: Animal Park

THE COFFEE LOUNGE AT HERITAGE

24 High Street,
Thornbury, Bristol, Avon.

Tel: (0454) 415096

Coffee Lounge & Shop

Dating back to the 18th century, No 24 High Street, Thornbury which houses the Coffee Lounge at Heritage, is regarded by the local civic society as being of special architectural interest. The shop, selling fine china, crystal and gifts has retained and incorporated the original black oak beams and low ceilings into its fittings. Built partly from local stone, as an extension to the rear some 15 years ago the Coffee Lounge allows superb views from two wide sets of sliding doors of the garden and beyond across the valley to the river and to Wales. The walled garden has been landscaped and contains numerous trees and flowering shrubs. In the summer there are hanging baskets and pots and troughs bursting with flowers.

The Coffee Lounge is a self-service, 'cold-counter' restaurant with seating inside for 40 and outside for a further 12. A ' Heartbeat' award for healthy eating has just been awarded by Northavon District Council. Smoking is not allowed - except outside. The very large sunny garden is one of the most attractive features of the restaurant. There is easy access to it through the sliding doors and customers are encouraged to take their food and drinks outside whenever the weather permits. Well behaved dogs are allowed in the garden.

The food is healthy, fresh and almost entirely home produced. Chips are not served! The emphasis is on salads, quiches, fish dishes, fruit juices, soups, filter coffee and special and herb teas etc at reasonable prices.

USEFUL INFORMATION

OPEN: Mon-Sat: 9.30-4.30pm (excluding Bank Holidays)
CHILDREN: Welcome. High chairs
CREDIT CARDS: None taken
LICENSED: Not applicable
ACCOMMODATION: Not applicable

RESTAURANT: Healthy, fresh, mainly home-produced
BAR FOOD: Not applicable
VEGETARIAN: Several dishes daily
DISABLED ACCESS: Level. Ramp to garden
GARDEN: Large & sunny

THE CAPTAIN'S CABIN
Public House & Restaurant

51 Birnbeck Road,
Weston-Super-Mare, Avon.

Tel: (0934) 620847

This lively hostelry was built circa 1850 and was originally known as the Claremont Hotel. Now known as The Captain's Cabin run by Mike Page, it is a Freehouse situated at the north end of Weston overlooking the Anchor Head rocks and close to the historic Birnbeck Pier.

The large bar has a pool table, the lounge is where you can enjoy the very tasty bar snacks and daily specials. The restaurant, which seats 60 comfortably, is frequently used as a venue for weddings and meetings. One of the most popular places in summer is the vast outside terrace overlooking Anchor Head and Weston Bay which has seating for 100 people. It is a magical place to be on a summer's day.

Real Ale enthusiasts will appreciate the way in which the beer is kept and you can also be sure of a first class pint of Draught Guinness. As one might expect fresh fish, crab, lobster, prawns, langoustine and scallops feature largely on the menu. However the steaks are as good as you will get anywhere and if you have a fancy for a perfect pizza, you have come to the right place. Speciality Seafood evenings are always popular, in fact this is probably one of the most visited pubs in Weston. A place in which to have fun, be well fed and enjoy a drink, and know that the prices are sensible.

USEFUL INFORMATION

OPEN: 10am-11pm
CHILDREN: Welcome
CREDIT CARDS: Access/Visa/Master /Euro
LICENSED: Supper hours. Full On
ACCOMMODATION: Not applicable

RESTAURANT: Steaks, seafood, specialities
BAR FOOD: Traditional home-made dishes
VEGETARIAN: At least 3
DISABLED ACCESS: Level entrance
GARDEN: Patio seating 100 plus

DAUNCEY'S HOTEL

Hotel

Claremont Crescent,
Weston-Super-Mare, Avon.

Tel: (0934) 621144

Dauncey's Hotel has an enviable position. It is beautiful and quiet, looking over Weston Bay. You can see across to the North Somerset coast and as far as Wales. One of the happiest memories you will take away having stayed here will be the sense of peace and tranquillity when you sit on the patio just off the bar on a summer's evening, enjoying a drink before dinner.

The Hunt family are the resident owners whose delight in life is ensuring that all the guests, whether they come for business or for a well earned holiday, have everything they need. It really is the ideal base and is constantly in use for conferences and bowls tours. There are 50 bedrooms, all are appointed to a good standard with colour TV, radio/alarm clocks and tea and coffee making provisions in all rooms. With the exception of only three single rooms, all bedrooms are en-suite.

The two passenger lifts make it easily accessible for those who may need assistance, the hotel is centrally heated and there are reduced rates for children. Open all the year it has a wonderful Christmas House Party. The menu is varied and on request they will cater for vegetarian meals and special diets. There is always a good selection of wines and a selection of sandwiches are available from the bar at lunchtimes and evenings. Afternoon tea with home-made cakes is served every afternoon and is included in the price of the accommodation.

USEFUL INFORMATION

OPEN: 7.30am until 12.30am
CHILDREN: Welcome as part of the family
CREDIT CARDS: Visa/Access/Master
LICENSED: Full On Licence
ACCOMMODATION: 50 rooms,
   mostly en-suite

RESTAURANT: Traditional & regional
BAR FOOD: Selection of sandwiches
VEGETARIAN: Yes & other diets
DISABLED ACCESS: Sorry, no
   facilities
GARDEN: Yes. patio seating
   overlooking bay

SMITHS HOTEL

Hotel

20-24 Knightstone Road,
Weston Super Mare, Avon.

Tel: (0934) 642159
Fax: (0934) 644228

Situated right on the sea front with easy access to all the many amenities and attractions that Weston-super-Mare has to offer, Smiths Hotel is an ideal place in which to spend a holiday. Even if you are not a resident you are more than welcome to come and have a drink in the comfortable bar and enjoy the nightly entertainment that is put on for everyone's pleasure. It is very much a family hotel under the personal supervision of the resident proprietors, and cousins Andrew and John. These caring men and their staff work hard to ensure that everyone who comes to Smiths is cared for and made to feel individually important.

All the bedrooms are ensuite and equipped with everything one needs including colour TV &satellite. There is a lift to all floors, ground floor rooms are available for those who prefer them and several rooms have balconies which look out over the splendid panoramic reach of the bay.

Everyone looks forward to good meals and here in the public restaurant a full a la carte menu is available throughout the day. If the weather is good there is nothing nicer than having a meal under the shade of an umbrella on the sun patio. One of the great advantages of staying in Weston apart from the pleasure of walking along the promenade or enjoying the sandy beach and the attractions, you are close to Bath with its Roman Spa Baths, or Wookey Hole and Cheddar's 50,000 year old caves. There are several National Trust properties nearby.

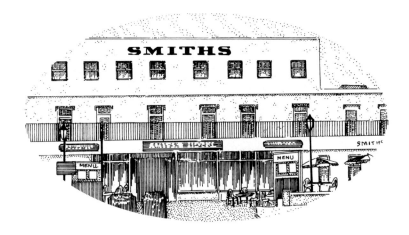

USEFUL INFORMATION

OPEN: All year, Mon-Sat: 11-11pm,
   Sun: Normal hours
CHILDREN: Welcome
CREDIT CARDS: Most major cards
LICENSED: Full On
ACCOMMODATION: 50 en-suite

RESTAURANT: Traditional English
   Open to non residents
BAR FOOD: From roasts to sandwiches
VEGETARIAN: 4 daily + specials
DISABLED ACCESS: Level, rooms &
   toilets
GARDEN: Large Terrace overlooking
   sea

TIMBERTOPS HOTEL & APARTMENTS

Hotel

8 Victoria Park,
Weston Super Mare, Avon.

Tel: (0934) 631178

Centrally situated in Weston in a sunny Victorian cul-de-sac close to the sea front and Grove Park, Timbertops comprises three separate properties which combine to make Timbertop Aparthotel. All three are grouped around the Timbertop gardens with sun terraces that face south with scenic views across Weston Bay. Sunshine pours in from morning until late evening.

Both the Hotel and the Apartments are available all the year. Rosemary Moncrieff owns the hotel and runs it with her children. What strikes one most is the relaxed, welcoming atmosphere which makes one feel instantly at home, especially female visitors on their own. This is probably because Rosemary Moncrieff lived in hotels for over 25 years and understands what people need and like when they are constantly travelling. Nothing seems to be too much trouble to ensure your comfort and every member of the staff is helpful with directions and local information.

Timbertop has acquired a reputation for excellent food, imaginatively presented with a daily selection of home-cooked food and a choice of desserts from the 'glass' fronted refrigerator in the designer carvery. The standard of hygiene and quality of food products is high.. The hotel buys fresh food and vegetables daily from only the most reputable and prestigious suppliers. Unique to Timbertop are 'family suites' comprising 2/3 bedrooms with en-suite bathroom/toilet which is located giving private access from each bedroom. All apartments are self contained with central heating, fitted kitchens and one, two or three en-suite bathrooms to accommodate up to eight guests.

USEFUL INFORMATION

OPEN: All year round
CHILDREN: Welcome. Highchairs, cots
CREDIT CARDS: Access/Visa
LICENSED: Residential Licence
ACCOMMODATION: Most rooms en-suite, laundry facilities, public telephone

RESTAURANT: High quality, plentiful
BAR FOOD: Not applicable
VEGETARIAN: On request
DISABLED ACCESS: No
GARDEN: Delightful ' secret' garden, tables, umbrellas, car parking (some off street)

INDEX TO PLACES AND VENUES

Longleat Safari Park

Invitation
Press
Ltd

I hope that you have enjoyed the selection of places in which you can lunch, dine, stay or visit. I have enjoyed researching and writing this book.

It would make the next edition more exciting if you would contribute by suggesting places that could be included and your comments on any establishment you have visited would be much appreciated. In return I will be very happy to send you a complimentary copy of one of the other books in the series or an 'Invitation' T-shirt. The choice is yours.

I enjoy corresponding with my readers and look forward to hearing from you.

Bon appetit!

Yours sincerely

Joy David

*24-26 George Place,
Stonehouse,
Plymouth,
PL1 3NY.*

*Tel: (0752) 256177/256188
Fax: (0752) 254314*

Company No:2816900

301

READER'S COMMENTS

Please use this page to tell us about PUBS, HOTELS, RESTAURANTS etc and PLACES OF INTEREST that have appealed to you especially.

We will pass on your approval where it is merited and equally report back to the venue any **complaints**. We hope the latter will be few and far between.

Please post to: Joy David, Invitation Press, 24-26 George Place, Stonehouse, Plymouth, PL1 3NY and expect to receive a book or 'T' Shirt as a token of our appreciation.

Name of Establishment:
Address:

Comments

Your Name (Block Caps Please) ....

Address: ....

....

READER'S COMMENTS

Please use this page to tell us about PUBS, HOTELS, RESTAURANTS etc and PLACES OF INTEREST that have appealed to you especially.

We will pass on your approval where it is merited and equally report back to the venue any **complaints**. We hope the latter will be few and far between.

Please post to: Joy David, Invitation Press, 24-26 George Place, Stonehouse, Plymouth, PL1 3NY and expect to receive a book or 'T' Shirt as a token of our appreciation.

Name of Establishment:
Address:

Comments

Your Name (Block Caps Please) ....

Address: ....

....

AN INVITATION TO
LUNCH, DINE, STAY AND VISIT

The following titles are currently available in this series:

To order tick as appropriate:

Devon and Cornwall, Edition II	☐ £8.30 inc p&p
Somerset & Avon, Edition II	☐ £8.30 inc p&p
East Anglia	☐ £7.30 inc p&p
The Mid-Shires	☐ £7.30 inc p&p
Heart of England	☐ £7.30 inc p&p
Wales	☐ £7.30 inc p&p
Southern England	☐ £8.30 inc p&p
North and East Yorkshire	☐ £9.30 inc p&p

To follow

Cathedral Cities of Southern England	☐ £12.20 inc p&p
Cathedral Cities of Northern England	☐ £12.20 inc p&p

*Also by **Joy David***

An Invitation to Devon   ☐ £7.30 inc p&p
(a very readable, gentle meander through Devon)

An Invitation to Plymouth   ☐ £10.20 inc p&p
(a contemporary, easily read book covering all aspects of the city)

Name

....

Address

....

....

Tel: (daytime)

....

Please make cheques payable to Invitation Press Ltd
**Invitation Press Ltd, 24-26 George Place, Stonehouse,
Plymouth, PL1 3NY. Telephone (0752) 256177/256188**